The Genetic Lottery

A Novel

Terri Morgan

Books by Terri Morgan
Junior Seau: High Voltage Linebacker
Ruthie Bolton-Holifield: Sharpshooting Playmaker
Gabrielle Reece: Volleyball's Model Athlete
Venus and Serena Williams: Grand Slam Sisters

Books by Terri Morgan and Shmuel Thaler
Photography: Take Your Best Shot
Chris Mullen: Sure Shot
Steve Young: Complete Quarterback
Capturing Childhood Memories: The Complete Photography Guide
for Parents

Silverdarts Press Paperbacks

Library of Congress Number 2011963355 ISBN 978-0-615-58279-5
Cover Design by Katja Coulter

What Readers are saying about The Genetic Lottery

"This book saved my life when my youngest was diagnosed with paranoid schizophrenia less than a year after I read it. I wasn't scared, I knew what questions to ask, and I knew what to stay away from. It is one of the most important books I have ever read, even though it's fiction. The fact that we can accept our child's illness can be laid squarely at the author's feet. I never would have understood the complexity of schizophrenia had I not read the book." -Dawn M.

"Thank you Terri Morgan for this special touching novel. This book has special meaning for me as my nephew is living with schizophrenia. You write wonderful and with passion and are not at all condescending. I stayed up all night and read it, and I loved every word." - Liz Vadset Olver

"Knowing that Terri usually writes non-fiction, I was curious how she could write realistic fiction about such a sensitive subject. But true to her reputation as a thorough researcher she has done just that. The episodes she recounts parallel the stories that real persons have shared with me. I recommended it to my Board and to others who have an interest in gaining insight into the life of a child living with schizophrenic parents. At the very least it is a riveting read and at best it exposes the reader to shocking truths and the silent suffering of so many." - Carol Kozlovich, President, NAMI Hawaii

"Although I have treated many schizophrenic patients and their families I still found this fictional narrative very touching and illuminating." Heather B. Cattell. Ph.D, clinical psychologist and author of *The 16: Personality in Depth*.

For Gary Neville Sandstrom,
Capitola's Water Dancer
TLA

The Genetic Lottery

A Novel

Terri Morgan

Introduction

Every morning when I first wake up I wonder and I worry. Before getting out of bed, before registering my full, aching bladder, before remembering what day it is and what responsibilities await -- I assess myself for signs of the disease. I roll my eyes around the room, looking for phantoms that may have appeared while I was sleeping.

For odd, moving sights, like my dresser transformed into a rolling automobile or roaring lion.

To make sure that the clock radio on my night stand or the framed photos on the bookshelves haven't cloned themselves overnight and morphed into twins or even triplets.

Then I listen carefully. I hear Jason snoring lightly beside me. I hear the ticking of the living room clock. I hear the jangle of Rosco's tags as he rolls over on his bed in the corner of our room.

I hold my breath and listen for mysterious voices or alien noises. Then, once I'm sure I'm not hearing any unusual, strange sounds, I ask myself--- silently so not to wake my sleeping husband----a series of questions.

Who am I?

What's my address?

Where do I work?

How old are my children?

What's my husband's name?

Who's the president?

Only after the correct responses to the first five pop into my mind, and I chuckle to myself after answering "Calvin Coolidge" to the sixth question because I know good and well that Barack Obama currently resides in the White House, do I know I'm safe for another day. If I still have my sense of humor, and apparently my faculties, I've still escaped it.

Escaped the mental illness that afflicted and consumed my mother, my father and my brother.

Escaped the schizophrenia that robbed them of their minds and me of a childhood.

I know that at 32 my chances of developing schizophrenia are miniscule and keep shrinking with every passing month. Despite that, I'm still obsessively terrified of developing the devastating mental illness that was an ever-present part of my formative years.

It's shaped who I've become, and I've worked for more than half my life to recover from its impact. My father, mother and brother all lost the genetic lottery, and their misfortune continues to ripple through my life even today.

My name, at least the name I go by now, is Caitlin.

That's the name I chose for myself 18 years ago when I fled my childhood home. I cast off the name on my birth certificate for the new one in hopes of casting off the madness that was my family.

Chapter 1

There are a lot of popular misconceptions swirling around about schizophrenia. Some people, especially those who are fortunate enough not to have had firsthand experience with this devastating, disabling mental illness, think schizophrenics suffer from a split, or two vastly different personalities.

I imagine they picture someone like a benevolent, beloved school teacher who bakes cookies for the neighbors in her spare time turning into a vicious profanity-spewing crone who butchers small cuddly animals with her bare hands during episodes.

Others, who are steeped in popular culture, believe all schizophrenics are geniuses, like the Nobel Prize-winning mathematician John Nash. These kinds of misconceptions are annoying, but not surprising, considering there are so many mysteries about schizophrenia that have yet to be solved.

Despite billions of dollars worth of research, scientists have not yet pinpointed the causes of schizophrenia, although they believe a combination of genetics, brain chemistry and brain abnormality are involved. They do know that there is a hereditary basis for the susceptibility of the disease, meaning that schizophrenia often runs in families. Unfortunately, it runs in mine.

My father, Keith, was 16 or 17 when he began changing from an outgoing, straight-A student into a foul mouthed chain-smoking punk who was afraid to leave his room for days on end except to steal cigarettes or use the bathroom because "they" were out to get him. My mother, Lisa, was diagnosed with schizophrenia when I was two, although I suspect she was afflicted long before that. After all, she named my brother, who was born three years before I was, Jondalar, after one of her favorite characters in Jean Auel's "The Children of the Earth" book series.

Although she was young, just 21 when she had my brother, and impulsive like many young adults, saddling your newborn with a moniker that would ensure he'd be the subject of relentless teasing throughout his school years isn't what I consider to be the actions of someone fully steeped in reality. Our father would sheepishly shrug his shoulders whenever my brother demanded to know why he didn't stop Mom from putting Jondalar on his birth certificate.

Dad also failed to stop Mom from naming me Ayla after the main protagonist in Auel's novels, a character I suspect Mom sometimes wished she was. Fortunately for me, my brother promptly nicknamed me Ava, as his young tongue struggled unsuccessfully to pronounce my given name. I returned the favor when I began speaking, shortening Jondalar to Jon.

While my nickname stuck, Mom refused to fully accept Jon's. When she was well, she would tolerate it grudgingly, and even use it herself occasionally, but when she wasn't well she insisted on correcting—and berating— anyone who dared use the diminutive version of his name within her hearing.

I don't remember the onset of Mom's illness, so I have to rely on family stories; mostly the memories and tales of my brother, grandmother, uncle and granddad. I've heard Dad's version too. But since his illness has grown steadily worse throughout the years, I've given up on trying to separate what's real and what's fantasy when it comes to his memories. What I do know is that Dad was stable and working at his father's hardware store when Mom got sick and was diagnosed. Mom was working night as a waitress at an old-fashioned all-night.

When Mom wasn't working, or busy taking care of Jon and me, she was painting. Like her mother, my Nana, Mom loved to paint. Both were very talented artists who enjoyed moderate success and renown while I was growing up. Their works were displayed and sold in several local galleries.

My earliest memories are of the reek of turpentine, oil paints and cigarette smoke, and the sight of my mother at her easel in the living room. She'd lean partially finished paintings against the walls and furniture, creating a colorful, ever-changing maze for us to negotiate to reach the couch, the TV, or the phone.

She'd work sporadically; at times with an energy and passion that led her to forget who she was, that she had children to feed until we started crying, or Dad came home from the hardware store and startled her with his arrival.

Throughout my childhood, these periods of artistic frenzy were usually followed by painting droughts. When they occurred, Mom would stand for hours with a brush in her right hand and a cigarette smoldering in her left staring bleakly at a blank canvas.

The painters' block periods, as Jon and I called them, were followed by long stretches where Mom would retreat to her bedroom and stay curled up in her bed, leaving Jon and me to fend for ourselves.

When Mom would re-emerge goofy phrases and nonsensical words would often come out of her mouth, which confused and frightened us kids. The longer those spells lasted, the less coherent she became.

Dad would ignore the fact that Mom was progressively getting sicker until some crisis occurred.

The first crisis occurred when Jon was five and I was still in diapers. After weeks of strange behavior, Mom came into the bedroom Jon and I shared and started ranting about Satan. I started crying, Jon recalls, which set Mom off. She began yelling that I was full of evil, and ordered Jon to cast me out of the house. Jon grabbed my hand, pulled me out of the room and together we fled out the front door screaming in terror. A neighbor overheard the ruckus and called the police after leading us into her home and locking the door.

Jon claims I cried the entire six weeks Mom was in the hospital being diagnosed and treated for the onset of schizophrenia. Nana, who took care of us while Dad was at work, never disputed his account, but would spare my feelings by diplomatically adding, whenever Jon brought the subject up, that "both you poor kids were pretty upset."

Family lore has it that I was a difficult child. I suffered from colic, apparently, and cried almost constantly during my first six months of life. The colic and the crying stopped suddenly one day, Nana remembers, only to be replaced a few months later, when I began to begin to talk, with a bad case of the "nos."

"You were a pretty stubborn kid," Nana told me when I was complaining to her that Kayla, my first-born, had a mind of her own. "She takes after you. Your terrible twos began when you were about 16 months old and didn't stop until you were in Kindergarten."

Fortunately for the rest of the family, Jon, who'd been pestering my parents for a brother or a sister since he began talking, adored me. Relatives said Jon loved to play with me, making faces and singing to me when I wasn't sleeping, eating or crying. And when I was crying, which was apparently quite a bit of the time even after the colic cleared up, to hear my mother tell it, Jon would interpret my needs, telling my parents "diaper," "hungry" or "ti-ti" when there was a physical reason for my howls. And when there wasn't an obvious reason for my unhappiness, Jon would entertain me until the tears stopped or his favorite cartoons came on.

"Thank God for your brother," Mom would say throughout my childhood whenever she was healthy, coherent and annoyed. "If I had had you first, you'd be an only child."

Whenever my sense of guilt gets so strong that I can't help but bring it up, Jason insists I wasn't responsible for my mother's illness. So do all the therapists I've seen over the years. But I know that stress can, and often does, play a role in triggering any latent disease. And after I became a parent for the first time, exhausted from the middle of the night feedings, and frustrated when Kayla would cry for what appeared to be no apparent reason, I found it harder to accept their reassurances.

Chapter 2

I've always loved to read, but Jon inhaled books. As a toddler, Nana recalls, he would pick up a book and head for her lap whenever she visited us, which was often as we lived in the same town —Cumberland. Cumberland is the county seat of Cumberland County, which lies in the Willamette Valley in Central Oregon. There are about 100,000 people living in Cumberland these days, up from the 75,000 or 80,000 souls who called Cumberland home when I was growing up.

Although I live in Washington State now, I was a true Cumberland native; third generation on my father's side, and second generation on my mother's. Growing up, that counted for something, as the locals sneered at anyone who dared move into their town. Unless you were born in Cumberland's Community Hospital, you were forever deemed an interloper and looked down upon with suspicion. Long before he was aware of his native status, Jon was obsessed with books and could hardly wait to break the mysterious code and begin reading on his own.

He learned the alphabet before his fourth birthday, and asked Mom almost daily how much longer before he could start going to school.

When the big day finally arrived, Mom put me in the stroller, took Jon by the hand and escorted him two blocks away to the elementary school. When we arrived on campus and found the Kindergarten classroom, Mom says there were at least a half-dozen kids clinging tearfully to their mothers outside the door.

Jon dropped Mom's hand and skipped through the door happily.

When Mom turned the stroller around and started home, I started crying. She claims I didn't stop until we returned to the school a few hours later and saw Jon come out of the classroom.

If Mom's memory was true, and not a figment of her exaggeration, as Jon and I used to dub many of her stories, I'm not sure if I was more unhappy to see Jon leave me behind as he headed off on a new adventure, or if I was afraid to be alone with Mom.

With Jon in school three hours a day, Nana recalls that Mom and I initially settled into a routine. We'd escort him to school after breakfast and escort him back home before lunch. In between, Mom would try to get some painting done. To keep me entertained, on mornings when I wasn't out with Dad, and to prevent me from interrupting her work, she bought me a set of little plastic pots filled with brightly colored and, presumably, non-toxic paint, and some fat handled brushes.

She'd set up a child-sized easel next to hers and sketch the outline of a person or object onto a piece of paper. She'd then tack it to the easel for me to color in with paint.

I'd splash away happily, getting more paint on my clothes and the floor than the paper, she'd concentrate on her artwork.

Jon's Kindergarten schedule, as I realized when Kayla started school, fragmented Mom's day. I'm sure she must have been frustrated, like I was years later, to have her day chopped into small windows of time bracketed with child pickups and deliveries.

As her creative time dwindled, her fuse must have shortened. Jon would steer clear of Mom after lunch, heading for our bedroom or the backyard, usually with me in tow, until Dad came home from work. When I was older, and he'd talk about that period of time, he'd remember it as the era when Mom was always mad. And she stayed mad, even after she stopped picking up Jon at school, and he began to walk himself home.

In those days, Dad worked at Granddad's hardware store. But his real vocation, the work he loved to do best, was woodworking.

He'd converted the tiny, one-car garage next to the house into a wood shop, where he'd spend hours sawing, planing and sanding wood. He turned tree branches and planks of oak, redwood and walnut into beautiful, conversation-generating pieces of furniture.

Mom still has some chairs he made, which are still gorgeous and sturdy despite years of rough treatment and countless moves.

I can remember playing in the sawdust on the floor of his workshop, smelling the scent of freshly cut wood, and Dad brushing curled wood shavings out of my hair and off my clothes with his hands before we'd go back into the house.

Dad was often clumsy, nicking his fingers and drawing blood when his chisel would slip. Years later I realized his clumsiness was most likely a side effect of his medication. But in those early days, I was blissfully unaware of his illness.

I only knew that Dad cut himself so often that he kept a First Aid kit in the workshop. When I'd hear him swear suddenly, I'd look up from whatever I was doing to see if he was bleeding. If he was, I'd help him clean up the wound with cotton balls dipped in hydrogen peroxide, squeeze some ointment out of a sticky tube onto the wound and cover it with a Band-Aid if it was a small cut, or bandage it up with gauze and adhesive tape if it was a large one.

Dad would say "thank you, Doctor Ava," when I was done, and reward me by applying a Band-Aid on my hand or finger to match his own. I don't know why, but I loved wearing Band-Aids, although when I endured an actual injury, I would shriek with pain and fear.

Dad would usually return to his woodworking after I finished nursing him. But sometimes, likely when the cuts were bad, he'd put his tools away and call it a day. When that happened he'd slip into a funk, and go in the house and either pick an argument with my mother, or go into their bedroom alone and close the door behind him.

Jon and I would steer clear of him for the rest of the day, puzzle over the sudden change in his mood, and wonder what we had done to set him off.

Dad worked weekends, because those were the busiest days at Swarthout Hardware, and had Mondays and Tuesdays off. Before I started Kindergarten, I'd often ride with him on Monday mornings as he went about his routine. First, we'd go to the clinic, where I'd stay in the waiting room playing with one of my dolls, which I carried everywhere, after the receptionist called his name, and he disappeared out of sight. He'd return a few minutes later and collect me. After strapping me back into my car seat, he'd say, "Well, I got shot. What do you say we go to the grocery store to celebrate."

I hated shots and couldn't understand how he could go so willingly, week after week, for an injection. But it didn't seem to faze Dad, although I realize now that his weekly injections were torturous to him for other reasons besides physical discomfort.

I'm not sure what anti-psychotic drug he was on at the time, what medication his psychiatrist had prescribed to helped keep Dad's paranoid delusions at bay. But along with quelling the voices in his head, the medication made him tired and clumsy.

On Tuesdays, Dad would see his psychiatrist, and usually took me with him, likely to give Mom a break, so she could paint, or depending upon her moods, stare blankly at the canvas without being interrupted by me. In retrospect, Dad was probably uncomfortable with his psychiatric visits, but I loved them.

The office had an entire room packed with toys.

Shelves lined three walls and were loaded with dolls and plastic figures in all sizes, shapes and colors. There were boy dolls, girl dolls and dolls that looked like grown men and women. There were plastic animals, plastic soldiers, plastic cowboys, plastic Indians and plastic women. There were a half dozen or more doll houses, with three sides so you could reach in through the open wall and rearrange the toy furniture and move the dolls from room to room. There were colorful cars, plastic tools and boxes and boxes of crayons. There were small boxes of fat crayons and large boxes packed with regular-sized crayons in more colors than I'd ever seen before. There were baskets of paper, both white and colored, on the shelves and large mugs holding sharpened pencils.

The receptionist would lead me into the room, pull down the toys I wanted to play with that day and set them on the low table in the room. I'd play so happily that I sometimes cried with frustration and disappointment when Dad came in the retrieve me.

Those tears would stop by the time we reached the car, because I knew the next stop was Swarthout's Hardware Store. All the employees there would fuss over me while Dad and Granddad disappeared into Granddad's office to talk. When they re-emerged, Granddad would let me pick out a candy bar from the impulse racks next to the checkout counter, making me promise to share it with Jon. Then Dad and I would walk to the bank, where he'd cash his paycheck.

Despite his treatments, Dad still had rough periods. Our weekly excursions ended when I started Kindergarten. So did my time playing in the workshop, because by then Dad had stopped working on his projects. At the time, I thought I had done something wrong, something to make

Dad so mad at me that he was punishing me by not spending time with me in the workshop. It was only years later that I realized it was his illness, not my behavior, that put an end to our special times together.

Chapter 3

L ike Jon, I was looking forward to starting school. And Jon was the one who first noticed the banner on the front of the elementary school advertising Kindergarten Sign Ups. We badgered Mom and Dad to enroll me for the upcoming school year with no success.

Mom was in one of her blank stages and unwilling to leave the house other than to buy cigarettes.

Dad was retreating to bed as soon as he came home from work and sometimes missing work, hiding behind the closed bedroom door for hours. So finally, Jon took matters into his own hands. He took my hand one hot, sunny late summer morning and walked me to the elementary school.

Although I'd been to Jon's classroom in the school annex, it was my first time inside the main school building. It was cool inside, and it smelled of dust and white glue. Our steps echoed as we walked down a long hall to a room with a colorful sign on the open door. A nice lady inside the room asked where our mother was. When Jon said she was sick, she gave Jon some papers to take home for our parents to fill out.

Back at home, Jon tried his best to get Mom or Dad to sit down and take care of the paperwork. Finally, he asked Nana to help, but only after he'd picked up a pen and written "AVA" where he should have written Ayla, thus sparing me the kind of teasing he endured each year the first time his teacher called roll and mispronounced his given name.

I was skipping with excitement when Jon and I walked to school together for my first day of Kindergarten.

"You'll like it," Jon said. "You've got Mrs. Beachman, and she's really nice."

Jon escorted me to my classroom, past a couple of kids clinging tearfully to their mothers. I bounded into the classroom, and looked around.

"Hi," I announced to the friendly looking woman standing in the middle of the room. "I'm Ava."

"Welcome," she said. "I'm Mrs. Beachman, and I'm your teacher."

"I know," I replied. "My brother told me. He says you're really nice."

She smiled and told me to sit down in one of the small wooden chairs that were arranged in a semi-circle in the middle of the room.

The first day was fun. We sang songs, and we colored pictures. Mrs. Beachman read us a story. We learned where to put our jackets, and that we had to stay in our seats unless we were told otherwise. We ate a snack and lined up at the door for recess. Time passed quickly, and I was surprised when the bell rang, and Mrs. Beachman said it was time to go home.

My classmates filed out and found their mothers, and in a few cases, fathers who had come to take them home. Neither of my parents had come, and Jon was still in class, so there was nobody to meet me. I stood uncertainly in the hall for a few moments, then turned around and went back into the classroom.

"Can I stay here with you?" I asked.

"Oh no," Mrs. Beachman said. "It's time for us both to eat lunch. And then I have to get the room ready for the afternoon Kindergarten class."

"There's another class?" I asked in amazement. She smiled and nodded, and led me out of the room.

I trudged home, where Mom was in a painting trance, and went in the kitchen and ate some cold cereal straight out of the box for lunch. Mom took no notice of me, so when I was through, I went outside and walked back to school. I was waiting by the closed door of the Kindergarten classroom when Mrs. Beachman arrived to open the room back up for the second session.

Gently, she explained that school was over for me for the day, and that I couldn't stay. When I started to cry, she walked me to the office. After a while, Nana arrived to take me home.

Chapter 4

"Jon-da-lar, Jon-da-lar, doesn't have a home, so he lives in a car." The chanting began behind us as Jon and I were walking home from our new school to our new home at the Golden Torch Trailer Park. It was November, and we were the new kids in our respective classes, arriving late enough into the school year that all our fellow classmates noticed us.

"Jon-da-lar, Jon-da-lar, doesn't have a home so he lives in a car."

Jon tensed up beside me and muttered "Ignore them Ava." I ignored Jon and whirled around angrily.

Two boys, presumably Jon's new fourth grade classmates, smirked and began chanting again, sure that their teasing had gotten under my skin.

"You'd better stop that," I yelled.

"Come on Ava," Jon said.

I could tell by the sound of his voice he was worried that I'd start a fight that he would have to finish.

The chanting continued, picking up in volume and no doubt attracting the ears of every other kid walking nearby. Jon stopped walking and turned uneasily to look back at me and his tormentors.

"I'm serious," I yelled at the pair. "You're in real trouble now."

The boys stopped chanting long enough to laugh. "What ya gonna do," sneered the taller of the pair. "Beat us up?"

"No," I said firmly, with an unexpected calm sweeping over me.

"I'm going to report you to the Swedish Embassy. Our great-great-grandfather Jondalar was the King of Sweden, and it's illegal to take the name of a Swedish King in vain."

The pair looked at me with confusion crossing their faces, obviously not expecting such a speech from a first grader. Before they could regain their voices, I put my hands on my hips and continued.

"You're in big trouble," I announced. "I'm going to call the Swedish Embassy when I get home. They'll have you arrested and thrown in jail."

"They can't arrest us," said the shorter kid. "They're not cops."

"They've got dip-lo-mat-ic imm-un-ity," I said repeating a phrase I'd heard my mother chant during her last breakdown. I had no idea what the words meant, but they sounded both scary and official, especially with all the syllables drawn out. "It's a very serious offense. You'll be sorry."

The two looked at each other, surprised perhaps, at the multi-syllabic words coming so confidently out of the mouth of a small girl. Jon took advantage of their speechlessness to move in for the kill.

"Aw Ava, you don't want to do that to them," he said.

"I have to," I stated. "They took the name of King Jondalar in vain. That's a major crime."

"I don't think they really meant it," Jon said, glancing at his two tormenters. "I don't think they deserve to be sent to the dungeon just 'cause they didn't know." The boys stiffened at the word dungeon, anxiety apparent in their expressions.

"I don't know." I said.

"Aw, let's give 'em a break."

"I don't know," I repeated.

"I'm really sorry," burst out the taller boy, whose name we found out later was Timmy.

"Me too," blurted out his companion, Ryan, who later became one of Jon's friends.

"Don't let it happen again," I snapped, then turned around and resumed marching home. I heard the sounds of the two scampering off, then Jon
snickering. He rested his hand briefly on my shoulder, and we began walking together.

Dad was in the hospital following a psychotic breakdown, so Mom had decided to save money by moving out of our house and into a camper her friend Joan loaned her. *The Dinosaur* as Jon dubbed our new home, was an ugly green vehicle that was old long before we were born. A door at the right side of *The Dinosaur* opened into an area maybe eight feet wide and 12 feet long. At the very front were two big bucket seats, separated by a flat-topped metal case that held the engine.

There was an L-shaped padded bench behind the passenger seat and running along the side of the rig. Nestled in the L was a Formica topped

25

table mounted on a pole that could be raised and lowered. The kitchen, such as it was, consisted of a small sink, a tiny refrigerator below the counter and a microwave oven mounted about a foot above the narrow counter top. Mom called it a galley, which prompted Jon and me to pretend we were living on a boat and not inside an aluminum-sided gas hog. There was a small narrow closet at the end of a row of plastic cabinets, and a door that led to a bathroom about the size of those found on commercial airplanes. The bathroom was actually just a shower stall, holding a toilet and a tiny sink. I liked it, because you could sit on the toilet while you bathed. Mom hated it, because it was hard for her to fit inside. She preferred using the toilet in the laundry room at the middle of the park and would go days without showering.

All the parks near our former house were full, so we ended up at the Golden Torch, about five miles away from our school and our friends. Joan's husband Tom drove *The Dinosaur* to the park, with Jon and me lying on our stomachs on the bunk above his head, looking out of the front and side windows while Mom and Joan followed in separate cars.

Jon watched intently as Joan's husband hooked up the water, electricity and sewer lines after first leveling *The Dinosaur* on orange-colored jacks. Then, to our amazement, Tom walked to the side of the rig, opened some latches, turned a crank, and pulled a little room out. We ran inside to investigate the new space, and almost broke it free from *The Dinosaur* by jumping on the floor before Tom had set up the legs that supported it.

The room, which was maybe six feet by six feet, could be sealed off from the rest of the trailer by a sliding, corrugated plastic door. Mom let Jon and me roll out our sleeping bags on the big bunk over the cab of the vehicle and threw sheets on the bed Tom set up in the extension for herself.

Jon and I quickly discovered how cramped our new living quarters were when we began literally tripping over our clothes and the few toys we were allowed to keep. At our old home, where Mom and Dad were notoriously lax at housekeeping, we were used to dropping jackets and other clothing on the floor when we removed them and leaving our toys wherever they had been when we stopped playing with them. *The Dinosaur* was so small, however, anything left on the floor became a hazardous obstacle.

Jon and I discovered we had to hang up our jackets and put our toys, clothes and books in our drawers when they were not in use. The drawers were small, and to fit all my clothes in, I had to fold them and arrange them neatly in stacks. Initially, I was irritated that this new chore had been imposed on me. Soon, however, I found I liked keeping my things in order and grew irritated when Mom's debris spread out of her pop out room and into the common area. I'd kick, or toss, the offending item in the general vicinity of Mom's bed to get it out of the way.

Nana was appalled when she first saw our new home. "This is not an acceptable home, Lisa," Nana said. "I can't believe you're going to make my grandchildren live here in this tin box."

"There's nothing wrong with this RV," Mom stated.

"Nothing wrong! How can you say that? This place is small, it's dingy, it's tiny, and it smells. You'll freeze in here in the winter. It's a hovel, and I'm ashamed to have anyone in my family live in a dump like this."

"It's not a hovel. It's a recreational vehicle! People spend tens of thousands of dollars on RVs like these because they enjoy the lifestyle. Some of the people in this park have lived in their RVs for years."

"I don't care about the other people! I care about my grandchildren. This is an absolutely unacceptable place to raise Jon and Ava. They don't even have a bedroom. I'm taking them home with me."

"Oh no you don't," Mom screamed.

Jon and I fled *The Dinosaur* at that point, but couldn't escape the argument entirely. Mom was so angry and yelling so loudly you'd think she was using a megaphone. We could still hear her voice even after running to the far end of the trailer park. Mom ultimately won the fight because she drowned out Nana while giving all of our new neighbors a preview of what type of drama they could expect from the occupants of *The Dinosaur*.

For the first few days, with the exception of Mom's and Nana's scream fest, it was fun living in *The Dinosaur*. Jon and I pretended we were pirates living on a boat, and every third phrase that came out of our mouths was either "aye aye, captain," "ahoy matey" or "land ho." We took cardboard tubes from the inside of paper towel rolls up to our bunk and used our makeshift telescopes to spy on the neighbors.

When we weren't on the lookout for other pirate ships, vessels to rob, or Navy ships trying to track us down, we were in the cab, spinning the steering wheel as much as it would turn and charting our course on the high seas. We didn't have bandanas to tie onto our heads, so we made do with a couple of my T-shirts.

Jon fashioned an eye-patch for himself out of cardboard and rubber bands and wore it proudly after using our black crayon to color the eyepiece.

We went outside hunting for sticks to use as swords and discovered there was not a single, living tree on the grounds of the Golden Torch.

There was, however, a small creek running behind the property. The creek was about eight feet wide, and the water was shallow, running slowly downstream carrying fallen leaves on its surface.

We waded across it, soaking our shoes, socks and the bottom of our pant legs, and had our pick of branches that had fallen off a small grove of beech trees on the opposite bank to use as swashbuckling sailors defending our ship.

We discovered there was a trail alongside the creek that led to our new school, which was about three blocks away. So instead of walking along the sidewalk, we pretended we were either Indians walking through the woods or pioneers blazing a way through the forest, depending on our moods, as we walked to and from school. Along the way, there were trees to climb, rocks to throw into the water, mud puddles to leap over and wildlife — well a few birds and some squirrels — to spot. We had so much fun exploring along our new route that we were late to school every day during the first week.

Our new school had a large playground and two sets of play structures; one for little kids like me and a second for older kids like Jon. There was an asphalt area next to the main school building, with hopscotch squares, a map of the United States and four-square courts painted on the ground in yellow, blue, red and green paints. There was a large cement rectangle with four basketball hoops and room for kids to play two full-court games at the same time. There was an enormous grass field rimmed with a dirt track. The field was big; it could accommodate either two baseball games or a soccer match.

Jon and I would stay after school and play until the streetlights behind the schoolyard came on, both on our own and with other kids who also used the school grounds as a park.

Between the creek and the campus, we spent most of our waking hours outdoors, and we both thrived on the abundance of playtime. Then it started raining.

The winter rains arrived early that year, and once the weather got bad, it rained almost daily, or so it seemed. The creek rose, and our dirt trail turned to mud that sucked the shoes off my feet when I tried to walk along it. At school, our teachers kept us inside for recess and held P.E. inside the gym. Jon and I would hang our wet raincoats in the bathroom when we got home.

The Dinosaur, which didn't smell very good to begin with, took on the same powerful and unpleasant odor that our laundry did the year before when Mom forgot to take the clean clothes out of the washer for two weeks.

The sound of the rain beating on *The Dinosaur's* metal roof got on Mom's nerves. So did Jon and me. Noises of any kind particularly irritated Mom once it started raining.

We weren't allowed to play the radio any more, and if we tried to watch the portable TV Tom had given us, we had to turn the sound down so low that we might as well have turned the volume off all together. We were ordered to use our "inside voices," and when we forgot and spoke in normal tones, Mom would shriek and holler "stop it, stop it, stop screaming" and clap her hands over her ears, scaring us into silence..

We tried to be as quiet as we could for as long as we could each day we were cooped up inside.

Jon and I would sit in the cab and do our homework, using the metal engine case as a table to hold our books. When our schoolwork was done, we'd pull out books that we had checked out of the school library and read.

I was still learning to read, and when I couldn't figure out a word, I'd either ask Jon or guess, based on the pictures on the page and the storyline. When we either got bored with our books, or the light in the cab grew too dim to read comfortably, we'd move into the back and play cards.

Sometimes Mom would join us at the table while we played. Other days she'd shut herself into the extension, and we'd hear her mumbling to herself through the plastic door. It frightened me when Mom shut herself away, and I would alternate between hoping she'd stay behind the plastic curtain and leave us alone, and wishing she'd come out and at least talk to us, if not take care of us.

I was confused, scared and would tremble more and more as each day passed with Mom hiding herself away. Afraid to speak and aggravate Mom, Jon and I would communicate with each other by writing notes and using a primitive form of sign language.

The tension inside *The Dinosaur* rose higher and higher each successive day. I could tell Jon was worried, and that worried me. Fortunately Nana, who kept a close eye on Mom and her moods, came to the rescue.

When we were back in our old house, Nana would drop by three or four times a week. Since we'd moved into *The Dinosaur*, Nana stopped by every day, often bringing cereal and milk, bread, lunch meats, sliced cheese and fruit with her. She also brought prepared meals that just needed to be reheated in the little microwave oven above the tiny counter.

A week or so after the rains came, Nana signed both of us kids up for after-school programs at our school. Jon was enrolled in the program for the big kids, and played basketball, indoor soccer, volleyball and other sports in the gym on rainy days, or outside on the rare day when the rain wasn't pelting down.

He also learned how to play chess, a game he tried unsuccessfully to teach me so he could practice for the program's weekly tournaments.

I was signed up for the little kids program, which operated more like a day care. It was held in a big, double-sized classroom that was filled with games, books and toys. Kids could play by themselves, with other kids, or take part in organized activities headed by the high school girls who helped the supervisor keep the chaos to the minimum.

I loved it.

Since we were new to the school, and Nana, rather than Mom or Dad came to pick us up, nobody knew our parents often forgot to bathe, comb their hair or dress appropriately for the weather.

The other kids, for the most part, accepted me as one of them, and for the first time in my life I had friends my own age to play with.

Nana must have also arranged for us to get breakfast and lunch at school, because around that time we started eating two meals a day in the cafeteria. Mom had always resisted what she called Nana's interference. But the crowded conditions in *The Dinosaur* must have annoyed her so much she was willing to accept Nana's help because it got us kids out from under her feet.

Chapter 5

"What are you looking at?" I demanded, shouting angrily at the girl about my age who was staring, drop-jawed at my mother as the two of us walked down the street. Dad was finally out of the hospital following a nine month stay, and we had moved out of *The Dinosaur* and into an apartment near the hardware store. Jon and I were thrilled when Dad returned *The Dinosaur* to Joan and her husband and excited to have Dad back in our lives.

"Nu, nu, nothing," the girl stammered, perhaps stunned by my venomous tone, or shocked by my mother's outfit.

"Then beat it," I snapped. "And don't you dare laugh."

If I hadn't been so angry and so humiliated by Mom's appearance, I would have laughed. In fact, I had laughed when I saw what Mom had put on. It was a warm, sunny, summer afternoon, and Mom was wearing a bright yellow slicker and dark green rubber rain boots as she clomped down the street.

She held an unfurled umbrella in one hand and had a firm grip on one of my hands with the other. A fluorescent orange sou'wester on her head, Mom was prepared for either a deluge or a circus tryout.

Unfortunately for me, neither situation was in her immediate future. Instead, she was headed to the grocery store with me, reluctantly, in tow.

I was mortified to be seen with Mom.

But I was also hungry, and, as usual, there was nothing to eat at home. Jon, Dad and I had learned the hard way not to let Mom go shopping by herself when she was ill.

Jon and Dad were both out, and I needed help carrying the groceries home, so reluctantly I tucked the food stamp booklet into my pocket, and Mom and I began walking to the market two blocks away.

Once inside, I managed to lose Mom when she became enthralled by the colored packages in the laundry aisle. I pushed the cart away, leaving her giggling at the displays, and tried to remember what groceries Jon had told me to buy earlier that day. Peanut butter, bread, grape jelly, cereal, macaroni, soup and milk. I counted my stamps, then tossed cans of chili, SpaghettiOs, and tuna into the cart. I was headed back towards Mom when I remembered Jon's admonition.

"Do NOT come home without coffee," he had said by way of reminding me how impossibly grumpy our parents were until they had caffeine in their bodies. I looped back across the store to the breakfast food aisle and looked on the shelves for Mom and Dad's preferred brand of instant. I spotted it on the top shelf and had to wait for someone to come by and reach up and retrieve the jar for me. Then I went looking for Mom.

I heard her before I spotted her, laughing loudly, maniacally, at something no one else could see or hear. Shoppers were avoiding her, turning around and backing out of the aisle to avoid going past her. I could feel people's eyes on me as I marched up to her and took her hand.

"Come on Mom," I told her. "It's time to go."

Mom was giggling to herself, but came with me willingly. I had to drop her hand to push the cart, but she followed me anyway to the check stand. The clerk looked nervous, ringing up our purchases, and avoided meeting Mom's eyes. She relaxed visibly when I counted out our food stamp coupons, handed them to her and accepted 43 cents back in change. The clerk bagged our groceries, set them back into the cart and told me to "have a nice day."

"Yeah right," I said, and Mom and I pushed the cart out of the store.

Mom was slipping deeper and deeper into her own world, while Dad was struggling to regain his equilibrium and adapt to life outside of the hospital. He wasn't talking to or arguing with people nobody else could see, but he was often confused. He'd spent nine months in the Behavioral Health Unit of Cumberland's Community Hospital, where all his needs were taken care of. Meals arrived regularly, his bed was changed, dirty laundry would disappear from his room and return as clean, folded clothing. He met with a psychiatrist daily, attended regular group therapy sessions and watched TV and smoked cigarettes the rest of the time. He was ill-equipped for running a household, especially one where his wife was acting stranger by the day.

Nana came over almost every day to make sure Jon and I were fed, bathed and safe, and to coax Mom, unsuccessfully, to take her medications.

33

Granddad, Dad's dad, came by regularly as well, to keep tabs on us and remind Dad he could come back to work at the hardware store whenever he was ready.

Jon and I did most of the grocery shopping, either walking to the store by ourselves, or waiting until one of our grandparents came over and could drive us. I thought we were doing pretty well; it was summer, and Jon and I spent most of our time outside playing.

Then one evening near the end of the August, we came home as the sun was setting, and the apartment was dark. Jon flipped the light switch as we came in the front door, but nothing happened.

Mom was sitting in the dark giggling, and Dad was in the kitchen banging around trying to fix something to eat. Jon and I figured the power had gone out and didn't connect the outage to the stack of unopened mail on the floor near the front door.

Nana diagnosed the problem the next morning, when she arrived and discovered several warning notices from the power company, threatening to stop service unless overdue payments were received.

Nana was upset when she realized that neither of our parents had paid the power bill, or any other bill that had arrived since we moved into the apartment, and that our phone service was on the verge of being shut off as well.

"This is no way to raise children," she lectured Mom and Dad, and threatened to take Jon and myself home with her.

Mom didn't respond.

Dad begged her not to take his kids away from him and asked Nana what to do.

Nana sorted through the pile of mail on the floor, then left, with Jon and me in tow, to go to make arrangements for the electricity to be restored.

Two days later Nana, Granddad and Granddad's wife Eileen, who was Dad's stepmother, came over at the same time to talk to Mom and Dad. They sent Jon and me out to play, so I don't know what they talked about.

I suspect, in retrospect, that they used us kids as bargaining chips to get Mom to start taking her medication again and to get Dad to return to work. Dad always did much better when he had a schedule; too much spare time seemed to confound him, while structure helped him shape his days and function better. Whatever was said, it had a positive impact on our lives.

Within a few weeks Mom started dressing more appropriately, leaving the rain gear in the closet on sunny days and wearing shorts and short sleeves on hot days. Once she started painting again, and Dad went back to the hardware store, Jon and I relaxed a little.

Chapter 6

School started up again, and Jon and I were at our third elementary school. I was in second grade, and Jon was in fifth. A month or so after classes started, Dad stopped going to work at the hardware store again and started spending more and more time pacing through the apartment, talking to someone neither Jon nor I could see or hear. The discussions grew more heated as the days passed, and Dad would frighten us as he argued with his demons, repeatedly, and loudly, insisting that they leave him alone.

Mom, on the other hand, was actually doing pretty well. Her doctor had her on a new medication, and although it made her gain some weight, it seemed to leave her healthier than she'd been for a long time. She was painting steadily, and she started picking up dinner shifts at a Mexican restaurant nearby. She was bringing home money again, along with left over chips and burritos that Jon and I would take to school for lunch.

Mom was at work, and Jon and I were in our bedroom, trying to do homework while Dad was stomping around the apartment yelling that we had to hide. Suddenly, the door to our bedroom was thrown open, and Dad barged in.

"Come on," he shouted. "Come quick."

He grabbed my arm and pulled me off my bed, my schoolbook and papers flying off my lap.

"We have to get out of here. They're after us."

Jon's eyes widened. "Dad, calm down."

"Don't tell me to calm down," Dad shouted. "This is an emergency. We have to get out of here. NOW!"

Dad was dragging me out of the room. My feet went out from under me, and I slid on my side as he pulled me towards the living room.

"Help me Jon," I screamed.

Jon rushed over and tried to knock Dad's arm away from me to loosen his grip on my forearm. Dad lashed out with his other arm and knocked Jon away. Jon's legs went out from under him, and he crashed onto the floor. By the time Jon got back on his feet, Dad and I were out the front door. Jon ran after us.

"Get in, get in," Dad screamed as he pulled me to the car. I was screaming too, and Jon was yelling "Stop it," at the top of his lungs.

"Both of you get in. They're coming to get us. We have to get out of here now."

Jon could have made a run for it while Dad was struggling to shove me into the back seat. I would have, if I had been him. I would have run as fast and as far as I could have from Dad's maniacal delusions. But my loyal, protective, older brother didn't abandon me. He climbed in the back seat behind me and pulled me close.

Dad fired up the engine and peeled out of the parking lot in reverse. The tires shrieked as he slammed the car into drive while we were still backing onto the road. He floored the gas pedal, and we took off.

"They're after us, Jon, they're after us. You have to help us get away."

Jon must have realized arguing with Dad was futile, so he took the only other option available, and pretended to cooperate. "OK, Dad. What do you need me to do?"

"Keep a look out the back window. See if you can spot 'em while I try to lose 'em."

"OK, Dad."

Jon turned and knelt on the back seat, peering over the back dash and out the rear window. "I think it's clear, Dad. There's no one behind us."

"They're too crafty, son. They're still there. Keep looking."

I strapped on my seat belt, certain we were going to crash and gripped the armrest on my left hand. I was still crying, but more quietly now, more confident that Jon would be able to reach Dad and get us out of this nightmare. That confidence began leaking away as Dad sped up, blasted through stoplights, took turns without slowing down, while continuing to rant.

"They're after us," Dad yelled. "They're trying to catch us."

Jon was gripping the back of the seat, but was unable to hold on when Dad abruptly turned to the left. He fell towards me and landed partially sprawled on my lap. We both yelped in pain.

The noise distracted Dad for a moment. He looked into the rear-view

37

mirror and began yelling again when he realized Jon wasn't in position to watch for our tail.

"Get back up there, son. You can't quit. They'll get us if you do."

Dad turned his head to see if Jon was complying, and the car began veering to the right.

We screamed.

"Watch the road," Jon shouted.

Dad turned his head back and jerked the steering wheel to the left. We were inches away from sideswiping a minivan. Then suddenly we were racing into oncoming traffic. "Look out," Jon screamed again, as horns blared. The other driver swerved in time, somehow, missing us by inches. Dad corrected and swerved back into his lane. Jon slid down onto the seat beside me and belted himself in.

Flashing blue and red lights filled the car. "Oh shit," said Dad. "It's a trick. They've got the cops in on it now, too."

"No, Dad," Jon said. "I can hear them on my radio. They're here to help us. Pull over."

"It's a trick," Dad repeated and sped up again.

"I'll lose them at the light."

He raced towards the intersection, where the traffic light signaled red.

"They think I'm going to stop," Dad said and started to laugh.

"I'll show them."

The last thing I remember was Jon screaming "NOOO."

Chapter 7

I woke up in a strange white room with the worst headache I've ever had in my life. I stared at a ceiling, which was made out of acoustical tiles, like the ones in my school classroom. My nose was filled with the faint, but pungent odor of Lysol disinfectant, and I could hear muffled voices and footsteps beyond the room. Something nearby was humming, and something further away was beeping.

I tried to sit up, but couldn't lift my head off the pillow. My legs, back, shoulders, neck and arms all hurt, although not as much as my head. My left arm was immobile, swathed in hard bandages that turned out to be a cast. I moved my right arm, which was on top of what was either a thin cotton blanket or a thick bed sheet, and saw the white adhesive tape on the inside of my elbow. There was a plastic tube coming out of the tape.

'Maybe Dad was right,' I thought, and then I started to scream.

A woman wearing light blue pajama pants and a brown pajama shirt rushed into the room.

"It's OK, honey," she said. "What's wrong?"

There was so much that was wrong, I couldn't even think of where to begin. Finally, I croaked out a question. "Where am I?" I asked.

"You're in Cumberland Community Hospital," she replied.

"You were in a car accident."

I tried again to sit up, but the room started spinning when I attempted to lift my head off the pillow. "Where's Jon?"

"Your brother? He's back at home. He was released yesterday."

Jon had a broken arm, broken nose, two black eyes, a set of six Frankenstein stitches at his hairline and bruises all over the right side of his body.

Dad was bruised too, but God, apparently, was smiling down on him because although he was sore, he wasn't seriously injured.

A pickup truck that had had the right of way and was tooling through the intersection when Dad blasted through the red light had T-boned our car, crashing into the left-rear door .

The driver had slammed on his brakes, Jon said, which slowed him down a little, but not enough to miss nearly crushing me to death. I had been in a coma for three days, had a broken arm, three broken ribs and too many bruises and abrasions to count.

I didn't realize it at first, waking up in the hospital, that I had finally won the Band-Aid lottery.

Unfortunately, I was too disoriented and injured to care.

Nana and Mom both cried the first time they saw me after I woke up. Jon looked battered but relieved and filled me in on the accident and its aftermath.

The cop who'd been trying to pull Dad over was out of his car and nearly got scalded when the radiator of the pickup truck started spewing steam and water.

Dad tried to fight him and ended up in handcuffs.

Three ambulances arrived and whisked Jon, who was conscious and clearly injured; me, who was unconscious; and the unfortunate driver of the pickup off to the hospital.

Of the three, I was the most badly injured, followed by driver of the pickup, then Jon. I never learned the extent of the other driver's injuries, but I understand he was in the hospital nearly as long as I was.

"It was really cool," Jon said. "These two guys put me on a bed and wheeled me to the ambulance. I lay down in the back, and they were hauling ass with the sirens going, and the lights flashing all the way."

Sometime after Jon and I were rushed into emergency surgery, the cop who'd corralled Dad arrived to have him checked out before being taken to jail. The doctors, however, admitted him to the Behavioral Health Unit on a 72-hour hold.

Dad was still locked up in the unit, which explained why he wasn't visiting me, and was being treated for acute, paranoid schizophrenia. Mom was distraught, literally wringing her hands constantly when she was visiting me.

Granddad Swarthout came to see me every evening after closing the hardware store for the night.

He and Eileen, the woman he'd married after divorcing Grandmom, the one who insisted she was NOT anyone's grandma and wouldn't tolerate being called one, had brought me the new Teddy bear that I found on the bed beside me when I emerged from my coma.

Eileen came to see me nearly every afternoon and read me stories to help pass the time. I'd fall asleep to the sound of her voice and wake up later, wondering if I'd been dreaming or if she had really been there. Nana hung the Get Well Soon cards made by my third grade classmates on the wall where I could see them when the bed was cranked up so I could sit comfortably. Nana spent hours with me each day, alternating with Mom, who mumbled and muttered to herself most of the time.

As my headache began to gradually fade away and the dizziness disappeared, I started noticing the steady stream of nurses and aides who came into my room hourly to take my temperature, blood pressure and pulse, change my IV bags and give me foul tasting pills to swallow. They were efficient, sure of themselves and friendly. Everyone who came in would smile and ask me how I was feeling, and if I would like some juice to drink or help getting to the bathroom. Everyone wore what looked like cotton pajamas, so it took me a couple of days to figure out different people had different jobs.

It finally occurred to me that the nurses were the ones who would explain what they were doing and patiently answer any questions I came up with. The aides were less talkative and always came in wielding a wheeled device that they promptly plugged in and used to measure what they referred to as my vital signs.

Every morning, a doctor would arrive, and mumble "hmm" while he or she read the clipboard attached to the foot of my bed. Unlike the nurses and aides, they wore white coats over their regular clothes and usually had a stethoscope looped around their necks or hanging out of their coat pockets. Then they'd pull out a thin flashlight and crouch down while they shined it into my eyes. Then they'd "hmm" again, jot something down on the clipboard, and drift out.

I liked being in the hospital. People brought me meals on trays three times a day, and I got to eat in bed, although the food wasn't very tasty. A volunteer wearing a pink jacket came into my room with a box of toys and books and let me pick out one of each to keep.

Nurses constantly fussed over me, asking me if I was hungry or

thirsty, bringing me juice boxes and pudding cups whenever I asked
for them. There was even a button I could push if I wanted something
and nobody was in the room to help me get it. Between Nana, Eileen,
Granddad, Jon and Mom, I was rarely alone. And when I was, I slept,
watched TV, or tried to read even though it was hard to hold up a book.

Apparently, the hospital officials weren't in a hurry to release me. Dad
was in the hospital still, and the hospital administrators were reluctant to
send me home with Mom.

A woman wearing high heels and a black skirt with a white silk blouse
came into my room and introduced herself to me as my social worker.
She said her name was Mrs. something something, that she was from the
County office of something something, and was helping to put together my
release plan.

She asked me questions, about Mom, about Dad, about the accident,
about my schoolwork and about Jon. She asked about Nana, and about
Granddad, and if I had any other relatives living close by. She wrote down
my answers and left. Eventually, I guess after calls were made, conferences
were held and various relatives of mine interviewed, I went to Granddad's
and Eileen's to recover.

It was nice at Granddad's house. It wasn't as much fun as the hospital,
with my own TV, people coming and going constantly and with nurses
coming every time I pressed a buzzer. But it was quiet, much quieter than it
generally was at home, and comfortable.

I got to sleep in the big double bed in the guest room, on clean, fresh
sheets that Eileen changed every other day, whether I had spilled anything
on them or not. The guest room was in the front of the house, next to
the bathroom, and was pretty, with pale yellow walls and bright yellow
curtains.

Nana came over every morning to keep me company, help me put
together jigsaw puzzles, fetch me drinks and give me sponge baths. Eileen
would read to me after lunch, and Jon would come over after school with
my schoolwork assignments. Jon would do his homework while I labored
with mine.

When I had trouble with it, which was often, either Jon or Eileen
would help me out. Mom would drop in, although I never knew when

to expect her, or what kind of state she'd be in. When she wasn't there, I would miss her terribly. But often, she'd be agitated when she came, pacing around the room restlessly and mumbling to herself, or distant, ignoring me completely, or confused, and I'd wish she'd leave again. I missed Dad, too. Jon said Dad was still in the hospital and was expected to be there for a long time.

Sometimes, after we finished our homework, we'd write him letters and urge him to get well soon.

Despite Jon and Eileen's tutoring, by the time June came and I was well enough to return to school for the last week of class, my teacher told me I had missed so much school that she couldn't pass me into the fourth grade if I didn't attend summer school.

I was crushed by the idea of spending my summer vacation in the classroom, especially since I was finally healed enough to start playing outside again. Once summer school began, however, my disappointment disappeared.

There were only 15 kids in my summer school class and most of them were pretty nice. Everyone knew I had been in the car crash and nearly half of them had been in my third grade class and had sent me Get Well cards. The elementary school rumor mill had been working in overdrive in the aftermath of the accident, and apparently my classmates considered my survival to be somewhat miraculous.

For the first time since I had started school, I was not the daughter of those crazy people, but the subject of sympathy and fascination. I was the miracle girl who everyone wanted to play with at recess, and nobody made fun of me when I gave wrong answers to even the easy questions.

With a small class, the teacher was able to provide me with a lot of attention. I quickly caught up with my classmates, and, after a few weeks, zoomed ahead. Then I was in demand as a helper, and more popular than ever. When I finished my work, I would help my classmates with theirs.

I loved the feeling that came when something would click for a classmate, and they would suddenly understand what I had been showing them.

For the first time in my life, I felt proud of myself.

Summer school turned out to be a blessing for another reason. Mom had been clamoring for me to return home. Since I had recovered enough to return to school, there was really no physical reason for me to stay with Granddad and Eileen, although I would have preferred to live with them indefinitely.

Midway through the summer, I moved back in with Mom and Jon. Both were glad to have me back home. I had missed living with them, too, but had grown to love the calm regularity at Granddad and Eileen's. I was glad to escape the chaos that surrounded Mom for the four hours a day I was in school.

Chapter 8

Dad was still in the hospital, so Mom moved us again. This time, it was to a funky little cottage that smelled like mold and dirty old socks in a rundown part of town. Once again, Jon and I were the new kids at school, only this time we were going to separate schools. Jon was in seventh grade, in junior high, and I was in fourth.

Money was tighter than usual with Dad out of commission and unable to bring in a paycheck, and Mom could only afford a two-bedroom place. So once again, Jon and I were sharing a room. I didn't mind; in fact I was more comfortable when Jon and I were together. But Jon must have found it awkward since he was going through puberty. He started getting dressed and undressed in the bathroom.

Jon and I were both worried, because Mom didn't even bother to set up her easel after we moved in. She wasn't sleeping well at night and started keeping what Jon dubbed "vampire hours." I'd wake up during the night to the smell of smoke from her cigarettes and the sound of her rustling around the house. She'd usually be fast asleep in the morning, however, and we'd tiptoe around the house while getting ready for school. Not necessarily because we were trying to be considerate, but because she'd erupt into a screaming rage if anyone woke her up. The first time that happened, she screamed so loudly that my ears rang for hours afterward.

We spent as much time as possible away from the house, nervously waiting for the next crisis to erupt. And it did, just before Christmas, about three months after we moved in.

BRREEEEEE

The high-pitched squeal woke me and Jon up at the same time.

"What's that?" I asked, sitting up in bed as Jon jumped out of his.

"The fire detector," he said, racing to our closed bedroom door. He put his palms against the door and quickly pulled them away.

"It's hot," he exclaimed. "We've gotta get out of here."

I scrambled out of bed and collided with Jon as he ran towards me and I ran towards the door.

45

"Not that way," he yelled, grabbing my arm. "The window."

We struggled to slide open the window, but the aluminum frame was warped, and the glass wouldn't budge. I was starting to panic when Jon grabbed the desk chair and told me to stand back.

It took three swings before the glass broke, and two more to punch out an opening big enough to crawl through. Jon grabbed the blanket off his bed, threw it over the jagged glass at the bottom of the window and hefted me up. I balanced for a moment on my stomach on the sill, trying to pull my knees under me when Jon shoved my legs, and I tumbled out of the window and onto the ground behind the house. It took a moment to catch my breath, and I was just getting to my knees when Jon landed on me, knocking me back to the ground.

"Come on," he yelled. "We have to get Mom."

Jon grabbed my hand, and we ran on cold aching bare feet around the cottage to the front. The window of Mom's room glowed orange, and there was smoke billowing out the open front door. Mr. Anderson, who lived next door, stumbled out of the house with Mom draped over his shoulder. A second man ran over to help him, and the two carried Mom away from the house and laid her gently on the ground.

She lay still. One side of her nightgown was charred, exposing her leg.

"I've called 911," someone, who we later found was Mrs. Anderson, shouted.

The sirens reached my ears before anyone had a chance to reply. The wail grew louder and louder as the fire truck raced up the street, which had grown brighter with the flashing red lights. The truck pulled up in front of the house, and three men in yellow coats jumped out. One ran over to Mom.

The other two began pulling out hoses. Then one headed for the house while the other shouted out to the gathering crowd, asking "is there anyone inside?"

"We all got out," Jon answered, as we ran over to Mom.

"Stand back," said the fireman tending her. Mrs. Anderson came to our sides and gently led us away.

"Is she going to be OK?" I asked anxiously.

The fireman placed a clear plastic mask over Mom's face, and moments later she started coughing. The fireman helped prop her into a sitting position, keeping the mask on her face. She coughed again, pushed the mask away and vomited.

Blue pulsating lights joined the bright red ones illuminating the street as two police cars turned onto the block and screeched to a halt in the middle of the street. The cops jumped out and ordered everyone to clear way for the ambulance, which arrived moments later. Two men in blue uniforms loaded Mom onto a stretcher and wheeled her to the back of the ambulance. The wheels folded up as they pushed the stretcher inside.

One man jumped in the back with Mom. The other slammed the door shut, climbed into the driver's seat and blasted the siren as he drove off.

I was shivering, both with cold and fear. Jon was trembling beside me as we watched the ambulance's taillights disappear. Mrs. Anderson went inside her house and came out with two blankets.

She wrapped one around my shoulders.

Jon bundled himself up, and we sat on the curb across the street watching the fire. By then I was crying, and Jon freed an arm from his blanket and draped it over my shoulder, pulling me closer.

The fireman who had tended Mom walked over carrying a plastic box and crouched down in front of us.

"Are you OK?" he asked.

We nodded. "Is our Mom going to be OK?" Jon asked.

"Yeah," the fireman said. "She inhaled some smoke, and it looks like she's got a little burn on her leg, so they took her to the hospital to get her checked out. But she should be fine in a couple of days. Do you know if your Mom is taking any medications?"

"Yeah. She's got schizophrenia," Jon said, using a word I'd never heard before.

"Skinzo what?" I asked. They both ignored me. Jon told him the name of the pills she took, repeating the names twice as the fireman, who was obviously unfamiliar with them, wrote them down on a small notebook he pulled out of his pants pocket.

The fireman pulled a radio off his belt and spoke into it briefly. Turning his attention back to us, he told us he needed to monitor our vital signs.

The fireman noticed we were both bleeding, from numerous small cuts on our feet, hands and knees. In the cold and the excitement neither of us had noticed. The fireman carefully brushed little pieces of broken glass off our pajamas, and cleaned out all our cuts with something that made me wince when it was applied.

He put Band-Aids on several of the cuts, the larger ones, and taped several gauze pads on a long scratch on Jon's right arm. I thought about how I used to bandage Dad's woodworking cuts and wished the fireman had used the soothing gooey ointment I used to use on Dad instead of the stinging liquid from his kit.

It took about 25 minutes for the firefighters to put out the fire. Jon and I were still shivering under Mrs. Anderson's blankets. One of the cops put us in his patrol car, which had the engine running and thankfully, the heater on, to warm up. A white sedan, with a red stripe and fire department logo on the side pulled up and parked in the middle of the street next to the fire truck. A man in a blue uniform got out and started talking to the cops and one of the firemen. Someone pointed to us, and he walked over and tapped on the car window. Jon opened the door, and the man introduced himself as the fire chief and asked us if we knew what had happened.

Jon filled him in on our great escape and tried his best to answer the chief's questions.

"Does she smoke?"

"All the time," Jon replied. "Is that what started the fire?"

"Probably," the fireman said. "My guys say it looks like she fell asleep with a cigarette burning. It's a good thing you two got out in time."

I was yawning by then, and Jon asked if we could go back inside and back to bed. No way, we were told. The house was a total loss, uninhabitable, although we could see the back of the house was still standing. Someone from social services would be coming to take us somewhere for the night where we'd be safe.

Jon asked if he could go inside to get our clothes. The fireman shook his head and glanced back at his colleagues. They conferred, briefly, then walked towards the back of the house. A few minutes later two of the firefighters walked up. One was carrying a pair of Jon's shoes in one hand and a pair of mine in the other.

Tucked underneath his arm was my Teddy bear. The other followed, carrying a big, bulging bag that turned out to be a bunch of our clothes gathered loosely in my bedspread. I reached out for my Teddy bear and held it close against my chest. The fireman put my shoes on my feet, even though I was way too old to need any help. Jon pulled jeans on over his jammies, wriggled into his sweatshirt, then pawed through the pile for my clothes. He handed me sweatpants, then a shirt. I put them on over my pajamas. The cop came back to his car and sat down behind the wheel, talking to us quietly while we waited for the social worker to arrive.

We spent the night in a foster home, me sleeping on the lower berth of a bunk bed with two strange girls in the room. Jon slept on a fold out cot in a room with another boy. The foster mother who met us at the door was wearing a robe over her nightgown and didn't seem annoyed at being woken up in the middle of the night to welcome in two strange kids. She made us hot chocolate to drink, showed us where the bathroom was, found us clean pajamas to wear and put us to bed.

We both slept late. I woke up to an empty room, clutching my Teddy bear and didn't know where I was or why my hair smelled like smoke. Then I remembered and got up to look for Jon.

I found him in the kitchen, eating bacon and eggs. Marion, the nice woman who had taken us in, poured me a glass of orange juice and asked me how I liked my eggs. I could hear a washing machine and dryer rumbling in the room off the kitchen.

After cooking me breakfast, Marion dug through dresser drawers in both bedrooms and came up with some clean clothes for us to wear. Everything we had on and everything the firemen had rescued for us reeked from the smoke of the fire. Jon took a shower, while I lingered over the breakfast table. He emerged from the bathroom with wet hair and wearing baggy jeans and a T-shirt that was a little too tight. Marion drew a bath for me, put a bar of soap and bottle of shampoo on the rim of the tub and left me to soak in privacy. I peeled off my borrowed pajamas and climbed in.

Nana was sitting on Marion's couch next to Jon when I came out of the bathroom wearing a stranger's old clothes. She had her arm around Jon, who was leaning into her side. I ran over to Nana and climbed on her lap.

She hugged me with her other arm and kissed the top of my head.

Mom was asleep when we tiptoed into her hospital room. A nurse was there, scribbling on the clipboard at the foot of Mom's bed.

"She's sedated," the nurse said. "She probably won't wake up."

I hadn't wanted to come to the hospital. I was angry, furious, with Mom for starting the fire that could have killed us all. But when I saw her, I was overwhelmed with relief. I threw myself on the bed next to Mom. "Careful," both Nana and the nurse said at the same time. Somehow I had missed dislodging the clear plastic lines running into her nose, the second set running into her arm and brushing against her bandaged thigh. Mom's eyes fluttered, then opened. Her eyes were glazed, covered with a thin film. She blinked several times, then focused them on me.

"Ayla," she said, reaching to grip my forearm with her hand. "My baby. Oh, thank God you're here."

"Hi honey," Nana said. "Jon and I are here, too."

"Jondalar," Mom said. "Come closer so I can see you." Jon sat down on the side of her bed. Mom let go of my arm and reached out for Jon. She mumbled something, then fell back asleep. The three of us watched her chest move up and down for about 20 minutes. Then we quietly tip-toed out of the room.

Chapter 9

The stress of the fire must have triggered a breakdown in Mom. The doctors kept her sedated until the tubes bringing her oxygen and intravenous fluids were removed. Then an orderly wheeled her over to the locked ward, the Behavioral Health Unit, where the mental patients were housed, reuniting her with Dad, who had been there for the past seven weeks. Jon and I went home with Nana and stayed with her until first Dad, then Mom was deemed stable enough to be released, and they found a new place for us to live.

Nana lived in a small, two-bedroom house not far from the elementary school where Jon and I had gone to Kindergarten. She had sold the big house Mom and Uncle George had grown up in after Grampa died, about two years before I was born, and downsized to what she called her retirement home. The house was small, probably no more than 800 square feet in size, but it sat on a big, deep lot.

The house was set near the curb, so the front yard was tiny. The driveway to the left of the house ended at a one-car garage. There was a covered breezeway leading from the garage to the kitchen door. There was a 30 by 20 foot cement patio at the back of the house, and beyond the patio, was a yard at least a half acre in size. The area nearest to the house was planted with grass and framed with flower beds on two sides; the rear area was filled with trees.

Nana's bedroom overlooked the back yard, while the front bedroom, which faced the south, had been converted into her painting room. Instead of carpeting, which covered the floors in the hall, living room and Nana's room, the painting room was floored with linoleum.

A big easel was set up in the center of the room with a stool in front of it, while low shelves on two sides held art supplies. An old easy chair, with a faded cover splotched with paint, rested in one corner of the room.

When we were little and got to stay overnight at Nana's, Jon and I would sleep in the living room on the couch. Nana would place pillows on each end, and we'd sleep with our feet pointing towards each other.

But we were taller now, so for the first two nights, I slept alone on the couch, and Jon on a pallet of blankets and pillows on the floor.

Then Nana bought a blue foam chair that folded out into a single bed on the floor, and I started sleeping on it with her in her room, while Jon moved onto the couch.

We enrolled in school. I returned to my first elementary school, and Jon went to the junior high.

I knew most of the kids in my class, and Jon was reunited with a number of kids he'd known at elementary school. Unfortunately, our classmates remembered not only us, but our Mom, who had embarrassed us on several occasions when she came to pick us up from school or watch us in school plays. The kids also remembered Jon's unusual first name, and Jon said the teasing began almost immediately. It was tempered, however, by our new status as the kids whose house had burned down.

News of the fire had been reported in the local paper, and the story named both Mr. Anderson and Jon as heroes for rescuing Mom and myself from the blaze. While most of Jon's classmates viewed him with new respect, the urge to taunt him for his unusual name was too strong for some kids to resist.

Jon and I loved living at Nana's. She would make breakfast in the morning and serve dinner each night at six. She washed clothes on Wednesdays and Saturdays, so we never had to wear dirty socks two days in a row, or go to school without clean underwear on.

She'd remind us to brush our teeth before going to bed and would tuck me in every night at 8:45 and tell me she loved me before I went to sleep. They were simple things, things I do regularly for Kayla and Taylor, things they take for granted.

For Jon and me, who had only known chaos at home, they were tremendous. We were grateful for her care and tried to be helpful.

We would clear the table after meals, without being asked, and wash the dishes. We did our homework every evening and brought home excellent quiz scores that Nana hung proudly on the refrigerator door. Every Saturday morning, we'd help her clean house before going out to play. We keep the box next to the fireplace filled with wood and carried in the groceries when Nana returned from the store.

We kept quiet and tried not to interrupt Nana when she was painting, which wasn't hard at all, since we'd had so much practice around Mom, who tended to blow up angrily if we bugged her while she was working. And when Nana held painting classes, as she did occasionally on weekends to supplement her Social Security checks, we'd help set up easels and art supplies for her students, clear out of the house, then return after the students left and help put everything away.

I was happy at Nana's but I missed Mom and Dad. I suspect Jon did too, although he never talked about it. What I missed, I realized later, wasn't Mom and Dad as they were at the time, but a fantasy of Mom and Dad as healthy parents.

I would daydream about Mom and me cooking dinner together, shopping and her fixing my hair. I fantasized about Dad playing catch with us, taking us to the park and building furniture while I played in the sawdust and wood shavings.

We were too young to visit Mom and Dad in the hospital. You had to be at least 16. Nana went to see Mom at least once a week, bringing her the cookies she and I would bake together. Nana brought Mom pictures of us and the homemade cards we'd make. I suspect it was hard for Nana to visit Mom and see her in a locked ward. And I suspect, at least during her first few months in the hospital, Mom wasn't able to communicate very well with Nana. When we'd ask how Mom was and if she had any messages for us, the answer was the same, week after week. "Your mother's getting the best care available, and she loves you both very, very much," was Nana's reply.

Granddad also visited Dad regularly and would call us after some of his visits to tell us Dad had asked about us and sends his love. Both reports made us sad, because we knew that both Mom and Dad were too sick to really communicate with us through their parents.

Christmas came, and Mom and Dad were both still in the hospital. Granddad Swarthout came over on Christmas Eve with shiny, brand-new bicycles for us. Jon's was royal blue, and mine was fire engine red.

Nana read us "The Night Before Christmas." We decorated the sugar cookies she had baked earlier in the day and stuffed ourselves silly. We watched "The Grinch that Stole Christmas" on TV, then went to bed. When she tucked me in Nana asked me if I was having a good Christmas.

"It's the best one ever," I told her. "I hope Mom and Dad are having a good Christmas, too."

Chapter 10

School was out for the year and our other Grandmother, the one who lived in Idaho, came to visit for two weeks. She stayed in a motel, along with her new husband. Jon and I rode our bikes from Nana's house to see her and to swim in the motel pool.

Mom was still in the hospital, but Dad was living in a halfway house. He seemed happy to see us, when we went to visit him with Grandmom, but didn't have much to say. He wouldn't, or couldn't, meet our eyes and would smoke one cigarette after another. He seemed nervous and would rock back and forth in his chair. Grandmom would talk soothingly to Dad and ask Jon and me questions to try to draw us into the conversation. I was always glad when it was time to leave. I think we all were. Jon would be quiet, quieter than usual, after the visits, and I often saw Grandmom blot her eyes with a tissue as we headed out of the facility. I suspect she was relieved when her vacation ended, and she left Cumberland.

At the halfway house, Dad was being taught how to live with schizophrenia. His program included family therapy, so Granddad, Jon and I attended group counseling sessions with him twice a week. I thought the sessions were stupid; Jon and I knew more about living with a schizophrenic person than the therapist did. And it wasn't Granddad's fault Dad was sick, so it didn't seem fair that he had to give up his afternoons and listen to Dad talk about his childhood over and over again. So I think all three of us were dismayed when Dad's therapist asked us to stay after the family therapy session and attend support groups. Granddad was sent into a room with other adults, and Jon and I were herded into a room with seven other kids and an adult facilitator. Each of the other kids had a schizophrenic parent; Jon and I were the only ones with two, which made us initially the center of the facilitator's attention.

The support group Jon and I were in was also an educational program. The facilitator spent the first half of the session talking to us about schizophrenia. I was surprised to learn that Jon knew almost as much as the facilitator. He never talked about Mom or Dad's illnesses unless he had to, like when he told the fireman what medications Mom was taking. I don't remember what the facilitator's name was, but I do remember quite a bit of the information he gave us.

"Schizophrenia is a disease that affects the brain," he said. "It's an illness that affects someone's moods and behavior."

'Well, duh,' I thought. Probably every other kid in the room had the same reaction. But the eye rolling stopped when the facilitator continued.

"People don't get schizophrenia because they're bad people, or weak," he said. "They don't get it because their parents were mean. It's an illness, like cancer or diabetes. It's not a disease someone gets because they did something wrong, and it's not someone's fault that they got sick. They get it because there is a chemical imbalance in their brain.

"Schizophrenia is a chronic disease, meaning there isn't a cure for it," he continued. "But it can be controlled and treated with medication."

"My mom's on meds, and she's still crazy," a girl blurted out.

"We don't use the term crazy," the facilitator said. "We use words like sick, ill or diseased instead. Not all medications work the same with different patients. So sometimes it takes doctors a while to find out what medication works best for a patient."

During the first few support group meetings, Jon and I, as well as the other kids, squirmed uncomfortably while the facilitator talked to us about schizophrenia and explained that although our mother or father may be sick, it didn't mean that they didn't love us. We all squirmed more when the facilitator asked us how we felt about things. It was an awkward experience until one day, when the facilitator left the room to take "an important phone call," and we kids started talking about how much the support group sucked.

We were laughing at Ricky, one of the older kids, doing an impression of the facilitator. "It's OK to be sad," he mimicked, "when Mommy or Daddy is sick and can't take care of you.

"And it's OK to be sad when Daddy is talking to the aliens, and they tell him to take off all his clothes and go outside," he continued.

"Is it OK to be sad when your Mom wears a metal bowl on her head to keep the aliens from reading your mind?" Marcus asked with a smirk.

"Your mom does that too?" blurted out Ashley.

"It's like so embarrassing when that happens."

"My Dad wears a pith helmet lined with aluminum foil," Sean confessed. "He won't leave the house unless he's got it on. I pretend I don't know him when we're out in public."

We were trading stories and laughing, until the door opened and the facilitator returned. The room went quiet, and you could almost see the light bulb going off over his head. "I'll just leave you kids to talk among yourselves for a while," he said, and backed out of the room.

"My Dad thinks someone's out to get him," I ventured. "He's always talking to someone I can't see or hear."

"My Mom does that," Ricky said. "She's always arguing with what my sister calls her phantom."

Swapping stories, I found out that almost everyone's sick parents were chain smokers like Mom and Dad. And the parents that didn't drink endless cups of coffee guzzled cola day and night. "I've seen my Mom eat instant coffee right out of the jar," Sean said. "Yuck," everyone answered in unison.

"That's gross!"

"If you want gross, you ought to smell my Dad sometimes. When he gets paranoid, he won't take a shower for days," Robin volunteered. Jon and I looked at each other knowingly. "When that happens, I don't bring my friends over to play."

"You bring friends over?" three kids blurted out together. "That's brave," Marcus added. "I wouldn't dare bring anyone to my house 'cause I never know what my Mom might do. Besides, it's always a mess. She never cleans the house."

"People make fun of my Mom when she's sick," I volunteered. "She dresses up in weird clothes, and she'll cry when people tell jokes. When we're watching TV, she laughs at the sad parts."

For the first time, I was disappointed when the session ended, and it was time to go home. It was a relief to hear other kids talk about the same embarrassing things we were going through with our parents.

It was a relief to realize Jon and I weren't alone.

I started looking forward to meeting with the group, because it was the only time I could talk freely about Mom and Dad.

I didn't have to worry about anyone laughing at what I said, or recoiling in horror.

I learned Jon and I were lucky, even though both our parents were ill. We still lived with them most of the time, even though life with Mom and Dad was often chaotic and upsetting. Five of the other kids in our group lived in foster homes.

Sean and Casey O'Reilly, the two red-headed kids whose mother was in the residential home with Dad, lived in separate foster homes. The only times they saw each other were when they were visiting her or attending the kids meetings. They would sit together, sometimes leaning against each other, during the support group.

Casey would sometimes cry when her foster mother came to pick up her. Each time that happened, it made me realize how lucky I was to have my brother help me negotiate our lives.

Chapter 11

Mom was out of the hospital. Dad had been released from the halfway house and was attending an outpatient program five days a week. We were living in yet another apartment, and money was tight, as usual. Mom and Dad couldn't afford to buy another car to replace the one Dad wrecked during the great escape attempt that landed him in the hospital. I didn't realize it until later, but Dad wouldn't have been able to drive even if we had had a vehicle.

His license was revoked after the crash.

Jon and I had our bikes, but Mom and Dad had to walk everywhere, ride the bus, or talk either Nana or Granddad into driving them somewhere. For the first few weeks we were all back together under the same roof, I held my breath, waiting for the next upheaval to begin. Even when things were going relatively smoothly at home, minor problems could turn into major incidents when Mom and Dad were concerned.

The first incident arose near the end of the month. Mom and Dad had run out of cigarettes and cash. Nicotine withdrawals made Mom cranky and irritable. Dad became agitated when he didn't have his smokes and started ranting that "they" were conspiring against him. I tried to ignore them both and vowed, once again, never, ever to take up their filthy tobacco habit. I heard them flipping up the couch cushions, looking for coins, and pulling out drawers seeking any cash that may have been hidden.

Eventually, they decided to go out and see if they could find someone to bum a couple of smokes from.

Jon was at soccer practice, and with Mom and Dad out, I had the house to myself a rare and welcome situation. I turned on the radio, something I could rarely do when Mom was around because of her hypersensitivity to sound, and danced around the living room. Tonight, I was going to my first sixth grade dance, and I wanted to practice my moves before displaying them in public. I let the music wash over me and pretended I was dancing in the arms of Jordan Meyers, my latest crush.

The sound of the door opening knocked me out of my reverie.

I scrambled to turn the radio down before Mom started screeching, but relaxed when I saw my brother, rather than my parents standing in the entry.

"You're not going to believe what they're doing now," Jon said.

I was afraid to ask, but did anyway. "What?"

"Picking up cigarette butts off the street and smoking them," he said.

My stomach turned at the thought. Having grown up with two chain-smoking parents, I thought cigarettes were gross. But the thought of smoking a used butt that had been in someone else's mouth then tossed onto the filthy ground made me feel sick to my stomach. So did the smell of the old, half-smoked cigarettes Mom and Dad came home with an hour later. Mom was clutching a crumpled paper bag reeking of burnt tobacco. She dropped it onto the kitchen table, and Dad pulled a pack of cigarette papers out of his pocket.

"Wait," Jon said, and grabbed a grocery bag from the space between the refrigerator and the pantry. He ripped it apart and spread the rough paper on the kitchen table.

"Thanks, son," Dad said, and dumped the contents of the bag onto the paper before sitting down.

Mom sat down across from him, and they spent the next hour or so pulling the butts apart, piling the loose tobacco and rolling cigarettes. I left the house before either of them could light up one of their homemade smokes, but couldn't escape the smell entirely. The acrid odor of burnt tobacco was still permeating the air when I returned home hours later. Mortified that one of my classmates might have seen Mom or Dad scavenging for cigarette butts, I stayed home from the dance.

The second incident was far more serious.

Dad's outpatient program ended at 5 p.m., and the walk home generally took 15 to 20 minutes.

Sometimes Dad would stop to chat with one of his fellow patients along the way, so Jon and I weren't worried when 6 o'clock rolled around, and he still wasn't home. We called Mom to the table, and Jon, whose turn it was to cook that night, served up his trademark spaghetti. Mom kept mumbling throughout dinner, something about ants in the belfry and that vixen who was after her man, while she ate.

Dad still hadn't come home, and Jon and I were getting concerned. He sat on the kitchen counter while I was washing the dishes, musing our options out loud. Calls to the treatment center, where Dad's program was housed, revealed nothing. Dad had left as usual at 5 p.m., the receptionist told us. Jon paged Dad's social worker. Mom was pacing around the house, talking to herself. Jon and I tried, unsuccessfully, to do our homework, while we waited for the social worker to call.

It was after 8 p.m. when Mr. Edwards, Dad's social worker, returned our page. Jon filled him in on Dad's absence, and Mr. Edwards agreed to make some calls and see if he could find him. We waited another 90 minutes or so, with Mom becoming more and more agitated, for news.

Finally, Mr. Edwards called back to tell us Dad was in jail.

A clerk at the 7-Eleven store had called the police after he caught Dad trying to shoplift a pack of cigarettes. Dad had gotten combative with both the clerk and the cop who showed up to take him into custody. The cop ended up with a black eye, and Dad ended up in handcuffs.

We found out the next day that Dad's stint in the County Jail had been short lived. By midnight, he had been transferred to the hospital on a mental health hold. It would be another 72 hours before anyone in the family was allowed to visit him and another six weeks before Dad was well enough to be released.

Chapter 12

Jon had been in junior high school when he was in seventh grade. Now that I was in seventh grade, all the junior highs had become middle schools. So I was in middle school, and Jon was a sophomore in high school. He had been working at Granddad's hardware store all summer and was planning to work after school there as well.

Jon wanted to go to college, and he was saving as much money as he could towards that goal. Granddad supported his efforts and offered to match every two dollars Jon saved with one of his own.

I wanted to go to college, too, and asked Granddad for a job as well. He told me I was too young, but when I got into high school, if I still wanted to work at the hardware store, he'd give me a job and the same deal he gave Jon. Granddad also reminded both of us that childhood was a time for fun. Knowing Jon loved playing soccer, Granddad suggested he take some time off from work and try out for the school team. There was a girls' team at my middle school, so I tried out for it as well, wearing the new cleats and shin guards Granddad had bought me.

Jon landed a spot on the junior varsity, and I made the girls team, mainly because the coach was too kindhearted to cut any players. I had never played organized sports before and wasn't fully familiar with the rules of the game. I didn't run very fast, and I got winded easily. My biggest asset was that I had a lot of experience kicking soccer balls, as Jon and I used to practice a lot together both at the park and by blasting the ball against the rebound wall at the tennis courts.

I had strong legs, good leg coordination, and I liked to kick hard. I was also aggressive, especially when I got mad.

And it didn't take much to piss me off.

On the soccer field, I would challenge anyone for the ball, even the eighth graders who outweighed me by 20 or more pounds. I got knocked to the ground a lot, either tackled or shoved, and knocked down my fair share of other players. My teammates hated scrimmaging against me, but later on loved me when I was terrorizing opposing players with my fearlessness.

We practiced every day after school except Fridays. After three weeks of drills and scrimmages against each other, it was time for our first game of the season; and my first game ever. It was exciting, dressing up in my silky shorts and jersey for the first time. In my blue shorts, blue and white shirt and white knee socks, I looked like the other girls on the team.

I didn't feel like them, though.

Most of my teammates had been playing organized soccer since they were in Kindergarten, and they looked confident at practice and during warmups on the field before the game started. I had butterflies in my stomach and was worried that I was going to throw up.

I was relieved when the coach named the starting lineup, and I wasn't on it.

I spent the first half of the game on the sidelines, watching my fellow second stringers, trying to blend in, and hoping I wouldn't get into the game. When they would cheer, I would join in. When they moaned in dismay, I tried to look sad. I tried to watch the action, but found I couldn't concentrate on both the game and my teammates, so I focused on my bench mates and pretending I knew what was going on.

At halftime, I huddled with my teammates while the coach talked about strategy and what we needed to do to "put the ball in the net." Then the whistle blew, the starters ran onto the field, and I settled back down to watch. I was day-dreaming when the whistle blew again, and our coach ran onto the field to help one of our players up off the ground and to the sidelines. My teammates were screaming "foul, foul," so I joined them in bellowing out the phrase, although I wasn't sure who I was yelling at.

The coach pointed to me as he helped the starter to the bench and said "Ava, you're in for Serena."

I froze for a moment in disbelief, then raced onto the field.

The whistle blew again, and the game was on. I wasn't sure what position I was supposed to be playing, so I raced after the ball whenever it got anywhere near me. I found myself getting angry each time a player in red beat me to my target. When I finally got to the ball first, I blasted it as hard as I could towards the opponent's goal. It felt wonderful to release my frustrations on the ball, and I was basking, briefly, in the sensation when I heard my coach yelling "control Ava, control."

After that first kick, I wanted the ball more than ever.

Determined to have it, I shoved a girl out of the way when it was clear she was going to get to the ball before me. She hit the ground, a whistle blew, and every one of her teammates started yelling angrily at me.

One of the referees marched up to me, pulled a yellow card out of his shirt pocket and waved it in the air.

I didn't know what it meant, until the other team started yelling at me to get off the field. I thought my soccer career had ended for good, and I started crying as I made my way to the sidelines.

My coach put his arm over my shoulder and explained what I'd done wrong, and that I wasn't being banned from the sport for life. I had been given a warning, a yellow card, for rough play and would have to stay on the bench for at least five minutes. I took a seat, still sniffling and wiping my eyes. Three of the girls on the bench got up and walked over to me. One said "good hustle," another said "way to go" and the third told me she was glad I was on her team and not playing against her. I didn't get back into the game, which we lost 2 to 1. But I didn't care. I had survived my first soccer game, and my teammates didn't hate me. That mattered to me more than winning or losing.

Shortly after soccer season ended, Mom's doctor put her on a new medication. I didn't know it at the time, but I did notice the changes in Mom.

The clouds in her eyes seemed to be dissolving. When she was ill, her eyes turned dark and flat.

Now the darkness had faded, and her eyes were bright, clear and hazel colored. She started showering every morning and changing her clothes regularly.

Her speech improved immensely.

Instead of mumbling, Mom was speaking clearly and talking at a volume you didn't have to strain to hear.

She became less and less agitated as the days passed. Jon, who generally picked up Mom and Dad's medications at the pharmacy, filled me in on the medication switch when it had become apparent to both of us she was improving.

We were afraid to hope, but as the days went on without a psychotic break, we began to think maybe, just maybe, she was getting better. Nana, who watched Mom's changes warily, was "cautiously optimistic."

I adopted Nana's sentiment the afternoon that Mom wandered into the kitchen where I was fixing dinner and offered to help.

Two days later, I returned home from school to find Mom cleaning the living room. She had removed piles of clothes from the couch, emptied the always overflowing ashtrays and cleared stacks of books, papers, dishes and other debris from the furniture. She was dusting the newly exposed tabletops when I arrived and asked me if I knew where the vacuum cleaner was.

Less than a week later, Mom began sorting through her art supplies. The next day, she got Nana to drive her to the store and returned with blank canvases, new brushes and over a dozen tubes of paint.

Chapter 13

"**O**ur cousins are here! Our cousins are here!" I looked towards the house and saw a small girl running down the walkway in excitement. She turned her head towards the open front door, and repeated her refrain. "Our cousins are here!"

I was standing beside Grandmom's car, yawning and stretching out the kinks after the long drive when Katie, my 10-year-old cousin, burst out of the house. We, Grandmom, Jon and I, had made the six hour drive from Cumberland, Oregon, to Wilsonville in Washington State, where our Aunt Beth lived with her husband Ben and their three children. I had been apprehensive about the trip, having not seen Dad's sister and her family for several years. Jon had been reluctant to go, too, for a different reason. It required him to miss the start of summer school. Jon was determined to go to college and was in a hurry to get there. He wanted to accelerate his move through high school by taking classes in the summer and by taking as many advanced placement courses as he could handle.

Katie reached the car and skidded to a halt in front of me. "I'm Katie," she said. "You must be my cousin Ava. Do you want to come inside and see my room?"

Before I could answer, we were surrounded by people. Aunt Beth was hugging Grandmom, and our two other cousins, Billy, who was a year older than Jon, and Julie, who was two years older than me, welcomed us warmly, albeit a bit more sedately than their younger sister.

Grandmom had driven out from Idaho shortly after Jon and I got out of school for the year. She spent 10 days in Cumberland, staying in a motel, and visiting us.

Dad was back at home, spending most of his time smoking cigarettes, drinking coffee, rocking back and forth in his chair and wandering the neighborhood. The medication he had been taking since his latest hospitalization seemed to have worked for him. He had stopped talking to himself, which meant he was no longer arguing with the voices in his head. He was showering regularly and spending more time in the living room than the bedroom during the day. In fact, Dad felt so much better that he decided he was cured.

Granddad, Jon and probably his doctor as well, tried to convince him otherwise, but Dad decided he didn't need to take his pills any more.

Within four days, the decline in his mental state was evident; within two weeks, he began arguing with his phantoms again. Grandmom, who had been planning to drive north to visit Aunt Beth after seeing us, decided it was high time Jon and I got to spend some time with the rest of our family. Jon and I reckoned she wanted to get us away from our crazy parents for a while.

Jon was afraid Dad would continue to deteriorate if he wasn't home to keep an eye on him. I was anxious about being around Dad as he headed for another full psychotic break, and my anxiety outweighed my apprehension about the trip. Granddad, Grandmom and I argued with Jon until he agreed to go as well.

What finally swayed him was the fact that Mom was doing a lot better. While she still matched Dad in his excessive smoking and coffee swilling habits, she spent a lot of time painting which generally meant she was feeling pretty good.

Mom promised Jon she'd look after Dad and told him he had nothing to worry about while she was in charge. We both knew that when it came to our parents, we always had something to worry about, but Jon decided to take her at her word and here we were in a new state, preparing to spend the summer in the home of relatives we barely knew.

Billy hoisted our bags out of the trunk, and he, Jon and Julie carried them into the house.

Grandmom was installed in the guest room, and Jon was staying in Billy's room and I was staying with Julie in her room. I hadn't anticipated how much fun I would have at the Johnsons'.

Uncle Ben was at work all day, so I didn't get to see him as much as I did Aunt Beth and my cousins. Aunt Beth was a schoolteacher, so she had the summer off. She relished her summer vacation as much as we kids did.

Billy said she spent her summers serving as the Johnson family activity director, planning fun things to do and driving her kids to various games and activities. Katie was taking swimming lessons, and Billy played baseball in a summer league. Julie was on a girls' softball team. Aunt Beth would drive my cousins, their friends and any neighbor kids that needed a ride to the pool, practice fields and ball games.

I imagine it was a challenge to add entertaining her mother and two additional kids, but she embraced her expanded activity director role with enthusiasm. I could tell she enjoyed Grandmom's visit, because they spent hours together, talking, going for walks, shopping, or preparing meals and snacks for a houseful of hungry kids. Sometimes I would eavesdrop on them when they were talking, hoping to hear something about Dad.

Other times, I would sit with them and look closely at both women, trying to see Dad's features in their faces. Aunt Beth shared his blue eyes, auburn hair and the shape of his nose. Dad had inherited Grandmom's height — she was 6-feet tall, and he was 6-feet, four-inches with a slim frame.

When I was with them, I would pretend Aunt Beth was my mother and would edge closer and closer to her until she draped an arm across my shoulder or pulled me in her lap. Grandmom was also affectionate, and if Aunt Beth wasn't sitting down, I'd lean on her and bask in Grandmom's love.

Jon and Billy got along great and spent most of their time together. Billy, who was going to be a senior in high school in the fall, had his driver's license and would borrow Uncle Ben's car most nights.

He and Jon would disappear, going to movies, concerts and parties with Billy's friends. I was so busy playing with Katie and hanging out with Julie and her friends that I barely missed him. Each day was an adventure.

At 13, I was a little too old to play outside with Katie, but I often did anyway. We would play hopscotch on the front walkway with her friends from the neighborhood for hours at a time. We would climb the big pine tree in the back yard, and come down with our fingers, palms and clothes sticky with pine sap.

We played foursquare, hide-and-seek and kick the can with the kids from up the block. It rained one afternoon, so we made forts out of the furniture and couch cushions in the family room and played with her Barbies. I felt self-conscious, sometimes, playing with Katie, but mostly I just enjoyed myself. I knew these games were too childish for a teenager and pretended I was playing them for Katie's sake, not my own. The reality, however, was they gave me a delicious taste of the childhood I'd largely missed out on.

I looked up to Julie and loved spending time with her as well. She seemed to like having me hang out with her, and took it upon herself to introduce me to teenage fashions. I had never given any thought to fashion before, as most of my clothes had come from second-hand stores or were hand-me-downs from Jon. The idea that clothes could be more than just something practical was a revelation to me. So was makeup. Julie taught me how to paint my fingernails and put on makeup, makeup I had to wash off before Aunt Beth or Uncle Ben spotted me.

She went through her closet and dresser drawers, pulling out clothes she had outgrown and showed me how to put different items together to make an outfit. We went together to the beauty parlor for haircuts, which was another first for me as Nana had always cut my hair. Julie and the hairdresser consulted together for quite some time before Julie allowed the woman to cut my hair. When I looked in the mirror after the towels were removed from my shoulders, I didn't recognize myself for a minute. I'd transformed from a little girl to a teenager over the course of a 20-minute haircut.

Before I knew it, it was mid-August and two weeks before the start of school. Grandmom had gone back to Idaho, so Granddad and Eileen drove up to retrieve Jon and me. They spent two nights in a hotel, visiting the house during the day and taking everyone out to dinner both nights. On the third morning, Jon and I loaded our belongings into the trunk of Granddad's car and said our good-byes.

Between hand-me-downs and Aunt Beth's generosity, both Jon and I had twice as many things to take home as we had had when we arrived. Uncle Ben gave Jon his old Army duffel bag, and Billy gave me one of his old backpacks so we could finish packing up our clothes. Uncle Ben had said good-bye to Jon and me the night before, as he had to be at work early on the day of our departure.

Julie, Katie, Billy and Aunt Beth hugged us all—me, Jon, Granddad and Eileen—in the front room of the house, then followed us out to the car. Jon was stoic and climbed into the back seat after a second round of hugs.

69

I started to cry when Aunt Beth hugged me and was still weeping when I got into the car. Katie started crying, too, and Julie, Billy and Aunt Beth all looked sad.

"We'll miss you," said Aunt Beth, with her arm around Katie.

"See you next year," Billy said.

"Write me," Julie said.

I nodded, Granddad started the car, and we pulled away from the curb. I turned in my seat and waved until we turned the corner.

Chapter 14

Despite Mom's assurances, Dad had landed back into the hospital by mid-August. He had started refusing to take his medication before we left, insisting he didn't need it anymore. By midsummer, however, Mom said he was convinced the doctor was trying to poison him. Without the drugs, his psychosis returned, along with his paranoia. A waitress at a nearby coffee shop had called the police when Dad began knocking dishes off diners' tables and screaming. Mom didn't elaborate, but I suspect that Dad fought with the cops when they came, because I saw a court summons on the kitchen counter.

Mom, on the other hand, was still doing well overall. The living room was full of paintings; floral scenes, landscapes and forests. She had shifted from oils to watercolor while we were gone, and her paintings were brighter and sunnier than before. The house was cleaner than it had ever been when we arrived, and there was food in the refrigerator and a plate of homemade cookies on the counter. I was startled, both by how comfortable and inviting our house seemed, and by Mom's weight gain.

She had put on at least 30 pounds while we were away and was wearing one of Dad's shirts and a wraparound skirt. When she hugged me, I could feel how big she'd gotten. Nana, who called us weekly when we were in Washington, had told us that one of the side effects of Mom's medication was making her fat and warned us not to call attention to it.

"She's very sensitive about her weight," Nana said.

Another side effect of her medication was dry mouth, and Mom was constantly sipping soda or water to try to alleviate the discomfort. When she wasn't sipping, she was sucking on lifesavers or other hard candies. She was annoyed with the dry mouth but distressed about her weight. So distressed, in fact, she often threatened to stop taking her meds. Jon and I lived in fear she'd live up to her threat and constantly reassured her that she was more beautiful than she'd ever been and that her weight didn't matter.

Unfortunately, we were wrong. Mom's weight did matter, and her chronic dry mouth turned into a constant thirst. She began drinking so much water that she had to pee all the time and was reluctant to leave the house unless she was going somewhere that she knew had a bathroom handy. She got tired easily, and her painting production slowed down, which wasn't necessarily a bad thing as she had so many paintings stacked up in the living room you could barely walk without knocking into one. A few days before Halloween, Nana took her to the doctor, who ran some tests and diagnosed diabetes. I was irate when I heard the news.

"That's just not fair," I railed "She already has schizophrenia. It's just so not fair."

Mom took the diagnosis with much more grace and acceptance than I did. She stopped drinking soda and learned how to prick her finger and test her blood sugar levels. She met with someone at the hospital twice a week for the next three months to learn how to manage the disease. She taped a chart listing what she could and couldn't eat onto the refrigerator and, next to it, taped a schedule of when she had to eat, medicate and exercise. She took the pills her doctor prescribed her to boost her insulin levels faithfully and vowed to do whatever she could do to prevent having to take insulin injections.

She even started exercising for the first time in my memory, walking around the block every morning and again in the evening.

In some ways, getting diabetes was good for Mom.

It forced her to focus on her health and structure her days. She had to test her blood at regular intervals, eat at specific times, take pills -- insulin and anti-psychotics -- every morning and evening, and exercise. She had a schedule to follow, which helped her mentally as well as physically. I had been worried that the stress of her new illness would send her into a breakdown. Thankfully, I was wrong.

By spring, Dad was back home, and Mom was painting up a storm. She was excited about her work and would call Nana each time she finished a painting and invite her over to see it. Nana was impressed with Mom's watercolors. She had produced a series of flower gardens, full of bright colors; deep greens, brilliant blossoms and lovely blue skies.

Her new works were soothing to look at. She painted a half-dozen or more landscapes, in a style that was partially realistic and partially not.

The images were slightly blurred, which made the scenes look soft and inviting. The longer you looked at them, the more you saw; details that were almost hidden would catch your eyes as you moved closer and farther away from the paintings.

When Mom had finished 20 paintings, she and Nana carefully selected 10 of them, loaded them into the back of Nana's car and went to the Cumberland Gallery, one of three local galleries that displayed and sold Nana's work. The gallery had also carried Mom's work in the past, when she had been well enough to paint. Mom was hoping the owners would let her sell her paintings there again, and she was very nervous about how they would react to her new medium.

Mom was ecstatic when they returned to the house. Tom and Marianne, the gallery owners, loved her work. They not only wanted to hang it in their gallery; they wanted to host a show for Mom.

Nana and Mom were giddy with excitement and danced around the room while they told me what Tom and Marianne had said. "They want at least six more paintings," Mom said. "I've got to get to work."

The show was scheduled for late March, two months away. Mom finished 12 paintings and was agonizing which ones to include and which ones to not. She and Nana brought them all to the gallery and managed to convince Tom to expand the show to include all her new works.

Mom went to and from the gallery almost daily to help with the prepa–rations for the show. Tom photographed her paintings and put together a brochure. Marianne had postcards printed, with one of Mom's landscapes on the front, and information about the show on the back.

Mom and Nana spent hours addressing the cards to everyone they could think of, as well as to everyone who had ever signed one the gallery's mailing list. I went with them one afternoon and went through three and a half rolls of stamps getting the cards ready to mail.

I was proud of Mom and caught up in the excitement. At the same time, I was a little nervous about all the attention she was getting. I was in eight grade, after all, and already embarrassed about everything, my skin, my clothes, my hair, speaking up in class or having any attention directed my way.

I was mortified when I learned the name of the show: Back from the

Brink. Marianne had chosen the name to remind art lovers that Mom was back at work following a serious illness. That mortification was nothing compared to how I felt after a reporter from the Cumberland Weekly came to the house and interviewed Mom about her art, her life, her family and her health. The following week there was a picture of Mom at her easel on the front cover of the paper, along with a headline reading "Healing Arts: Local Woman Paints Her Way Back from Mental Illness." The newspaper was distributed free from racks in front of every grocery store, shopping center, clothing store and movie theater in town.

Everywhere I went for the next week, I saw Mom's picture and that ugly headline. I was sure people were staring at me, having noticed my resemblance to Mom or recognized our last name and were wondering if I was crazy, too. The day after the paper came out, I told Mom I had an earache and refused to go to school.

I couldn't hide in my room forever, so I returned to school the following day, hoping against hope that none of my classmates had seen the article. I knew from social studies class that most kids only read the newspaper when it was assigned, so there was a chance nobody knew I was the daughter of a crazy woman. Those hopes were dashed when I was walking to second period, and Ronnie Jenkins, a boy from my math class, came up to me in the hall and asked if I was looney like my mom.

I slugged him in the jaw so hard that my hand ached, and he dropped to the ground like he'd had his legs cut out from beneath him. I could hear kids chanting "fight, fight, fight" while I kicked him as he covered his face and head with his arms and tried to roll away. Someone, a teacher, grabbed me from behind in a bear hug and pulled me away.

I was hauled off to the vice principal's office, where I was lectured, reprimanded and told I had anger issues. I managed to keep my mouth shut for once, and not say what I was thinking, which was 'if you had parents like mine you'd have fucking anger issues too.'

I was suspended for five days, threatened with expulsion and sent home in disgrace. The vice principal ordered me to attend the school district's anger management program and told Granddad, the only relative with a car who was available that morning to pick me up, that I would be on probation until the end of the school year. I was glad soccer was over for the year, because I was prohibited from any extra-curricular activities while on probation.

The anger management program met twice a week at the school district headquarters downtown.

I had to take the bus there after school Tuesdays and Thursdays and spend two hours in a stuffy classroom with 10 to 12 other young hot heads learning how to control our tempers.

The instructor of the "damn right I'm pissed" classes, as I called them, irritated the hell out of me, because she didn't seem to have any insight as to why her students were so angry.

At our first class, we all had to introduce ourselves and tell everyone why we were there. Jim was a high school senior who had been sentenced to a semester of anger management after his third suspension for blowing up at his teachers. Shad, a shy seventh grader, was ordered to come by a juvenile court judge, because he'd been caught throwing river rocks at windows and had smashed 14 of them.

Karen, a freshman in high school, was signed up by her parents, who she fought with regularly. It didn't take me long to figure out everyone in the class had bigger, more serious problems than the ones that prompted some authority figure to force them to enroll. And it didn't take me long to figure out that the class wasn't going to help any of us.

After our introductions, the teacher passed out a handout listing seven tips. After each tip there was space for us to fill out how we could have used each tip to control our tempers in recent situations.

I interpreted the assignment differently and described why each tip wouldn't have worked when Ronnie asked me if I was crazy like my mother. Counting to 10 before reacting, like Tip 1 recommended, would have answered Ronnie's question in the affirmative.

Only a lunatic would have responded that way to such an insulting question that dissed my Mom in front of an audience of our schoolmates.

Take a break from the person you're angry with would have given Ronnie a green light to keep hassling me.

Walking away from an insult like that would have guaranteed Ronnie would keep mouthing off.

Get some exercise? Well, I did just that. Kick boxing is a sport, and that's essentially what I did to Ronnie. Think carefully before you speak.

That tip I had followed.

I didn't say a word before I slugged Ronnie in the face. Identify solutions to the situation. I did that too. I seriously doubt Ronnie will ever come near me again, let along taunt me. Use "I" statements to describe how you feel. I wrote, "I think Ronnie Jenkins is an asshole."

The teacher wasn't pleased with my answers, nor anyone else's for that matter. She told us all we were a bunch of smart alecs, which I guess proved she had her anger under management.

I knew she really meant we were a bunch of smart asses, another "well, duh" observation. Still, she was determined to work with us and spent the rest of the class giving us tips like "whistle a happy tune to turn around your mood" and "when life gives you lemons, make lemonade."

We were instructed to "take a deep breath," before reacting to anything unpleasant, and if we were really angry, to "find a safe spot away from everyone and yell out our ire."

We were told to talk to a parent, counselor or other trusted adult about our issues, advice that was pretty much worthless to me. My parents had been in and out of mental hospitals for years, and my school counselor had conspired with the asshole that was requiring me to waste time in this stupid class. The only trusted adults I knew were Granddad, Eileen and Nana, and they all knew all about my parents' problems, so I didn't think there was anything I could talk to them about that would be news to them. The only tidbit of advice that did make sense was to buy a punching bag and take your anger out on it, or throw a tennis ball against a wall as hard as you could, for as long as you needed to.

Jon and I had already figured out our own version of that tip, which is one reason we both liked playing soccer and both spent so much time practicing our kicks against the rebound wall at the park.

We were also instructed to keep a log of things that made us angry. I skipped that assignment because I didn't want or need any reminders about what pissed me off.

I was given an incomplete for not turning in my log and threatened with having to repeat the class unless I complied. So I made up a series of incidents, not getting invited to a school dance, missing my favorite TV show, breaking out with pimples and getting a B+ on my essay paper when I knew I deserved an A.

I guessed, correctly, as it turned out, that the teacher wasn't going to actually read our logs, so I added attending the stupid anger management class as well.

Despite my gripes, the class wasn't entirely useless. I got to know some of my fellow students and realize I wasn't the only kid with serious problems.

Jim, for example, had an alcoholic father who tried to choke him to death one night when he left a bowl of tuna fish on the counter instead of putting it back into the refrigerator. Shad's parents had both died in a car crash two years earlier, and he was living in his fifth foster home. Karen had been molested by her stepfather.

In an odd way, it was comforting to know I wasn't the only kid with serious problems. I felt sorry for the other kids, but it was nice to know I wasn't alone in struggling to cope with situations kids shouldn't have to face.

Chapter 15

Granddad kept his word and right after I started ninth grade, he gave me a job at the hardware store. At first, it was just half days Saturday and Sunday, so I could adjust to high school and try out for the girls' junior varsity soccer team.

I made the squad as a starter and when the fall sports season ended, I began working at the store after school Tuesday and Thursday afternoons as well. Granddad believed in starting new employees out at the bottom. For the first couple of months, the only thing he had me do was to dust the store shelves and sweep and mop the floors, both throughout the store and upstairs. There were four small apartments above the hardware store and one of my jobs was to sweep and mop the hallway and empty the trash. Like Jon, Dad, and even Granddad had to do way back when his father owned the stores, I had to prove myself before I was given any responsibility.

When my first payday arrived, Granddad presented me with an envelope with my name showing through a rectangular opening and told me he was proud that I was doing such a good job. I tore it open and pulled out my paycheck gleefully. Later, at break time, Granddad and I walked down the block to cash it. I opened a savings account, my college fund, and deposited $150, getting $27.85 back in cash. Granddad matched it, 50 cents to each dollar, like he had been doing for Jon, and my account swelled to $225. I was thrilled and started daydreaming about the classes I'd take and the sophisticated friends I'd make when I went off to the university.

Mom was still painting, still taking her meds and still monitoring her blood sugar regularly. She had lost some weight, although she was still heavy, but hadn't had a psychotic episode in nearly two years.

She seemed happy.

She had sold five paintings during her first show, and that spurred her to keep painting and working hard to stay healthy. Dad had been back home since midsummer and was going to an outpatient clinic five days a week. A van would pick him up weekday mornings before Jon and I left for Cumberland High School and would deliver him back home in the late afternoon. Dad seemed befuddled and was easily confused, but he hadn't had a psychotic break since he'd been home which was a blessing.

Jon was a senior, taking three advanced placement classes, and practically counting the days until graduation. I was so worried about being home alone with Mom and Dad that I made Jon promise not to abandon me. I knew he was eager to leave home, but he agreed to stay and to do his first two years at Cumberland Community College.

"If you go to summer school and graduate early we can go to the university together," he told me.

We worked together, lived together and attended the same school. So I was the first one to realize Jon was slipping away. It was subtle at first. Jon had decided not to play soccer, saying he'd been on the varsity team for two years and didn't have anything left to prove. Then slowly, Jon's eyes lost their sparkle. If you didn't know him well, like I did, you might not notice. But the bright light that seemed to emanate from my brother's eyes was dimming. He was quieter than normal, talking less and with less enthusiasm.

At home, he would stay up in his room for hours at a time, listing to music and, I assumed, studying. I worried a little, but was so busy with work, where I'd been promoted to stock clerk, and school I didn't give it as much thought as I should have.

I'm sure I was in denial, a trait that I probably inherited from Dad, who always pretended there was nothing wrong with Mom when there clearly was. So I was shocked when our first quarter report cards came out in mid-November. Jon, who had been an honor student in junior and senior high, brought home the first D of his academic career. Actually, it was two Ds, one in calculus, the other in chemistry. Jon got a C in French, another in history, and an incomplete in PE. Jon told Granddad he was just having a bad case of senioritis, and that he'd buckle down again and bring his grades back up. I didn't believe him, and I don't think Granddad did either.

Jon wouldn't let Granddad, or Nana, take him to the doctor. He also wouldn't talk about his schoolwork or what was bugging him. He stopped hanging out with the few friends he had and started skipping work. He would rarely talk to me anymore, which distressed me greatly. So I was surprised one evening, a few days before Christmas, when he came into my room to confide in me. He told me he was scared.

"I've been hearing voices," he told me.

"I think they're in my head because nobody else seems to hear them. And they scare me."

"What do they say?" I asked fearfully, sure the answer wouldn't be good. It wasn't.

"Bad things," Jon said. "Very bad things. The voices say they want me to die. They keep telling me to kill myself."

I felt like the floor had dropped out from underneath me. Once, when I was flying to Tucson, the plane hit some turbulence and suddenly dropped down several feet. I had a plastic cup full of soda in my hand and had just lifted it off the tray table. Suddenly, I was holding it up over my head, as my hand held steady while the rest of me plummeted with the plane. I was hit with a sense of deja vu when that happened, because it reminded me vividly how I felt when Jon told me he had lost the genetic lottery and inherited the disease that had consumed our father, the illness that our mother fought daily to control. When I caught my breath, I tried to speak, but could only cry. Jon started crying too.

"Help me Ava," he whispered. "Help me make the voices stop."

I called Granddad. Jon was still crying when Granddad arrived. Dad looked confused, he wasn't sure what was going on. Mom was anxious, wringing her hands and pacing around the house. I was hugging Jon, holding him close, and he was literally crying on my shoulder. His head was drooped, and I could feel his warm tears soaking through my blouse.

"Granddad's here," I told him.

"We're going to take you to the hospital."

I thought we were heading to the emergency room, but Granddad pulled up in front of the Behavioral Health Unit; a place where Mom and Dad had been so many times. He must have called ahead, because two men dressed in matching pale blue scrubs came out immediately and helped lead Jon into the building.

They whisked him through the double glass doors and across the lobby. A woman behind a reception counter pressed a buzzer, and a door leading into the main part of the facility opened up.

80

The two half led, half carried Jon through the door. I could hear Jon crying as the automatic doors shut behind them.

I sat down on a chair in the waiting room, while Granddad talked to the receptionist. After a few minutes, he sat down next to me, holding a clipboard in one hand and a pen in the other. He was still filling out the forms when a bell rang, and I saw Mom and Nana standing outside the glass entry doors.

"They're with us," Granddad said, and the receptionist buzzed them in.

Mom, Nana and I sat there weeping, while Granddad struggled with the forms and tried unsuccessfully to comfort us. Finally, a man in a white coat came out and introduced himself as a doctor.

"What happened tonight?" he asked, the first of many questions that couldn't ever be really answered. I described what Jon had told me, and he nodded.

"Has he ever displayed symptoms like this before?"

"Not really," I replied. "But he's been acting funny for a while."

The doctor blanched when I told him, in response to his question about family illnesses, that both our mother and father were schizophrenic. Mom, Nana and Granddad all met his eyes and nodded sadly. Mom told him what medication she was taking, what Dad was supposed to be taking but rarely did and answered a number of other questions about her and Dad's illnesses. I zoned out mentally, suddenly so exhausted I could no longer think. Finally, the doctor thanked us all, said Jon had been sedated and was being kept overnight for evaluation.

"Call me in 24 hours for an update," he told us.

"Go home now and get some rest."

It was a bleak Christmas. Jon remained in the hospital for 10 days. He was heavily sedated and could barely speak when Mom and I went to visit him every afternoon. I was too young to visit, but Mom and I lied and told everyone I was 16 so they let me in to see Jon. He met with a psychiatrist every morning, we were told, and was being given an anti-psychotic drug, in conjunction with a powerful tranquilizer in an effort to stabilize his symptoms.

Five days after he was admitted, the doctor we had met on that first, horrible night told us Jon had been diagnosed as a paranoid schizophrenic. I demonstrated what I thought was tremendous restraint and didn't say either 'duh' or 'what took you so long to figure that out.' Instead, I nodded, and asked what Jon's prognosis was, not really expecting an answer. I got one, sort of a non-answer.

"We don't know yet," the doctor said. "It's too early to tell."

I returned to school after the winter break like a sleepwalker. It was difficult to concentrate on my classes when my world, my beloved older brother, my best friend and protector, was disintegrating.

It was even harder to care about my classmates concerns and gossip. Whether or not the Cumberland High School basketball team made the playoffs, or if some senior dumped his girlfriend for some freshman just didn't matter to me. I snapped at people more easily than usual. After a few weeks my few friends, mostly soccer teammates from junior high school, stopped defending me when other kids wanted to know "what's wrong with her?"

It was worse after Jon was released from the hospital.

He spent his days in bed, either sleeping or staring at the ceiling.

Mom would sit with him in his room for hours to keep him company. He mostly ignored her. Nana came by the house every afternoon to visit and help keep our household running. Three times a week she drove Jon to his appointments; to see his psychiatrist and attend group therapy sessions. Once a week, Mom, Dad and I went with Jon to family therapy, where even I knew more than the therapist about schizophrenia.

Finally, I begged Granddad to let me work more days at the hardware store, so I had a legitimate excuse not to participate. After he agreed, on the condition I keep my grades up, I threw myself into my studies to avoid having to think about what Jon was going through and about how terrified I was that I would become schizophrenic, too.

By late spring, Jon began recovering enough, or became used to his medication enough, to get out of bed most days. He still wasn't well enough to return to school, and his concentration was so poor he couldn't even read more than a page or two of anything at a time. He spent most of his time watching TV, while I spent most of my time at home watching him for signs of recovery or relapse.

Chapter 16

Summer came, and I signed up for summer school. Going away to college took on greater urgency in my mind, and I wanted to get through high school as quickly as possible. It sure didn't look like Jon would ever make it to college, and I was afraid the family disease would claim me, too. If I was to be cursed, like the rest of my family, with schizophrenia, I wanted to experience as much of life as I could before my mind was taken.

From mid-June to the second week in August, I went to class every weekday morning, to work at Granddad's store every afternoon, and to Nana's for dinner every night.

She'd be coming home from my house about the time I'd arrive, having helped fix the family dinner, taken Jon for one of his appointments, or consoled Mom about Jon's condition. After dinner, I'd do my homework until Nana was ready to drive me home.

Granddad insisted I take weekends off from work, so Saturday I'd usually ride my bike to the library and read until my eyes were blurry.

Sundays I'd go for long bike rides exploring the countryside, stopping sometimes along the river to wade and watch the water rush by.

We had all hoped Jon would be well enough to return to school in the fall. Instead, he retreated even more into lethargy.

I started my sophomore year, while Jon continued his decline. He wasn't eating much and had lost weight. His skin was pale, from staying inside so much and his muscles slack from a lack of exercise. His hair was limp and long, because he refused to have it cut. It was often greasy, because Jon rarely washed it anymore.

I made the soccer team again and got called up the varsity squad midway through the season when several girls went down with injuries. I took 10 weeks off from work to concentrate on soccer and schoolwork, then returned to my job at the hardware store.

Granddad let me work three afternoons a week, instead of just two, and my college fund account was growing steadily.

On the afternoons I wasn't working, I'd study in the library to avoid going home and seeing the stranger that had been my brother.

Mom wasn't painting much, but I knew she was still taking her medications, as I was the one who went to the pharmacy to pick them up, now that Jon wasn't capable of doing it anymore. Jon was either taking his meds, or flushing pills down the toilet daily, because I had to pick up refills for him, too, each month. Dad was still going to the outpatient clinic five days a week. I was trying to stay as busy as I could to avoid thinking about my family, but it didn't stop me from worrying constantly that one of them would have a relapse.

When it did come, it started slowly. In February, Jon started waking up from his stupor. He still wasn't talking much, but he seemed a little more energetic. His appetite returned, and he started eating regular meals again. A week or two later, he walked to the store with Mom. After that, he began venturing out of the house, although no one was sure where he was going or what he was doing.

Foolishly, I let myself become optimistic. 'Jon was getting better,' I thought. 'Maybe the medication was working.'

I was partially right, and way wrong.

Jon's changes were due to medication, but not in a good way. He wasn't taking his meds anymore. The upside to that, as far as Jon was concerned, was that the side effects that kept him lethargic and apathetic disappeared. They were replaced by a return of his demons; the voices that only Jon could hear; the voices that told him he was worthless, stupid and would be better off dead.

Somehow Jon managed to fool, not only me and the rest of the family, but his psychiatrist as well. He told everyone he was doing great, absolutely great, and feeling better than he had for months. He started disappearing from the house for hours at a time. When asked, he'd say he had been going for a walk, or looking for a job. In reality, he'd been hanging out in the homeless encampments down by the river, trading his prescription tranquilizers and anti-psychotic medication for marijuana.

I suppose Jon started smoking pot to try to quiet the voices in his head. And it may have worked, temporarily, because once Jon started, he wanted to smoke it all the time. In the long run, however, it was one of the worst things he could have been doing.

I learned later how dangerous marijuana is for schizophrenics.

While smoking pot won't make someone schizophrenic, it generally does make a schizophrenic person more ill. And it certainly had that affect on Jon. In March, he started talking back to the voices in his head.

A few weeks later, he began accusing Mom and Dad of using radio waves to control his thoughts. That was followed by a period of time when he stopped eating again, claiming we were trying to poison him, but he was too smart to let that happen.

Jon stopped going to his appointments, saying the doctor's office was bugged. I called his doctor several times and pleaded in vain for him to help Jon. To my distress, the doctor said there was nothing he could do. Jon had turned 18 in January and was legally able to make his own decisions regarding his medical care.

"Unless he becomes a threat to himself or others, there's nothing anyone can do," the doctor told me. I slammed down the phone and cried with frustration.

Easter vacation was in early April that year, and I was exhausted from school, work, household responsibilities and worrying. Granddad offered to let me work more hours during my vacation, but I turned him down, even though I would have loved to earn some extra cash.

I planned to sleep late all week and get up only in time to go to work in the mid-afternoon. For the first few days, I'd wake up at 6:15 a.m., the time I normally got up for school. Then I'd remember I was on vacation and would roll over and go back to sleep until 10, 11 or even noon when I'd finally get up. So I was still in dreamland, late that Thursday morning, when Jon had a full-blown psychotic episode.

I woke to a loud thump, followed by a crash. I heard another crash as I was sitting up. It sounded like my soccer team was practicing in Jon's room, which was next to mine, and kicking furniture instead of soccer balls. It was Jon, in a frenzy, tearing through his belongings looking for the bugs.

"I know they're here. I know they're here," I heard Jon screaming.

"Nobody spies on me and gets away with it."

"Stop it," I heard my mother yell.

"They're spying on me," Jon screamed. "They planted devices in my room, and they're reading my mind."

"No, Jon, stop," Mom yelled.

I heard her footsteps pounding down the hall and jumped out of bed.

I ran to the door of my room and flung it open just was Mom was opening the door to Jon's. A book flew out of the door at her, dropping behind her in the hall. It was followed by another that smacked Mom in the stomach and doubled her up with pain. She screamed and tried to scramble away as Jon kept hurtling books in her direction. I grabbed her arm and half led, half dragged her into the front of the house. Dad was nowhere in sight, and I hoped he was somewhere safe.

"Come on Mom, we have to get out of here," I pleaded. I threw open the front door and ran out. I raced to the house next door and pounded on their door shouting

"Brent, Val, I need your phone. It's Ava from next door, and it's an emergency."

The door opened, and my neighbor handed me his cordless phone. My hands were trembling so much it was hard to punch in the number. Mom was behind me on their porch, trembling and crying. It rang once, twice, three times, and I was just about to hit end and try again when I heard a voice.

"9-1-1, what's your emergency?"

"My brother is a schizophrenic, and he's having a psychotic breakdown,"I said, trying to speak slowly and calmly even though I was trembling violently.

"He's going berserk, and he needs to be restrained before he hurts himself or someone else."

Chapter 17

"**M**iss, miss, you need to get up. We're at the end of the line."
I woke up from a deep sleep and saw the bus driver standing in the aisle next to my seat.

"We're in Portland, ma'am," he said.

"The bus will be heading back south in a few minutes. Isn't this your stop?"

I staggered to my feet, groggy from napping on the bus.

"Thanks," I mumbled. The driver reached up and pulled my backpack down from the overhead rack.

"Do you have any other luggage?" he asked.

"Just this," I replied, leaning down and dragging my small red duffel bag out from below the seat.

I stumbled off the bus and looked around to get my bearings. It was misting and chilly. I zipped my coat up and walked into the Greyhound Terminal looking for the ladies' room. After washing my face and combing the tangles out of my hair, I took a deep breath and gazed at my reflection in the piece of polished metal that hung on the wall over the sink and served as a mirror.

My eyes were still red from crying, and the skin below my eyes still puffy. I soaked a paper towel in cold water and held it over them for a few minutes. When the towel began to feel warm, I tossed it in the trashcan, washed my face again and patted it dry, trying not to irritate my eyes any further.

Then I shouldered my backpack, the one Billy had given me at the end of that wonderful summer in Washington, picked up my duffel bag and went to find someone who could tell me what city bus I needed and where to catch it.

It took me about 45 minutes to get to Uncle George's house. His car, a minivan that looked like it belonged to a carpool driving mom, not a bachelor musician, was gone, and nobody answered the door when I knocked, so I settled down on his porch to wait.

I shrugged off my backpack and leaned it against the wall. I pulled a paperback book out of my duffel bag, then tucked my bag behind the backpack. Leaning against the backpack, I opened the book and prepared to wait for who knows how long.

The sun was a lot lower when Uncle George, King George, came home with a woman I'd never met before and found me sleeping on his porch with my book on my lap.

"Ava," he exclaimed. "What in the world are you doing here?"

I burst into tears.

"Jon's in the mental hospital," I blurted out.

"He's crazy, like Dad. I just can't take it anymore."

"Well, come on in then," George said calmly.

George's companion, who he introduced as Tiffany, made tea while I cried and tried to tell George about Jon's breakdown. He held me, awkwardly, in a hug and kept mumbling "It's OK, Ava."It wasn't, and we both knew it, but I let him try to soothe me.

Tiffany poured us herb tea after I finally stopped crying.

"It's chamomile," she said. "It will help you relax."

She took off shortly after we finished drinking, and Uncle George carried my backpack into his extra bedroom. The room was filled with guitars and musical equipment; I counted six acoustic and two electric guitars, three amps and two folded up music stands leaning in a corner. There were coils of thick black cords on the floor, an elaborate stereo system on a bookshelf along with hundreds of CD cases and stereo speakers mounted high up on the wall.

There was a love seat along the wall opposite the bookshelf and several hard-backed chairs in the middle of the room. Posters of musicians, guitars and a snowboarder soaring in the air above a half pipe were tacked up on the walls.

"This folds out into a bed," George said, gesturing to the love seat, which held a skateboard and a basketball.

"Let's make some room."

I dragged the chairs, one at a time, into the living room, while George moved things out of the way. Three of the guitars he carried into the living room, along with the skateboard. The others he lined up along the wall.

He shoved two of the amps into the closet, along with the cords and the basketball. I helped him scoop up the soda cans and papers littering the floor. George flipped the cushions off the love seat and pulled out the bed.

"Here you go," he said. "Welcome home."

One of the reasons, the main reason actually, I'd come to Uncle George's was because he was so calm and undemanding. I had considered, briefly, calling my grandmother in Idaho, or Aunt Beth, and asking if I could come stay with them. I didn't, though, because I knew that both would be overly concerned about me and would flood me with attention and questions.

I just wanted to escape from Cumberland, from Jon's breakdown, from Mom and Dad and from schizophrenia, both physically and mentally. I was so emotionally depleted that I wasn't even ready to take measure of what I thought or how I felt, let alone talk about it.

So I came to Uncle George's.

I knew he wouldn't pressure me to talk about anything until I was ready to. And I knew that when I was ready, he'd be the best person to talk to.

My uncle was the least judgmental person I'd ever known. I could tell him anything, about anyone, and he would just nod and take it in without feeling the need to analyze what I'd said.

My uncle was also very much a live-and-let-live kind of guy. I know he wouldn't mind me showing up unannounced, like I did.

I wondered though, as I flopped down on the foldout bed in my new, temporary home, if he was worried about how long I'd stay. As if he knew what I was thinking, I heard his voice from the other room.

"Hey Mom, it's me. Ava's here."

"Oh about like you'd expect, really bummed about Jon."

"No, no, physically she's fine. What about you?"

"Wow, Mom, I'm sorry to hear that. Are you gonna be OK?"

"Oh good. How's Lisa?"

"Oh man, I'm glad I'm in Portland and not Cumberland. No wonder Ava bailed."

"No, she's taking a nap. I can tell her to call you when she gets up if you want."

"I don't know, as long as she wants to. Days, weeks, months, years, I don't care. It'll be nice to have a housemate for a change."

"OK Mom."

"I love you too. I'll talk to you later."

Chapter 18

I was exhausted, depressed and spent most of the first week at Uncle George's sleeping 12 to14 hours a day. When I was awake, and when George was home, we'd listen to music, chat, eat and go for walks. Uncle George loved to hike, and when he had time, we'd go to one of his favorite city, state or national parks and wander the trails. When he didn't have much time, we'd walk around his neighborhood so he could stay in shape; good hiking trim as he put it. Whatever you wanted to call it, it felt good.

I liked the way my body relaxed when I went for a walk, and I really liked the way a long, challenging hike would leave me pleasantly tired. We went on a 12-mile hike the second week I was there that left my legs wobbly, my feet sore and my mind temporarily at ease.

Like most musicians, my uncle was a night owl, leaving the house around seven most evenings to play lead guitar with one of his bands in one of the many clubs in Portland and returning home in the wee hours of the morning. He played regularly with two bands and filled in every few weeks with a third. He was in demand and sometimes had to turn down gigs because he was already booked, or he wanted a night off.

George also worked as a studio musician and would get called for what he referred to as commercial jobs, playing jingles and background music for radio and television shows and ads. In addition to his career, my uncle had an active social life, with so many women calling and dropping by the house I stopped trying to remember their names after the first week.

The first four days I was there, however, Uncle George stayed home in the evenings. His band mates called several times a day, trying to talk him into joining them for gigs. Finally, I told him I didn't need a babysitter.

"I'm 15 for Christ's sakes. I've been taking care of Mom, Dad and Jon for the past year and certainly can to take care of myself for a few hours."

I could tell by his expression, he felt like he should be arguing with me, but after a few minutes a look of relief crossed his face, and he smiled and said "OK."

I talked to Nana on the phone almost every day and called Granddad at least twice a week. But I wasn't ready to talk to my parents or Jon, who was still in the hospital. I changed the subject when Nana or Granddad tried to talk about them and eventually they got the hint. I could tell they were both worried about Jon and about me. Nana asked me several times if I was getting enough to eat and if George was taking good care of me. I thought her questions were kind of funny, since I had been taking care of myself and my family back in Cumberland for the past year.

"That's just her way of letting you know she cares," George told me when I told him what she'd said.

"Besides, she's a mom. She can't help herself."

Granddad asked me a number of questions about my uncle, trying to gauge whether or not he was a suitable guardian. He also told me several times that if I wanted to come back to Cumberland, I could stay with him and Eileen. Eventually, when it became obvious to all of us that I wasn't going to return to Cumberland anytime soon, both Granddad and Nana began urging me to enroll in a high school near Uncle George's house. By then, I had missed nearly six weeks of school and was afraid I'd have to repeat my sophomore year.

One of George's girlfriends suggested I get my GED instead, saying she'd gotten her diploma by passing a test instead of finishing high school.

It turned out that you had to be 18 to take the GED, and at 15, I was way to young. I was disappointed and about to hang up when the man on the other end of the phone said there was another program available that I might be interested in. It turned out the Adult Ed school also offered a high school diploma program where students could earn the high school credits they needed to graduate.

Like the GED program, it was designed for people over the age of 18, although there were exceptions that would allow younger people to enroll. I could qualify if my school counselor would contact them and recommend me for the program. When I told him I had dropped out when I moved to Portland, he suggested I schedule an appointment with a program adviser and explain my situation and request admission.

My adviser was a serious woman in her mid-20s who looked like she'd never smiled in her life and wasn't likely to start smiling anytime before the turn of the century. She made me fill out several forms and sign a waiver authorizing the Adult Ed school to request and receive my transcripts from Cumberland High School. The forms were a little confusing, and the woman looked so formidable that I was afraid to ask her for assistance. Fortunately, Uncle George had come to the appointment with me, and he helped me figure out what to write on what line and which boxes to check.

Once the uptight adviser was satisfied all the blanks were successfully filled in, she asked me why I had dropped out of school. I wasn't sure how to answer her and made a couple of false starts.

"I didn't mean to. It just happened. I had to leave Cumberland because my brother, uh. I moved in with my uncle and, uh."

George came to my rescue.

"My niece came to live with me because of a difficult home situation. Both her parents have serious health problems and were unable to provide a stable environment for Ava."

I thought he had come up with a good answer and was impressed by his ability to sound so formal and adult, but the adviser wasn't satisfied, and she wanted more information. It pissed me off to have her ask for details, but once again George intervened before I said something that would have certainly not helped my case.

"My sister and her husband are both disabled due to acute schizophrenia, and my niece was forced to leave home suddenly when things there became extremely chaotic."

"I see. And are you her legal guardian?"

"Yes," George lied.

"Why haven't you enrolled her in high school?"

"We thought that things would settle down back at home, and that she'd be with me only temporarily. But it looks like she'll be here for some time, and since she's missed so much school this semester, we both thought the high school diploma program would be the best option for her."

"I see."

"Especially since she's eager to get into college. We thought this program might speed things along for her."

"I see."

I was starting to wonder if I that unsmiling woman was actually a robot, and her voice box had gotten stuck on "I see" when she finally decided to let me enroll in the program.

"First you'll need to schedule an appointment for an assessment. This is an individualized program designed to meet the specific needs of each student, and we need to know where you fit before you start."

"OK," I said. "Can I schedule an appointment now?"

"You need to talk to someone in the counseling department."

"I see," I said sarcastically. George elbowed me and asked where the counseling department was.

"Geez, what an uptight bitch," I said as we walked down the hall to make my assessment appointment.

"I hope my instructors aren't anything like her."

Two weeks later, after my grades from Cumberland High had arrived, and I'd completed my assessment, I started classes.

I introduced myself to my teacher and new classmates as Caitlin. I'd been thinking about changing my name ever since I'd fled from home. I wanted to distance myself from my past. Since I was starting a new life in a new city, I figured it was a good time to try out a new identity.

I picked Caitlin for no real reason other than the fact that I had always liked the name. Uncle George called me Caitlin when he could remember, but often slipped back to Ava.

Granddad and Nana didn't even try.

I still wasn't talking to my parents or Jon, but I knew Mom especially wouldn't be pleased with the change and would be calling me either Ayla or Ava forever.

The adult education school was way different than high school. Instead of five classes each semester, each class met for three hours a week, once a week, for eight weeks. That sounded like a light schedule to me, until I learned that you had to do about 12 hours of homework each week for each class. There was a learning center at the school where you could work on your homework, or you could take it home with you and do it there. I liked working at the learning center because there were tutors available who would help me when I got stuck and because it was easier to work there than at home.

At home, there were too many temptations, TV, music, video games, hanging out.

At the learning center, there wasn't much else to do but study.

At the end of each course you had to take a test. If you passed, you were awarded 2.5 high school credits. If you flunked, you got zip and had to take the class over again. I wanted to start with three classes, but my counselor said it would be best to begin with just one or two.

I signed up for English and American history and planned to take geometry and biology after I passed the first two courses.

I was the youngest person in the program and probably the most determined. I checked out my textbooks as soon as I enrolled and had already skimmed through the first three chapters in both books by the time school started. Once school began, I started my homework as soon as class ended, and when I would finish, I would read ahead in the textbooks and take the practice quizzes at the end of each chapter or section.

Shortly after I started school, Uncle George helped me get a part-time job at a coffee house managed by one of his girlfriends, and I learned how to make lattes, cappuccinos, mochas and other fancy, overpriced coffee drinks. There, too, I was the youngest, although no one knew it.

Uncle George and I had both lied and told my new boss I was 16, the same age of two of my co-workers.

I thought it was fun working at the coffee house and especially liked bantering with my co-workers and chatting with customers.

I'd come home with my clothes and hair reeking of coffee and a pocketful of coins representing my share of the tips customers dropped into the jar on the counter by the cash register.

My co-workers would cash in their coins for bills after the tips were divvied up, but I liked to feel the weight of the coins in my pocket. Between class, work and hanging out with Uncle George when we were both at home, I was starting to relax and enjoy myself.

I stopped worrying constantly about Jon and wondering if Mom and Dad were taking their meds and doing OK and started having fun.

George had taught me and Jon to skateboard years ago, and although I wasn't that good at it, I loved the sensation of gliding on four wheels. Sometimes we'd drive to the skate park, and after I got tired of skating, well, tired of wiping out, I'd use Uncle George's video camera and film him while he rode. We'd watch those videos sometimes for hours, with George constantly stopping and freezing the action with the remote to show me how maneuvers and tricks were done.

George and I were watching the Seattle Mariners play the Boston Red Sox on TV when the phone rang.

For the first time in weeks, I didn't feel a jolt of fear, a jolt of adrenaline with the ring in anticipation of bad news.

George picked up the cordless phone and said "hello," while I watched the Mariners' pitcher walk the bases loaded.

"Hi Mom," I heard him say, as he walked out of the room to avoid competing with the television.

His expression was pained when he came back into the living room, holding the phone in his right hand

"It's your Nana," he said. "She wants to talk to you."

"What's wrong?" I asked.

"It's Jon. He's in the hospital."

Chapter 19

J on had tried to kill himself by overdosing on tranquilizers. Apparently he had been squirreling away his pills instead of taking them as directed and swallowed his stash one morning when he thought he had enough for a lethal dose. Mom heard a loud thump coming from his room when he either collapsed or fell off the bed and found him unconscious on the floor.

When she couldn't wake him up, she called 911.

Paramedics rushed Jon to the hospital's emergency room, where doctors pumped his stomach in time to save his life and, I believe, gave him something to counteract the sedatives in his bloodstream.

Nana was a little unclear on the details, but the upshot was once Jon's life was out of immediate danger, he was wheeled across the parking lot from the ER to the Behavioral Health Unit and admitted on a 72-hour hold. Nana said he was asking for me and urged me to come back to Cumberland and see him.

I was shocked, scared and then angry.

Shocked because I had finally pushed my family's mental problems into the back of my mind, and Jon's suicide attempt brought them rushing back in a most unwelcome manner.

I was scared, because Jon could have easily died, and because I knew he was smart enough that if he wanted to try it again he would probably succeed.

Then I was just angry; angry at Jon for putting everyone through this trauma; angry at whatever unfair force had inflicted a horrible mental illness on my brother and angry because I once again had to face my family's problems. I was angry, too, that I'd have to miss work and school, to go back home, and I was even angry at Nana for asking me to.

I didn't see any need to rush to Jon's bedside, because in my experience, when it came to someone in my family, a 72 hour hold translated to at least two months in the hospital and usually more. Nana was insistent, however, so I agreed, reluctantly, to come the next day, mainly just to get her off the phone so I could swear loudly and repeatedly without her paying long distance charges to listen to my temper tantrum.

George dropped me off at the bus depot the following morning, and Nana was waiting at the bus stop in downtown Cumberland when I arrived. We got in her car, and before she started the engine, she turned to me and said it was really Mom and Dad who were asking for me, and not Jon.

"They need you Ava," she said. "They're devastated."

I was upset, too, and wasn't sure I could take on the extra burden of my parents' emotions. I didn't have much time to brace myself for what was waiting at home, since Mom and Dad were living less than a mile from the depot.

Mom was watching for us and ran out of the house when she saw Nana's car pull up to the curb. She wrapped her arms around me in a bear hug when I got out of the car, before I even had time to close the car door, and told me over and over and over how glad she was to see me.

After what seemed like hours, but was probably less than three minutes, Mom let go, and the three of us went inside the house.

The TV was on, but Dad was gone, out collecting bottles and cans to cash in at the recycling center, something he did when he either ran out of cigarettes or was upset. Mom wept as she told me what had happened, how frightened she was when she found Jon and how guilty she felt for not being a good mother.

"Forgive me, Ava," she said. "Please forgive me for being so sick when you were growing up."

Before I could answer, Mom started crying harder and turned to Nana.

"Oh Mom," she said. "I'm so sorry for everything I put you through. I had no idea how horrible it is to have a mentally ill child."

Mom and Dad had been to see Jon earlier, going into his room one at a time because the psychiatric hospital prohibited multiple visitors during a patient's first 72 hours. Jon was sedated, she said and very groggy. Nonetheless, Mom urged me to go and see Jon. "He needs you, Ava," Mom said.

"He loves you more than anyone, and it would do him a world of good for you to visit."

I didn't think Jon was anxiously awaiting me, or that visiting him would have much of an impact, especially if he was still sedated. I wanted to see him for my sake, to see that he was still alive, but I was scared that he would be psychotic and impossible to communicate with.

I also bristled at Mom's exhortations. I felt like she was putting a lot of pressure on me, relying on me to snap Jon out of his suicidal depression, and it pissed me off.

I was seething while Nana drove me to the hospital. Mom stayed home to wait for Dad to come back from his scavenging. Nana offered to wait in the parking lot, but I had no idea how long I'd be, and she looked exhausted. I told her to go home, and that I'd ride the bus back to her house after I saw Jon. She put up a brief argument before she agreed and drove off.

I took a deep breath, walked up to the front doors and rang the buzzer. When a disembodied voice came out of the speaker next to the door, I gave my name and said I was there to visit my brother Jon Swarthout. Half a minute later, there was a buzz, and I pushed open the door and walked into the waiting room. The man behind the reception counter was typing on a keyboard, and I waited for several minutes until he stopped and looked up. He asked me my name, even though I knew he had been the one who buzzed me in, and why I was there.

He told me to take a seat and wait while he called the doctor to authorize my visit and picked up the phone. I heard his one-sided monologue, realized he was talking to an answering machine and looked around for a comfortable seat in case I was in for a long wait.

Glancing around the room, I saw I wasn't the only visitor awaiting to see a patient.

There was a guy about Jon's age, sitting on one of the padded chairs against the wall. He had blonde hair, a short but scruffy beard and the saddest look on his face I'd ever seen. He was staring down at the floor in front of his feet.

His eyes were glazed, with shock, sadness and worry. It was an expression I was all too familiar with from too many trips to the emergency room with Mom, Dad and Jon; the look of a relative who doesn't know if their loved one will live or die.

I don't know what possessed me.

I was near that glazed look myself and wanted to retreat into my own head until it was time to see Jon.

Something about his expression touched me, and, perhaps the memory of all those children of schizophrenic support group sessions I had attended made me walk over and sit down in the chair next to him. As soon as I opened my mouth, I realized I had an intense need to share what I was going through with another human being.

"My brother's in there," I said, gesturing to the door next to the reception counter. "He's schizophrenic, and he tried to kill himself yesterday."

The boy, the young man, looked up and turned his gaze towards me. His blue eyes were red rimmed, and his expression weary. "My best friend tried to kill himself," he said. "We're roommates, and I came home last night and found him in the bathtub with blood everywhere. It was horrible."

A tear rolled down his cheek. "He's my best friend," he repeated, as he wiped his face with his sleeve. "He slashed his wrists with a razor blade. I thought he was dead when I found him."

I reached over and put my hand on his shoulder. "My brother ate a bunch of pills," I said softly.

"My mom thought he was dead when she found him."

"We grew up together," he said.

"I don't know what to say to him when they let me see him."

"I don't know what to say to my brother either," I said. "He's been psychotic for a couple of years now. I moved to Portland a couple of months ago to get away from him."

We talked until my last name was called.

"I'm Caitlin," I said as I got up.

"I'm Jason," he said. "Thanks for talking to me."

Jason was still sitting in the same chair when I came out after a frustrating 30 minute visit with my brother. Jon had been sedated and wasn't interested in talking. I could tell he was angry, but didn't know if he was mad at me or at the fact he was in a locked mental ward. He wouldn't meet my eyes and wouldn't reply to any of my questions.

I gave him a rambling monologue, telling him about my life in

100

Portland and finally gave up and left, wiping tears from my eyes.

"You still waiting to see your friend?" I asked Jason as I walked into the waiting room.

"No," he said. "I'm waiting for you. Alex won't see me. He told one of the aides to tell me he's pissed that I called 911 and didn't let him die."

"That's totally harsh," I said. "My brother wouldn't talk to me. I almost wish he had refused to see me."

"That sucks," Jason said. "Do you want to, like, go somewhere and get some coffee and talk?"

I wanted to go home to Nana's, lay down on her couch and pull a blanket over my head.

"Sure," I said, surprising myself again.

"That sounds good."

We walked to a coffee shop a block and a half away from the hospital. There was a cafeteria in the main hospital building, but I figured it would be crowded and noisy, so I steered Jason to *The Ugly Mug* instead. I called Nana from the pay phone to let her know what I was doing so she wouldn't worry while Jason ordered us coffee and snacks.

We sipped our steaming drinks. "Not bad," I said. "Almost as good as the coffee we make where I work."

Jason asked me about my job, and I told him how Uncle George had helped me get hired and how I was being trained to be a "barista."

"That's just a fancy name for someone who makes fancy and expensive coffee drinks," I added.

I asked Jason if he was working.

"Not right now," he replied. "I worked all summer as a busboy at a Mexican restaurant in Salem, but I quit when I came to Cumberland at the end of August to start school."

Jason told me he and Alex had moved to Cumberland together so they could go to CCC, which everyone in town called Cumberland Community College. It was the same school Jon had agreed to attend instead of Oregon State University, which was his first choice, after I talked him into staying home so I wouldn't be alone with Mom and Dad. Jon and Jason might have been classmates, I mused, if things had turned out differently for Jon.

Jason asked me about my brother.

I told him how close Jon and I had been growing up, and how Jon was best big brother a girl could ever dream of. I told him how everything had changed when Jon got sick and choked up a little when I described Jon's first two psychotic breaks. Jason reached across the table and took my hand.

"I'm so sorry," he said quietly. "That must have been horrible."

"It was totally fucked," I said, wiping my eyes with a paper napkin. "I couldn't believe it was happening."

I asked Jason about Alex, and he told me how they had met in preschool when they were just three or four years old.

"We became friends, probably because we both liked to play with the same toys. There was a fire engine there that you could sit on and push around with your feet. That was our favorite thing to do, and we'd play with it for hours."

Unlike most kids with a favorite toy, Jason said he and Alex would take turns riding the truck.

Whoever wasn't on the truck got to wear the plastic fireman's helmet and wave the plastic ax around, Jason said with a smile.

Jason and Alex lived a block away from each other and went to all the same schools together.

"We were in the same classes all the way through elementary school," Jason said. "We took a bunch of the same classes together in junior high and high school, too. He's been my best friend forever."

Having switched schools so often during my childhood, I was astonished. I couldn't think of any classmate I'd known continuously since Kindergarten. When Jason asked who was my best friend growing up I had to admit we moved around so much that I didn't have one, unless I counted my brother.

"Wow. I lived in the same house all my life until I came here, unless you count all the nights I spent at Alex's house over the years."

Jason wanted to know why our family had moved so often. Normally, I would have given a vague answer, but since I figured I'd be going back to Portland in a few days and wouldn't see Jason again I was honest. "We were really poor, and my parents were both in and out of mental hospitals," I said.

"Oh man, that really sucks," he said, reaching for my hand again. "Are your folks OK now?"

I shrugged.

"My Mom's doing pretty good, at least she was until Jon tried to off himself, but my Dad's kind of fried."

I halfway expected the news about my parents would scare Jason off, and he'd rush out of *The Ugly Mug* as soon as he finished his coffee. Instead, we ended up talking for hours; about Alex, Jon, ourselves and dozens of other subjects. We both liked hiking and playing soccer, and both of us loved to read. We both had been planning to go to college since elementary school, and we both liked classic rock and roll and hated, absolutely hated, heavy metal. We both loved the Beatles and both swore we knew the words to every song. We tried testing each other; taking turns humming a tune and having the other sing the lyrics. We talked and laughed for so long that it was dark when we came out of *The Ugly Mug*. Jason offered to drive me home so I wouldn't have to wait for the bus. We walked back to the hospital together and got into his 10-year-old Volvo station wagon. "Nice car," I said.

"It was my Mom's," Jason answered. "My folks gave it to me when they got a new car last year."

I gave Jason directions to Nana's, where I was planning to stay while I was in town. He pulled up to the curb, and I thanked him for the ride and the coffee.

"No problem," Jason said. "Thanks for hanging out with me."

He paused, then asked, "are you going to visit your brother again tomorrow? I get out of class at 3 p.m., and I could give you a ride."

"Visiting hours tomorrow don't start until five, but I'd love a ride," I replied.

"Great," Jason said. "How about I pick you up at 3:15, and we hang out until it's time to visit your brother."

"Cool," I said. "See you then."

Chapter 20

Jason was sitting in his car in front of Nana's house when we arrived back home about 3 o'clock in the afternoon. He waved as we pulled up and got out of his car and watched us park in the driveway.

"Hi," he said to Nana as he opened her door for her. "I'm Jason Kane. You must be Caitlin's grandmother."

"You mean Ava?" Nana replied.

Jason looked quizzically at me. "I changed my name after I moved to Portland, and my family hasn't gotten used to it yet," I explained sheepishly.

"I can relate," Jason smiled. "My mom still calls me Jay-Jay."

"You're early, Jay-Jay," I said. "Come on in while I help Nana put the groceries away."

"My class got out a little early," Jason said and smiled. "Well actually, I got out of class a little early. The rest of the class is probably still there."

"Are you related to the actor Michael Caine?" Nana asked.

"No, but I get asked that a lot. My family spells our name with a 'K.'"

Nana opened the trunk, and Jason reached in to grab two bags of groceries. I picked up the third, and Nana smiled.

"It's nice to have some help," she said. "You two better watch out, I might get used to this and decide to keep you."

We brought the groceries into the kitchen and set the bags on the counter next to the refrigerator. Nana waved me away when I tried to put things away, so I went into the bathroom to change my clothes and brush my hair. I could hear Nana and Jason chatting when I came out and paused to listen. Nana wasn't grilling Jason, but I could tell by the way she was leading the conversation that she wanted to know as much about him as she could.

I came into the kitchen to rescue him, although he didn't realize he needed rescuing. "Your grandmother is really nice," he told me as we headed towards his car.

"She's the best," I replied.

We drove down to Ramsey Park, which bordered the river and parked by the empty tennis courts. Ramsey was the biggest park in town, covering about 40 acres, and the nicest. It was well maintained and had sports fields and ball courts, playgrounds, walking paths, grassy areas and lots of clean restrooms. We wandered past the basketball courts, where several half-court games were under way and walked past the playground, where a handful of mothers were sitting on a bench facing the swings and sandbox, chatting while watching their kids play.

We ended up on the crushed gravel path along the river and followed it until we found a nice shady spot. We left the trail and flopped down on the grass. I asked him if he had any news about Alex.

"He still won't see me," Jason said. "I talked to his mom this morning, and she said the doctors want to keep him in the hospital for at least another week. She sounded kind of cold, like maybe she thinks it's my fault Alex tried to kill himself."

"That's harsh. Did she come out and say that?"

"No, but she seemed like she was kind of pissed off at me. She's been like a second mom to me, and I've never had her talk like that to me before."

"She's probably just upset about Alex," I said. "I know I'm flipping out about Jon."

"Maybe," Jason replied. "I'm flipping out about Alex myself. Speaking of Jon, is there any new news about him?"

"Not that I know of," I said. "I think my Granddad went to see him this morning, but I haven't heard anything yet."

Jason talked about Alex. "I didn't see this coming," he said, shaking his head in dismay. "I thought I knew everything about him. We've been friends forever. We spent so much time at each others' houses, it was like we both had two sets of parents."

Jason and Alex had graduated from South Salem High School and moved to Cumberland last August to go the CCC. "I could have stayed at home and gone to Capitol," he said, referring to the community college in Salem, "But CCC has a good environmental studies program, and I want to go into solar power and renewable energy when I finish school. Besides, I wanted to move away from home and spread my wings a little.

Alex hadn't decided what he wanted to major in, but he wanted to come here, too, so we could go to college together and be roommates.

"I loved it here from the first day," Jason continued. "But I don't think Alex did. I don't know if he was homesick or bored or what, but he never seemed happy here. It's weird. He seemed really excited about going away to college last summer. He talked about it all the time, the different courses he wanted to take and how cool it would be to live away from home.

He got so amped about it that it was starting to drive me crazy. It was all he talked about all summer. He was sure he was going to get on the Dean's list and get a scholarship to Oregon State. When we first got here, he was still pretty gung ho, for the first month or so, but then kind of lost enthusiasm I guess. He cut a lot of classes and got pretty crappy grades in our first semester. We went back to Salem for Christmas, and to tell you the truth, I was kind of surprised that he came back to Cumberland with me after the break. But I didn't think he was gonna do anything like he did."

Jason asked me if I liked growing up in Cumberland.

"I guess," I said. "I never really thought about it."

We talked for a while longer, and then it was time to go visit Jon. Although visiting hours were officially under way when we arrived a little after 5 p.m., I still had to sit in the waiting room for 20 minutes or so until I was escorted in to see Jon. Jason sat with me, and we played tic-tac-toe while we waited and watched other visitors come and go.

A police car pulled up to the No Parking Zone in front of the entrance, and we watched two cops get out and help a tall, skinny man with long, ginger brown hair tied back into a ponytail and a long, bushy beard out of the back of the patrol car.

They each had a hand on one of his arms as they led him to the front door and rang the buzzer. The receptionist activated the intercom, and we heard one of the cops say they bringing a potentially suicidal man in for observation.

The counter clerk buzzed them in, and the cops walked to the counter with the man, who looked like he was in his mid to late 40s and old enough to be their father, between them.

"Can I have your name, sir, and proof of insurance?" the clerk asked the man.

106

"Calvin Coolidge," the man replied.

"Excuse me," said the clerk.

"Calvin Coolidge," the man repeated.

"I've seen all the movies. You're supposed to ask me who the president is and what's the date. Calvin Coolidge, Aug. 3, 1923."

Jason and I stifled giggles and looked away from each other to keep from laughing out loud.

"Take a seat," the clerk said, who immediately picked up the phone and punched in several numbers.

The cops escorted the guy to a chair along the wall opposite us and sat down on either side of him. A minute or two later, a man, probably an aide, nurse or medical assistant, came out with a clipboard in his hand and walked towards them.

"Can I have your name sir?" he asked.

"Haven't you seen the movies?" the man replied. "You're supposed to ask me who is the president. It's Calvin Coolidge."

This time, I could see the two cops fighting not to smile.

"OK," the guy with the clipboard said. Turning to one of the cops, he asked if he would sign the patient in on a 5150. The cop agreed, signed the forms on the clipboard, and the two officers left as the man was being led into the main part of the unit.

After another long wait, I was finally allowed in to see Jon. Once again, Jon was uncommunicative, leaving me frustrated and annoyed. After 20 minutes of being ignored, I gave up and left. Jason jumped to his feet when he saw me coming out of the main unit and touched my arm. I was frowning and trying hard not to cry.

"Come on, Caitlin," Jason said kindly. "Let's get out of here."

I wasn't ready to go back to Nana's and tell her that Jon still wouldn't even look at me. Jason suggested we go for a walk and then get some coffee. We wandered around the hospital grounds for about 45 minutes, then walked the block and a half to the coffee house we'd visited the previous day. Yesterday, *The Ugly Mug* had been nearly empty. Today, half of the tables were taken, and there was a line at the counter. We stood at the end of the line and were reading the day's specials written out on a chalkboard propped up near the counter when we heard the door open. I looked up and saw the man the cops had brought to the Behavioral Health Unit walk in and get into the line behind us. Jason spotted him too and said,"hey, it's Calvin Coolidge."

The man looked at us quizzically for a moment, then grinned.

"Oh yeah," he said. "I saw you two in the waiting room at the nut house."

"Ten-four Captain," Jason replied with a smile. "And I've seen the movies, too. You're supposed to ask me what the date is and who's the president."

"Damn right," the man joked. "Calvin Coolidge, Aug. 3, 1923."

"Why Calvin?" I asked.

"Why Calvin Coolidge?" he replied. "The man blamed by most political scholars for triggering the Great Depression by encouraging widespread speculation in the 1920s, which led to the stock market boom and then the crash? I just like the sound of his name. I thought of using Herbert Hoover, but Calvin Coolidge rolls off the tongue better."

"I mean, why did you tell everyone that?" I asked.

"Well, it's a long, sad story. But basically, my bitch of a soon-to-be ex-wife came home from Seattle yesterday morning and announced she'd just met the love of her life and now she wants a divorce. Naturally, I wasn't too thrilled to hear that, so we've been arguing about it for the last 24 hours. She started packing up her stuff, and I think she wanted me out of the house so she could clean me out. But whatever the reason, that egotistical bitch called the cops and said I told her I couldn't live without her, and she was afraid I was going to kill myself because she was leaving me. I told the cops that it was bull shit, but they said they were required by law to take me to a shrink to get checked out. I didn't want to get stuck there while the bitch packed up everything I owned along with her stuff, so I decided to tell everyone the president is Calvin Coolidge."

"So what happened at the hospital?" Jason asked.

"They put me in an exam room, and when the doctor came in he said 'I hear you think the president is Calvin Coolidge.' I said yes, I've seen the movies, and he asked me a couple of questions and about 10 minutes later said it was obvious someone who was displaying a sense of humor like that wasn't about to kill himself and did I want a bus pass or to call someone to pick me up. So I called my buddy Mark at work and told him I'd wait here until he got off and could come by and give me a ride home."

We chuckled. "What's with the date?" Jason asked.

"Aug. 3, 1923? That's the day Calvin Coolidge was sworn into office. He was Harding's vice-president and took over after Harding died. He was visiting his parents at the time and was sworn into office in their living room in Vermont by his father who was a notary public, because there wasn't anyone else around qualified to do it."

"You sure know a lot about Calvin Coolidge," Jason noted.

"I was a history major in college," the man said. "And I'm into politics."

"So who really is the president?" Jason asked.

"It's Calvin Coolidge if someone is trying to lock me up," the man said with a grin. "And if my freedom isn't at stake, it's that horn-dog Bill Clinton."

We placed our order for coffees and some cookies and found an empty table to sit at.

"So," Jason asked me rhetorically. "What do you think, Caitlin? Is he crazy or not?"

"Absolutely not," I replied. "I'd say he's expressing an appropriate response to his situation in a healthy and appropriate manner."

We both laughed.

"I like you, Caitlin," Jason said. "And I like Calvin Coolidge."

Chapter 21

Mom was waiting for me at Nana's when Jason dropped me off. I was in an OK mood when I walked into the door after having spent the last few hours laughing and joking with Jason. My good humor evaporated when I saw her. Mom was needy at the best of times, and with Jon in the hospital, this clearly was one of the worst of times our family had experienced to date. Mom rose from the couch when I walked in and rushed to embrace me.

"Hi Mom," I said, trying to disentangle myself from her hug. "What's up?"

"Oh, Ava," she replied. "I'm just so glad you're here."

My guard instantly went up. Mom was a master manipulator, and one of her tactics was to lavish attention and praise on her victim to soften them into doing her bidding.

"Uh, thanks, Mom," I said cautiously.

"I don't know what I'd do without you," Mom said. "You're a God-send."

I decided to ignore her comment.

"Any new news about Jon?" I asked. "He wasn't talking to me when I visited him today, and his doctor wasn't around."

Mentioning Jon was a mistake. Tears began welling up in Mom's eyes, and she reached for me again saying "oh, Ava." I sidestepped her and asked "where's Nana?" while starting towards the kitchen.

Nana was out in the backyard, watering her flower garden. I spotted her through the kitchen window and went out through the back door with Mom following close behind.

Nana had a beautiful garden.

Her house was built on a former farm, and the rear of her deep backyard still held the remnants of a cherry orchard. There were eight trees that produced sweet and tasty Bing cherries every summer, and four smaller apple trees that had obviously been planted years later that produced hundreds of Red Delicious apples each fall.

There was a lawn between the orchard, or the back 40 as we called it, and the patio off the kitchen. Two sides of the lawn were bordered with deep flower beds. There was a long double row of roses on one side and a bed full of what Nana called her English cottage garden. It was jammed with flowers of all sizes, shapes, colors and smells. Nana was watering the roses and turned when she heard the back door open.

From the look on Nana's face, I realized she had come outside to escape Mom's dramatics, just like I was trying to do. Nana turned her attention back to her roses as we approached. I quickly filled Nana in on my visit with Jon and asked if she had heard anything new.

Mom's eyes welled up again. Nana and I both ignored her.

Nana said the only thing she had heard was that the doctor had decided Jon needed to stay where he was for at least a few weeks. Before I could reply, Mom started wailing.

"Oh, my poor baby," she cried. "My poor Jondalar. I just don't know what I'm going to do."

Once again, I ignored the advice I'd learned in the anger management class two years earlier and spoke before I thought.

"Shut up, Mom," I snapped. "This isn't about you. It's about Jon. And if you don't shut the fuck up, I'll end up in the mental ward, too."

Mom was momentarily shocked speechless. Then she started yelling at me. "How dare you speak to me like that," she shouted. "I'm your mother."

"Then why don't you start acting like one," I shouted. "You did a really shitty job of taking care of Jon. No wonder he's in the hospital."

By now, Mom was crying harder and louder.

"How dare you," she wailed.

"How dare you try to dump everything on me," I screamed. "I'm not going to take care of you like Jon did."

Mom didn't answer. She looked at me, then at Nana, who was still holding the hose. I think she was waiting for me to apologize or for Nana to comfort her. When neither of us moved, she shouted, "How can you be so heartless?" and ran back into the house.

Nana looked at me in surprise.

I was still furious. I knew it was unfair, but I blamed Mom and Dad for Jon's illness, and for his suicide attempt.

"They drove him crazy," I said to Nana, even though I knew rationally that that wasn't possible. "And they should have been doing more to help him," I added. "They know all the tricks. They should have been making sure he was taking his meds and they should have made him see his doctor."

I stomped my foot in anger.

"And now Mom is trying to get me to come back and take care of her. I just know it."

Nana just shook her head sadly. "Oh, Ava, I'm just so sorry," she said. "I know this is terribly hard on you. I think you had the right idea when you ran off to Portland."

I apologized, grudgingly, to Mom when Nana and I went back into the house about 30 minutes later, even though I was still angry. Her feelings were still hurt, even after I told her I was sorry, and she avoided my eyes all evening. I was still upset when Nana drove Mom home after dinner. I didn't ask about Dad, but Nana told me when she returned that he'd been at Granddad's all afternoon and evening. Nana and I were both exhausted and went to bed early. I thought I'd drop right off to sleep, but found myself tossing and turning for hours, unable to get my mind to stop thinking about Jon, Mom, Dad and poor, poor pitiful me. Finally, I turned on the light and rummaged through Nana's bookshelves until I found something to read. I read until my eyes felt like they were bleeding and finally dropped off sometime after 2in the morning.

I slept late the next morning, and Nana was already in her art room and engrossed in painting when I finally got up around 10:30 a.m. I didn't want to disturb her, so I made myself breakfast, cleaned up the kitchen and decided to go to the hardware store to see Granddad. I wrote Nana a note, letting her know where I'd be, then walked to the bus stop.

It was busy at the store. Two clerks had called in sick, and Granddad was manning one of the registers when I arrived. I put on a smock and helped restock shelves, straighten displays and help customers find things until it was time to go back to Nana's to meet Jason. Before I left, Granddad said Eileen had offered to make my favorite macaroni and cheese tonight if I wanted to come by their house after visiting Jon.

I smiled and said, "Most definitely."

I was still edgy when Jason arrived to pick me up around 2 p.m. Since we didn't have anything specific planned for the next three hours, until I could visit Jon, I suggested we go back to the park and work out. I had him swing by my parents' house and told him to wait in the car while I ran in.

I was relieved to find both Mom and Dad were out. I looked all over and finally found an old soccer ball in Jon's closet. I grabbed it and left.

Jason asked me if I wanted to go find a pickup game.

"No," I said. "Let's find a rebound wall. I need to kick the shit out of something and that might help keep me from killing someone."

Jason laughed and said, "that's fine with me."

We spent about an hour kicking the ball. He had quick reflexes, decent footwork and used finesse to put the ball where he wanted it. I just blasted away until I was sweaty, red-faced and tired; tired enough to feel the frustration drain out of my body. I got a drink of water from the fountain next to the restrooms, then came back, flopped down on the grass beside the asphalt and rolled onto my back.

Jason lay down next to me on his side, propping his head up on his palm.

"Thanks for humoring me," I said. "I needed that."

"It was a great workout," Jason said. "I think I needed that, too. Alex's mom says he still won't see me, and I'm getting worried. "

"Worried he'll try again?"

"Oh shit, I hadn't thought of that. Now I'm worried about that, too, along with being worried he'll never talk to me again."

"Sorry I brought it up."

"That's OK. I probably should be worried about that." He paused for a few seconds, then asked, "Are you worried about your brother? Are you afraid he'll try again?"

"Yeah," I admitted. "I know he's miserable."

Jason reached over and put his hand on mine. "I'm so sorry, Caitlin," he said. "That really fucking sucks."

Jason was wearing a different shirt when I came back to the waiting room after another frustrating attempt to communicate with my brother. "Did you go home and change?" I asked him as we walked out to his car.

"No," he said. "I had it in my car."

113

I looked through the side window of his Volvo after we walked out and realized for the first time the back seat and the way back were both cluttered. Blankets, a pillow, clothes, textbooks and note books filled the rear of the car. The front, however, was clear and clean; with a trash bag the only thing on the floor in front of the passenger seat.

"It looks like you're living in here," I said.

"Well, just sort of camping out," he said sheepishly. "It's just too creepy back at the apartment."

"Does it remind you of finding Alex?"

"Yeah. It's hard enough to get that image out of my mind as it is. Whenever I think about it all I think about is all that blood all over the bathroom and thinking Alex was dead. It just freaks me out. I know I have to go back there and clean up the mess, but I just can't deal with it."

"That would freak me out, too," I said, reaching over to touch his arm.

"No wonder my Mom's so freaked out, I mean more freaked out than normal. I'm glad I wasn't the one who found Jon."

I felt a huge pang of guilt about being so mean to Mom the day before.

"Oh God," I said, my eyes welling up with tears. "I'm such an asshole."

Chapter 22

I decided there wasn't any point in staying in Cumberland since Jon still wasn't talking to me. Granddad and Eileen agreed when I told them I was going to go back to Portland the next day. I didn't say anything to them about the fight I'd had with Mom, the fact that I'd been avoiding Dad, and that I was probably upsetting Nana with my pissed off attitude. So I felt kind of bad when Granddad and Eileen were so supportive.

"You need to live your own life," Granddad said. "Right now, you don't need to try and take care of anyone but yourself. Your brother and your parents are not your responsibility."

Granddad said he was sorry that he and Eileen hadn't asked me to move in with them when Jon got sick. "You can always come back and live with us," Granddad said.

I thanked them both and said I'd keep that in mind, but for now I really needed to get away from Cumberland. They told me that they understood and would keep the offer open if I changed my mind later on.

I had planned on taking the bus the next day, Wednesday, but Jason insisted on driving me to Portland. I protested when he offered, reminding him he had school. Missing a day or two won't matter, he replied. Besides, he added, I haven't been able to concentrate on anything since I found Alex. And I want to go home to see my parents.

I felt a brief pang of envy when he said that. Ever since Kindergarten, I'd been jealous whenever I saw other kids with their parents. It seemed like everyone's parents except mine were normal, and I'd longed for parents that didn't attract attention for bizarre behavior. The idea that parents could be a source of emotional support was so foreign to me I was taken aback for a moment.

When I regained my voice, I offered to take the bus from Salem to Portland, to spare Jason from driving further north than he had to.

He said he'd think about it, but when the time came he drove past all of the Salem exits. Before leaving town, I asked Jason to drive me over to see my folks.

He waited in the car while I went in and told Mom and Dad I was going back to Portland. I hugged them both and apologized again to Mom for being such a bitch. She let me off the hook, saying this was a difficult time for us all. Dad looked confused, more confused than usual, and didn't say anything other than good-bye.

Jason and I were both lost in our own thoughts as we drove out of Cumberland and onto the interstate. I was thinking about Jon, and I'm sure Jason was thinking about Alex.

We drove in silence for about 20 minutes.

It occurred to me later, when I was back at Uncle George's, that I was completely comfortable riding with Jason with neither of us talking. The further away we got from Cumberland, the more I relaxed. I suspect Jason felt the same way, because once we had some distance between us on the Behavioral Health Unit we started chatting about the scenery, movies we'd seen, the Seattle Mariner's prospects this year and other lighthearted topics. Jason told me about his family, and how his older sisters, twins who were now 21, had teased and tortured him so relentlessly when he was growing up that he referred to them as the evil twins.

"Andrea and Annette aren't identical," he said. "In fact, they hardly even look like each other. Most people are surprised to hear they're even sisters when they first meet them."

"Are you the youngest?" I asked.

"Now I am. I had a little sister, Kayla, who was three years younger than me. She died of leukemia when I was eight."

"That's horrible."

"Yeah, it was really horrible, especially for my parents. Kayla was in the hospital so much I hardly ever saw her. I don't remember much about her, except that she was always sick, and my parents were always freaking out. They were gone a lot, too. It seemed like they were always at the hospital with Kayla, or taking her to specialists trying to find something that would make her better.

"I spent a lot of time at Alex's," he added. "His parents took care of me whenever Kayla was really sick. I was at their house when she died. Alex's dad was the one who broke the news to me. I hated him for a while after that, even though he was always so nice to me."

116

We rode in silence for a while.

"Kayla was always sick, and I never was," he said. "I never even missed a day of school all the way through elementary school."

"Wow. I wish I could say that."

"Were you sick a lot as a kid?"

"Not really, but I was in a car accident in third grade and missed nearly half the school year."

"Whoa, that's gnarly. What happened?"

"My Dad ran a red light, and we got T-boned by a pickup truck," I said, suddenly flooded with memories of that awful night. I could feel the anxiety in my stomach turn to rage, and I rolled down the window as fast as I could. I leaned my head out and screamed.

"I hate schizophrenia, I hate schizophrenia," I yelled as loudly as I could into the wind.

"I just fucking hate it!"

Jason looked worried when I finally pulled my head back into the car.

"I'm sorry," I said. "I just lost it, thinking about the accident. My father is what they call a "paranoid schizophrenic," and he was really delusional the night of the wreck. He thought someone was out to get us and drove like a maniac, a real maniac, trying to get away from who knows what. It was terrifying. We could have died a dozen different ways. We had so many close calls until we finally got creamed. The other driver nearly died, and both Jon and me ended up in the hospital."

"Jesus, Caitlin, that's totally fucked. If I were you I'd hate schizophrenia, too, like the way I fucking hate leukemia."

We stopped a couple of times, once at a rest stop so I could use the bathroom, then an hour later for gas. We decided we were both hungry, so we stopped a third time at a deli for some sandwiches and drinks. It was warm and sunny, so we took our food to one of the tables outside and ate leisurely. I was in no hurry to get to Portland; even if we'd rushed, it would be too late for me to make it to class that day, and my boss at the coffee house wasn't expecting me back until next week. Jason didn't seem to be in a hurry to get home either. His folks both worked, he told me, and wouldn't be home until after 5 p.m. So we went back into the deli for dessert and returned to our table to eat it slowly.

Even with all our delays, we got to Uncle George's house by 3 p.m.
There was a car I didn't recognize in the driveway behind George's, so
Jason pulled up to the curb in front of the house.

"Well, he said. "I guess this is it."

"I guess so," I said, not making a move to get out of the car. "Thanks
for the ride. Do you want to come in for a drink or something?"

Jason smiled.

"That would be great Caitlin. I'd love to."

Uncle George and one of his buddies, Rick, were in the living room
playing a video game. George paused the game when we came in, and
I introduced Jason to him and Rick. I made coffee for me and Jason,
remembering to load his up with sugar, and the two of us went into my
bedroom to drink it.

Before he left, about an hour later, Jason asked if he could stay
in touch.

"I really like talking to you. Can I call you?"

"Sure, that would be nice."

I wrote down Uncle George's phone number on the back of an old
envelope and handed it to him. Then I walked him out to his car, thanked
him again for the ride and told him I hoped he'd have a good visit with
his parents.

I was already missing him by the time I got back in the house. I sat
down in the living room and watched George and Rick play for a while,
then went into my room to lie down and read. I must have been more tired
than I realized. Not only did I fall asleep after drinking a cup of coffee, but
I slept for hours. It was dark when I woke up to the sound of the phone
ringing. I heard Uncle George answer it, then knock softly on my door.

"It's for you, Caitlin," he said. "I think it's Jason."

It was, and I was glad.

"I just wanted to call and say thanks for hanging out with me," Jason
said. "I think you're the only person in the world who really understands
what I'm going through right now."

Chapter 23

I had thought I would feel good once I got back to Portland, but I didn't really. While it was a relief to get away from my parents, especially my mom, and not to have to endure the frustration and heartbreak of try-ing to find my brother inside that non-communicative shell he had retreated into, I was far from feeling good, or even OK. I remember how dizzy, dazed and disoriented I felt when I woke up in the hospital after the car wreck.

Emotionally, I felt like that, like I had just survived, barely, the emotional equivalent of a car wreck. It was disconcerting, to say the least, and I wasn't sure how I would make my way through it. I didn't know what else to do but go through the motions of my life, wait for the anguish to fade and try not to dwell on what had become of my brother.

I wasn't expected back at work until Monday, and other than school on Friday, I didn't have to do anything or be anywhere for the next four days. I slept late on Thursday and lay around watching TV and eating popcorn. I was bored, but lacked the energy to do anything, even read.

Friday started out the same, but when I got up, George made me breakfast and invited me to go hiking. I didn't want to go but didn't have the strength to muster up an argument. I put up a couple of feeble excuses, and the next thing I knew, we were in his car heading for Jack's Peak.

We walked the three-mile loop trail, mostly in silence, and got back to the house in time for me to take a shower and head off to catch the bus to get to class. I had only missed one class while I was in Cumberland, but it seemed like I'd been gone for weeks. I struggled to follow the teacher as she explained the new material.

All I could think about was Jon and how horrible he looked inside the locked mental ward.

Uncle George was waiting for me outside. I was scared, initially, when I saw him, thinking that something had happened to Jon or Nana, until I saw him smile.

"I thought you might like a ride home," he said.

George said he was hungry, so we stopped at Mama's Mexican Kitchen for dinner. We were halfway through our burritos, when I turned to him and asked what Mom was like before she got sick.

"She was smart and funny," he said. "She was really popular, especially in high school and had a lot of friends. There were always a lot of different guys calling her and asking her out. She broke a few hearts, let me tell you."

"Did she always paint?"

"Oh yeah, for as long as I could remember. She was also really good at drawing. It seemed like she always had a pencil or a paint brush in her hand when she was home."

"Did you guys get along?"

"We liked each other, but we weren't tight, like you and Jon. Lisa is four years older than me, so we had our own sets of friends and didn't really hang out together much. I looked up to her, and she tolerated me I guess."

"It's funny to think about Mom having a life before me and Jon."

"Yeah, I know what you mean. I can't imagine my mom as anything beside my mom."

"When did my mom get sick?"

"I'm not sure," he replied. "Once she and your Dad got married, I didn't see her all that much. I knew your Dad was sick, of course, although he was kind of in remission in the early days, but I didn't know Lisa was sick until she ended up in the hospital when Jon was in Kindergarten."

"Doesn't it bother you?" I asked.

"Of course it does," he said. "It's horrible; it's completely fucked. I feel like I lost my sister, at least the sister I grew up with. I mean, she's still alive, but she's not the same. But I realized a long time ago that there's really nothing I can do about it.

Somewhere along the line enough time passed, and I learned to accept it for what it is. She's mentally ill, and unfortunately, that's just the way it is. It's a drag, it's a bummer, it's totally fucked, but it is what it is. Stressing out about it is only going to make things worse for me, so I had to adjust to the new reality."

I wasn't sure I'd ever adjust to the reality of Jon's illness, or to the dread that I might lose him to a successful suicide attempt. So I just tried to focus on staying busy and getting through the days.

120

The passage of time helped him to adjust, George had told me, and I was hoping it would do the same for me.

Some days were harder than most.

A few days after I went back to work, I was carrying a pot of boiling water when the handle slipped out of my hand.

The glass pot broke on the floor, and the scalding water splashed onto my legs. I was wearing blue jeans, but the water soaked through the denim and left angry red blotches on my shins and calves.

I ran into the back room to run cold water on my lower legs, but they still throbbed and stung. I limped back behind the counter, and the assistant manager chewed me out for being so clumsy and ordered me to clean up the glass.

A week or two later, I got a D+ on a practice test and was so discouraged I wanted to drop out of school. At work, I had a hard time joining in with the banter, and one afternoon, I overheard one of my co-workers complaining that I was snotty.

Jason was having a tough time, too. He called me the day after he got home and said he almost wished he had stayed in Cumberland. He had been hoping his parents would be supportive and help him put Alex's situation in perspective. Instead, he said, they were both really upset that Alex had attempted suicide, and they were drinking more than usual.

They spent a lot of time on the phone with Alex's parents, analyzing everything the doctors had said and talking over and over about possible missed signs.

"They're acting like they did when Kayla was sick," he said. "They don't have any time for me, and the way they're acting is stressing me out."

Jason was also frustrated that there wasn't any change in Alex's condition. He was still in the Behavioral Health Unit, still not communicating much with his doctors or parents, and still didn't want to have anything to do with Jason.

"He's still pissed off at me," Jason said.

"His mom's still kind of cold to me, too, but my mom said it's nothing personal, that she's just upset."

Jason called again two days later, after he returned to Cumberland.

Someone, either the firefighters who responded first to his 911 call,

121

or maybe the apartment manager, had cleaned up the blood from the bathroom.

"It still creeps me out to be here," he said, adding that he was planning to camp out in his car for the next few days.

"I hope you don't think I'm a wus."

Alex's father had gone back to Portland, as he had to go back to work, but his mom was still in town. She was staying in a motel near the hospital and was apparently frustrated with the lack of Alex's progress. She complained to Jason that the doctors weren't telling her anything and kept wanting to know why Alex had changed so much since he'd gone off to college.

"She keeps asking me what happened to Alex, and there's nothing I can tell her," Jason said. "I don't know what happened to him, and I don't know why he slashed his wrists. I just wish he'd start talking to somebody, so we can all get some answers."

"You might not want to know," I told him.

"I know why my brother tried to kill himself. He's a paranoid schizophrenic, like our Dad, and he was trying to stop the horrible voices in his head that were controlling his mind. We grew up watching our father struggle with the same thing, and I know Jon doesn't want to spend his life either like Dad or horribly sedated on some medication that turns him into a zombie. Thinking about what he's going through makes me want to puke."

"Damn," Jason said. "I guess I don't really want to know."

"Ignorance is bliss," I joked. "You should try being ignorant. Or coming to my coffee shop and ordering the purple bliss smoothie or a double low fat latte with extra foam like the yuppies do. They always looked blissed out. Or at least smugly content."

Jason laughed and told me about the blissed-out hippie kids at his school.

"They must not know the 60s are over," he said. "They probably think the LBJ is still the president. Or maybe Calvin Coolidge."

Chapter 24

I don't know what I would have done without my uncle, or without regular calls from Jason. He'd call every couple of days to chat, and I really looked forward to our talks. He was the first real friend I'd ever had, the first person outside of my family I felt totally comfortable with. We'd share the latest news about Alex and Jon, when there was any, and talk about our days. We'd end up laughing over something silly, like Jason mimicking his math teacher's phoney English accent, or my description of one of my co-workers' latest hairstyles.

Most of the kids who worked at the coffee shop dyed their hair, with blue and orange currently being the most popular colors. But one of the girls took hair coloring to the extreme.

She'd shave everything off her head except for a Mohawk strip in the middle, which she dyed in rainbow colors. I thought her hair looked like rainbow sherbert and have no idea how she was able to attain that look or why.

Jason and I would talk for an hour or so at a time, especially on the weekends. George didn't mind me tying up the phone, but some of his girlfriends did.

Sometimes they'd show up and complain that our phone was ALWAYS busy and glare at me. George would just smile and tell them that's what teenagers did and to chill out and get used to it.

Naturally, that made me unpopular with some of his female friends, but it didn't bother me enough to cut down on the length of my phone calls.

George was extremely patient with me in other ways as well.

He never bugged me about doing my homework, or nagged at me to do something productive if I felt like slobbing out around the house all day and watching TV.

He invited me to tag along with him when he ran errands or shopped for groceries, and when he and his buddies went to the park to play soccer or shoot hoops.

He would coax me into doing something fun with him almost every day, even if it was just going out for ice cream. If it wasn't raining, he'd invite me to go skateboarding. We went so often that I started getting pretty good, especially on the streets and sidewalks.

There was a fairly new industrial park not too far away from our house that had an enormous parking lot that was built on a slope. We'd go there on weekends and after five on weekdays, when the parking lot was mostly empty, and ride on the smooth asphalt. The site was popular with other skateboarders, so there were usually other riders there. I got to know most of the regulars, and they got to know me.

I stood out both because I was one of the few female skateboarders and because of Uncle George. He was always one of the best skateboarders at the parking lot, as well as one of the most popular.

Just the fact that I was with him made the other riders accept me without question, even though I wasn't very skilled when I first showed up. Others liked to carve wide turns all the way down, the style of skating I preferred. I loved the feel of centrifugal force on my body as I squatted low and carved a wide, arching turn.

Other days we'd go to the skate park and ride on the half pipes and in the bowls that were shaped like the ends of backyard swimming pools.

The cement there was smooth, and you could glide high up on the inside of the bowls and go up and down in the pipes. It was scary at first, dropping down steep ramps to get the momentum you needed to ride in the bowls.

As I got used to it, the fear turned into excitement, and I loved the sensation of defying gravity and racing up a steep surface. I got so into skateboarding that I started using my skateboard for transportation, riding it to and from the store, the bus stops and to work and back.

The more I rode, the more confident I became, and the more fun I had. Some days, I'd have so much fun I'd forget about my brother and parents for a couple of hours.

Living with Uncle George was like living with a combination of a father and an older brother.

George was 22 when I was born, so technically he was old enough to be my dad.

124

He was much more fun loving than the average dad, though, and youthful and spirited enough to be an older brother. Nana said he was suffering from Peter Pan syndrome and would never grow up. I thought he was great, and I was glad I was living with him.

Uncle George seemed to like having me around, too.

I kept the house pretty clean, which he liked once his friends commented on it, and he realized there were always clean dishes in the kitchen, and that the bathroom was no longer scrotty and disgusting. I did a lot of the cooking, too, mainly to give myself something to do.

George kept telling me I didn't have to do so much housework, and that I wasn't his mother so I shouldn't feel like I needed to clean up after him. I would just nod and keep on tidying up, because the messier the house got, the more it reminded me of living with Mom and Dad, and the more stressed I became.

I liked keeping things in order, because it made me feel good, so I kept on doing so. Even if I hadn't been handling a lot of the domestic duties, I knew I still would have been welcome at my uncle's.

As the weeks went by, he started spending more and more time at home, hanging out with me and his buddies. His guy friends, the ones we went skateboarding with and the ones who came over to play music, video games and watch TV, treated me like one of their pals. I wasn't so popular with his female companions, however.

When I first started staying with George, he had so many women coming in and out of the house that I couldn't keep track of who was who. I just called everyone "girlfriend" and smiled when I said it like we were longtime friends.

After a couple of weeks, however, the parade of women in and out of his bedroom slowed down. I knew he still saw some of the women regularly at his gigs, largely because his band mates would tease him about his groupies, but the traffic in our house diminished.

I realized, too, that not all the women were happy about it.

I heard some of the messages they left on our answering machine.

A couple would leave what I'd call serial messages; the first would ask him to call them, the second would want to know what was up and why he hadn't called back, the third would get a little more heated and desperate.

Occasionally, there would be a fourth message, a really angry one. That would sometimes be followed by a slightly apologetic message. Every once in a while thought, it would be followed by an even angrier message, calling George names I'd never heard before.

It certainly was an eye opener for me, or perhaps I should say an ear opener. I learned a lot of about relationships, hook-ups and what not to say or do to a guy to convince him to spend time with you.

Chapter 25

There's an old saying that when one door closes another opens. For me, it seemed like I was living in a warped, parallel universe where when one problem ends, another begins. I was relieved when my uncle's ex-girlfriends stopped calling and coming over and vibing me.

What I didn't realize, however, was that my uncle's new lifestyle—cutting back on the babes he entertained in his bedroom —meant he stopped sleeping with my boss.

Melissa, who managed the coffee house, had hired me as a favor to George. I wasn't aware of it at the time, but she also showed quite a bit of favoritism towards me and was very patient, much more patient than she should have been, with my work transgressions. Although I quickly mastered the basic skills required to make fancy coffee drinks, heat up scones, serve snacks, work the cash register, wipe down tables, empty the trash, sweep and mop the floors and refill the cream and sugar containers, I was slow to master another important skill.

I didn't believe, as all retail employees are taught, that the customer is always right. And thanks to my failure to embrace the skills taught in the "damn right, I'm pissed class" I had attended against my will, I occasionally let a customer know when I thought they were wrong. If someone snapped at me, I wouldn't take a deep breath, count to ten and think of something pleasant. I'd snap back.

If Melissa overheard the conversation, she'd pull me aside and gently remind me to treat all our customers politely and professionally. If I encountered another pissy customer that day, she'd take me off the register and relegate me to tasks that didn't entail dealing with the public.

Looking back, I realize that her preferential treatment was probably one of the reasons I wasn't very popular with most of my co-workers. If I had been in their places, I wouldn't have liked myself either. So I imagine no one I worked with was heartbroken when my pet status ended along with Melissa and George's relationship. Once that occurred, Melissa stopped tolerating my outbursts, which I found difficult to control.

I certainly can't blame her for firing me when I refused to serve a woman who demanded, not asked, for me to remake her low-fat mocha double latte because I put too much whipped cream on the top.

By that I mean as an adult reflecting on my termination 17 years later, I acknowledge I deserved to have been fired.

As a hot-headed 15 year old, however, I did not take the news well. I had a temper tantrum and spewed out a few profane phrases that confirmed to Melissa I was definitely not an asset to the coffee house.

I managed to refrain from crying until after I was escorted off the premises but just barely. I was so angry I walked all the way home in the rain, rather than riding the bus, kicking a flattened soda can in front of me the entire time.

By the time I got home, I was soaking wet, my right foot was sore, and my anger had dissipated somewhat, only to be replaced with depression. I knew I had screwed up and was humiliated by getting fired. I was worried that George would be disappointed in me, since he had hooked me up with the job, and that he would lecture me about the behavior that got me canned. At least those fears weren't realized when he came home and found me watching TV instead of working.

He shook his head sadly when I told him I was unemployed and why. The only thing he asked me was if I learned anything from the experience. I nodded, and he said that was good.

I was so bummed out by the experience that I wasn't in a hurry to try to find another job. I didn't think any coffee shop or restaurant would hire me without experience, and I certainly wasn't going to tell prospective employers about my short stint as a barista.

I could have looked for a job in a store, with more than a year of experience at Granddad's hardware store under my belt, but I was still just 15 and thought store owners would be more likely to require a work permit, which I couldn't obtain until I turned 16. Besides, I didn't have the confidence I would need to land an interview.

So I moped around the house for a couple of weeks, getting more and more bored, and farther and farther ahead in my schoolwork. When I got tired of studying, and George wasn't able to do something with me, I'd grab my skateboard and ride around the neighborhood.

I started meeting some of the neighbors and discovered there were a lot of people home during the day, especially mothers with young kids. The neighborhood was a little run down, with every third or fourth house needing a new coat of paint or roof repairs.

The homes were small single story cottages on little lots, which translated to a lot of young families as affordable. Most of the people were friendly and eager to chat.

When I had my daughter Kayla, and was home for hours on end with her, I would become nearly desperate for the company of someone whose age was in double digits.

I guess many of the parents in our neighborhood felt that way too, but at the time I just assumed they were friendly and interested in getting to know me. Once they found out I was attending adult school and wasn't a truant or a total slacker, neighbors started asking me if I would babysit their kids. Not having had any younger siblings, I kept saying no thanks, that is until Jason clued me in to how lucrative babysitting could be.

His sisters, the evil twins as he called them when he was annoyed with something one or the other had done, which was often, had worked as babysitters before going off to college and brought in big bucks.

Apparently in Jason's neighborhood it was hard to find reliable teenagers who would take care of kids, so his sisters' services were in high demand. They could pick and choose the best babysitting gigs, the ones with the best-behaved kids in families that provided the best snacks and the highest wages.

On weekend nights, when parents were desperate for sitters, people would offer to pay more than the going rate.

"I don't know how much they were raking in, but they were always bragging it was more than their friends, and they both swore they'd never work a minimum wage job," Jason said.

"But I don't know anything about babysitting," I complained.

"Then take a babysitting class. That's how my sisters got started. Besides most people won't pay top dollar for a sitter unless they have their Red Cross certification."

Jason's advice was good. I looked up the Red Cross in the phone book, called them and signed up for the next class.

I was looking forward to Jason's next call, so I could tell him about my plans, but when he called three days later he sounded so sad I forgot about my news. Alex was still in the hospital, still very depressed and still refusing to see Jason, but he had finally been diagnosed.

"His parents told me he's bipolar. I'm not sure exactly what that means, but his mom started crying when she told me. The doctors want to keep him in the hospital for a while, because they think he'll try to kill himself again."

"Jeeze, that's terrible."

"Yeah, I know. I'm really bummed, and my parents are really upset about it too. My Dad said he had a cousin who had manic depression, which is what they used to call it in the old days when my dad was young, and that it's incurable."

"That's fucked."

"Yeah tell me about it. I don't know if Alex will ever get out of the hospital."

"There's got to be something they can do. Schizophrenia isn't curable either, but my Mom's doing OK. Well, not OK but she's not as fucked up as she used to be."

"Gee, that's a ringing endorsement for psychiatry."

"Hey, sorry. I'm just trying to cheer you up."

"I know, and I appreciate that. But I'm really bummed, and I wish I knew what's gonna happen to Alex. I don't know shit about biopolarism."

"Why don't you ask somebody?"

"Who? My Dad doesn't know hardly anything about it, and his cousin had it. My mom doesn't know anything about it either, and Alex's mom just cries when she talks about it."

"What about his dad?"

"Who, Alex's? I don't think he wants to talk about it either."

"Can you ask the doctor?"

"I don't think so. They probably won't talk to me because I'm not officially family."

"Well, why don't you go look it up."

"What, in the dictionary?"

"No, at the library. There's got to be a book or something about it."

130

"That's not a bad idea. I think there's a medical library at the hospital."

"No, don't go there. Everything will be written in doctor speak, and it won't make any sense. Go to the Cumberland Library."

"Hm, that's a good idea. I can go tomorrow after school. I'll let you know what I find out. How's your brother?"

"He's still in the hospital, too. Nana told me two days ago, the last time she called, that the doctors don't have any plans to release him in the near future. But it sounds like Jon's starting to talk to people again. Nana said she brought him some oatmeal cookies when she went to see him, and he told her he'd rather have chocolate chip cookies instead."

"What an ingrate!"

"Yeah, but at least he's finally talking, even if it is just to complain. I think it's a step in the right direction."

"What, he has to get grumpy to get better?"

"Maybe."

"If that's the case, I hope both Jon and Alex start acting like assholes real soon."

Chapter 26

I was in no hurry to go back to Cumberland, but uncle George talked me into going with him to celebrate Nana's birthday. I agreed even though I was a little nervous about going back to Cumberland. I missed my grandmother and Granddad and Eileen.

I missed Jon, who was still in the hospital.

I even missed my parents, in the weird way I usually did when I hadn't seen them for a while. I knew it wouldn't take long, maybe just a few minutes, when I was back in their presence for them to get on my nerves. But I was looking forward to seeing them again and hoping against all common sense and experience that this time things would be different, and my parents would be healthy and acting like the loving, supportive adults I pictured most parents of being.

Uncle George and I had been planning Nana's birthday celebration for a few weeks. He wanted us to take her out to dinner at her favorite Italian restaurant, then meet Mom and Dad back at Nana's house for cake and ice cream. We ordered a carrot cake at the bakery near our house and bought birthday candles at the grocery store.

We went to the nursery, and George bought Nana a new pair of pruning shears, and I used some of the money from my last coffee house check to buy her a new rose bush for her garden.

George wanted to stay for at least two days to help Nana fix a few things around the house. He planned to stay at Nana's and sleep on the couch, and I had called up Granddad and made arrangements to stay with him and Eileen.

We left Portland by noon, after a quick stop at the bakery to pick up the cake, and figured we'd roll into Nana's driveway around 3 or 3:30 p.m. The traffic south of Portland was heavy, however, and we didn't get to Cumberland until after 5 p.m.

We stopped at the grocery store, and I called Nana from the payphone to let her know we were in town and would be there soon while George went inside to pick up some ice cream.

Mom was at Nana's house when we arrived and smothered me with hugs when we walked in. Then it was Nana's turn. As soon as she was finished hugging me, Mom flung her arms around me for another hug. I was holding the bag with the ice cream in it, while George carried in the cake. I was afraid the ice cream would melt before Mom finally let me go, but eventually she let me get past the foyer and into the house. George, who had put the cake on the dining table, reached for the bag and took it into the kitchen.

"Happy Birthday, Nana," I said.

"Thank you, Ava. It's so wonderful to see you and George. I'm so glad you two came all the way down here to see me."

"We wouldn't miss it for the world, Mom," George said, as he came back out of the kitchen. "You don't turn 65 every day."

"Ohhh, don't remind me how old I am!"

"You're only as old as you feel," George said.

"Mom, you look beautiful," Mom said. "And it's so nice to see my brother and my daughter again."

"Are you coming with us to the restaurant, Lisa?" George asked.

"If that's all right with you."

"It's fine with me. What about Keith? Does he want to come, too?"

"I don't think so," Mom said, giving Nana a funny look and shaking her head slightly.

George and I looked at each other and shrugged. Something was up, but neither of us wanted to delve into it just yet. I, for one, was hoping to be able to celebrate Nana's birthday without any family drama.

Mom had to have a little snack before we left, to keep her blood sugar stable. While she was eating a piece of sliced turkey, Nana put the flowers we had bought her into a vase. I went to the bathroom to pee and wash the traveling grime off my face, and George wandered into Nana's art room to check out her latest works. I heard him whistle in appreciation, so I joined him in there when I finished drying my hands. There was a row of paintings leaning against one wall of the room. They were a series of mountain landscapes. Lined up together as they were, they formed a panorama of the Cascade Mountain Range. Taken individually, each depicted a separate mountain or mountain scene.

133

"Whoa," I said.

"Whoa is right. These are awesome. Mom, when did you do these?"

Nana walked into the room and beamed. "Do you like them? I've been working on this series all month."

"Like 'em? Mom these are fantastic! Do you have a show coming up?"

"No, these are for a commission. A dentist in town saw my work at the gallery and asked me to do this series for her office."

"Mom, that's wonderful."

"Nana, that's awesome."

"Thank you. I'm really pleased with the paintings, and I hope the dentist likes them."

"She has to, Mom, they're incredible."

Mom crowded into the room with us. "I've got some new paintings at the gallery. You'll have to come see them while you're here."

"Sure, Lisa, that would be great."

"You, too, Ava."

"Sure, Mom, that would be cool. Aren't these new paintings of Nana's great?"

"They're OK, if you like schlook."

My jaw dropped. For once, I was shocked speechless. My damn right I'm pissed" instructor would have been proud, because it took me more than 10 seconds to come up with a response. It turned out I didn't have to because George beat me to it.

"Jeeze Lisa, you're not jealous or anything are you?"

"Quit picking on me," Mom snapped. "I'm just telling it like it is."

"Don't get pissy and ruin Mom's birthday. Speaking of which, are you all ready for dinner?"

"I have to do my exercise now," Mom said. "I have to go for my walk before I do anything. My doctor has me on a very strict regimen to control my diabetes you know."

"I'm hungry now," I said.

"Well, if you can't wait 20 minutes for me to follow my doctor's orders, why don't you all just go off without me."

"We'll wait, Lisa," George said. "We wouldn't want to do anything to jeopardize your health. Go ahead, and we'll wait."

It took another 10 minutes to convince Mom that we would really wait for her, and yes, we really thought it was wonderful she was taking such good care of herself. And no, neither George nor I wanted to walk with her, even though we'd been in the car for so long. And of course, that didn't mean we didn't care for her. It just meant we were tired and hungry and wanted to stay with the "birthday girl" while Mom got her exercise in.

Finally, about the time I was halfway wishing Mom would go into diabetic shock and shut up, she laced up her sneakers and marched out.

"Don't say it," Nana warned us both as the door closed behind Mom. "It's my birthday, and I don't want to hear it."

George and I just shook our heads and said "OK."

Then we went out to his minivan to get his duffel bag and the acoustic guitar he'd brought and vented to each other.

"What a fucking bitch. What's her fucking problem?"

"Don't call your mother a bitch."

"What should I call her then?"

"A fucking prima donna bitch."

We both laughed. "Seriously, though, what's her problem? Is she jealous of Nana or something?"

"I think so. When we were growing up, Lisa always wanted to be the center of attention. I think that's gotten worse since she got sick."

"That sucks."

"Yeah I know. She can be difficult sometimes. But let's both try to ignore it for Nana's sake. Remember, we're here to celebrate her birthday. Let's try not to let your mom ruin it for her."

"My mom? Like she's my problem? She was your sister first."

He laughed. OK, let's not let Nana's daughter ruin it for Nana."

We weren't exactly smiling when we went back into the house, but we weren't on the verge of exploding either. George sat down in the living room with Nana, while I went into the kitchen to call Granddad and tell him we made it safely to town, and that I'd be over later that evening.

"Mom got back from her walk and took 15 minutes "freshening up" in the bathroom before we could leave for the restaurant.

I was famished when we sat down and wolfed down half of the bread in the basket the waitress brought us with our menus before she came back to take our orders. Nana, George and I all were ready to order, but Mom had to ask the waitress questions about the menu before she would make her decision.

The food was great when it finally came, and I stuffed myself full of lasagna and salad. Nana said her mushroom ravioli was excellent and asked the waitress to box up what she didn't finish so she could take it home.

George cleaned his plate, then leaned back in his chair and sighed with pleasure.

Mom left half her entree uneaten and said "no thanks" when the waitress asked if she wanted to take the rest of it home.

It was nearly 8:30 p.m. when we left the restaurant, and Nana suggested we call it a night and save the cake, ice cream and the rest of her birthday celebration for the next night.

I was too stuffed to argue and wanted to get to Granddad's and Eileen's so I agreed. George was fine with the idea, too, and since desserts weren't on Mom's approved food list, she didn't offer up any objections. So George dropped me off at Granddad's.

I said good night to everyone, grabbed my pack, my skateboard and walked up to the door.

I turned and waved good-bye when I got to the front porch.

George gave the horn a little toot and drove off.

Chapter 27

Walking into Granddad and Eileen's house after spending the evening with Mom was like walking into another world, a calmer, quieter world. Eileen was reading, and Granddad was watching TV when I arrived. They seemed genuinely happy to see me, and I could feel my guard dropping along with my shoulders, which tended to tense up when I spent too much time with Mom. I lugged my pack and skateboard into the guest room, to give myself a moment to get reoriented, then returned to the living room.

"It's so nice to see you, honey," Granddad said.

"You look great, Ava," Eileen said. "Portland must be agreeing with you."

"Thanks. It's great to see you too."

We chatted for a while. Granddad and I talked on the phone at least twice a week, so there wasn't anything we needed to catch up on. They asked about Nana and how the birthday celebration went.

"Good, weird, I don't know. Nana was really glad Uncle George and I came down, and we went to Bella Roma for dinner. Mom was there, and she was being a pain in the, uh she was being difficult, so we didn't get to the restaurant until really late. We didn't get to do the birthday cake, so we'll do it tomorrow night I guess."

"That's too bad," Eileen said. "But at least you'll have something to look forward to tomorrow."

"That's true, I guess. Maybe Dad will want to come over to Nana's for cake. Mom said he didn't want to go out to dinner with us, so I didn't get to see him yet."

Granddad and Eileen exchanged glances.

"What?" I asked. "Is there something wrong with Dad?"

"I guess your mom didn't want to mention it," Granddad said.

"Mention what? Is he OK?"

"He's in jail," Granddad said.

"Fuck!" I said before I could control myself. "I mean, I'm sorry, I didn't mean to say that. What happened, why's he in jail?"

"He got picked up again for shoplifting, and apparently he assaulted the police officer who took him into custody," Granddad said sadly. "He was arrested last week."

"Was he stealing cigarettes?"

"I believe so."

"How come nobody bailed him out?"

"Well, he's in the jail infirmary, and that's probably the best place for him right now. He wasn't doing really well before he got arrested. At least while he's in jail, he'll be getting the treatment he needs."

I felt like someone had punched me in the chest and knocked the wind out of me. It took me a moment to start breathing again. After sucking in air, I asked if Dad had been taking his meds.

"I don't think so, judging by the way he was behaving," Granddad replied. "He was being very evasive with me, so I can't be sure, however."

A thought occurred to me, and I felt a wave of guilt wash over me. 'This is all my fault,' I thought. "I should have stayed home," I said.

"No," Granddad said firmly. "I know you mean well, and I know you love your father. But nobody could have helped him but himself. That's why I think it's good that he is where he is right now. Because while he's in jail, he'll be forced to comply with his doctor's orders. Right now it's the best place for him."

"I hate it," I said.

"I hate it, too," Granddad replied. "Unfortunately, things don't always work out the way we want them to."

I knew in my heart the Granddad was right, that I wouldn't have been able to help Dad even if I had stayed home. But I still felt guilty about leaving, and I felt even guiltier about being glad that I was living in Portland instead of with my parents.

I was still feeling guilty and conflicted when I got up the next morning, but pretended everything was all right when I sat down for breakfast. Granddad asked me what my plans were for the day. I told him I wanted to try to see Jon, that I had told Jason I'd call him and that Uncle George was planning do some repair work at Nana's house and I had offered to help.

While we were eating, Granddad and I decided to go visit Jon together.

I thought visiting hours were only in the late afternoon, but Granddad said Jon's current treatment program included a break between nine and ten in the morning, and we could see him then.

"I usually go see him in the morning before work," Granddad said.

"How's he doing?"

"Better, much better than he was doing when you saw him last. The doctors seem pleased with his progress."

I was glad Granddad was with me when the buzzer sounded, and the doors to the Behavioral Health Unit unlocked for me. Walking through the door made me sad, nervous, scared and anxious all at once.

My last visits with Jon had left me depressed and worried, and I could feel those emotions returning when I entered the waiting room.

Fortunately, we didn't have to wait very long before we were let in to see Jon, so I didn't have time to let my thoughts overwhelm me.

During my previous visits, I'd gone to see Jon in his room.

This time, we met him in the day room, a big, sunny room with couches, comfortable chairs and tables where people could play games or do jigsaw puzzles and a TV set. Four other patients were sitting with visitors, a half-dozen other patients were playing cards and watching TV when we came in.

Jon dropped his book when he saw us and led us to the far end of the room away from the TV so we could talk without competing with the sound coming out of the idiot box.

He put his hand on my arm when I approached and gave me a sheepish smile.

"It's good to see you, Ava."

"It's good to see you, too, Jon. How are you feeling?"

"Medium rare. Better than the last time I saw you, but not as good as I'll get."

"How are they treating you in here?"

"The food sucks, the other inmates are crazy, and the TV's always on. But some of the doctors are pretty nice, and there's some really good-looking female aides here, so it could be worse."

I was relieved just to hear Jon talking so it took me a moment to realize he was actually joking.

Not making the kind of jokes he used to, but joking nonetheless. That made me smile.

Jon wanted to know what was new, so I told him I had changed my name to Caitlin.

"No more Children of the Earth for you? I like that. Maybe I should change my name, too," he said.

"I still can't get used to your new name," Granddad said.

"I think it's cool," Jon said. "I just hope I can remember to call you that from now on. You won't be mad if I still call you Ava once in a while will you?"

"No, not at all. I don't really expect anyone who knew me as Ava to call me Caitlin, but they can if they want."

All too soon an orderly came up to remind Jon it was time for his group therapy session.

Granddad and I said good-bye and promised to come back the next morning.

Granddad drove me to Nana's house and dropped me off.

Chapter 28

Uncle George and I made three trips to the hardware store, once to buy plumbing supplies to fix Nana's kitchen faucet and the leaky shower head, and twice to return the new parts that didn't fit for the correct pieces. Granddad followed us to Nana's after our third visit and came inside to see exactly what we needed. He called the store and Jamie, one of the guys who worked there, showed up about 20 minutes later with the right parts.

Granddad headed back to work, while Jamie stayed and helped us with the repairs. Actually, to be honest, Jamie did the repairs while George and I looked on and passed him tools when he asked for them.

When he was finished, Jamie asked what other projects we needed done. George took him around the house and showed him the sagging hinges on the art room door, the broken window latch in the bathroom, the ripped screen on the back door and the leaky water heater. Jamie made a list and sent us back to the hardware store while he stayed and drank the tea Nana made him.

Jason and I had planned to go to the park, and he was at Nana's when George and I got back. Jason politely offered to help with the repairs. George and Jamie said they could handle everything and told us to go out and have some fun. We didn't argue and headed out to Jason's car before they could change their minds. I was surprised to see a black and white dog sitting on the driver's seat and drooling on the outside of the halfway opened window.

"What's that? Did you get a dog?"

"That's Charlie, my neighbor's border collie. My neighbor just hired me to dog sit and exercise him."

"Dog sit? Do you have your Red Cross dog-sitter certification?"

"No. I just lied during the interview. Besides, I had a dog when I was a kid, and Charlie likes me, and that's all the qualifications I needed."

Jason opened the front door and told Charlie to get in the back. The dog obediently hopped onto the bench seat and sat down.

I looked at him warily.

"What's the matter, Caitlin? Don't you like dogs?"

"I don't know. I've never spent any time with one. Will he bite?"

"Charlie? Naw, he's a lover, not a biter. He might lick you to death though."

"What?"

"Just kidding. He loves people, and he's really friendly. If he really likes you, he might kiss you unless you tell him not to. Come on, get in the car. He won't bother you."

I opened the passenger door, and Charlie looked up at me expectantly.

"Come on, Caitlin, it's OK."

I sat down and closed the door. I was fastening my seatbelt when I felt Charlie's nose on my arm. He was sniffing me, and I could hear his tail thumping against the back seat.

"See, he's wagging his tail. He likes you. He'll like you even more if you throw the stick for him when we get to the park."

While we were driving, Jason asked me if it was weird being back in Cumberland.

"Kinda," I replied. "Everything looks the same, but it feels like I've been gone for years, instead of just a few months. I don't know, I feel kind of nervous being back here. Like I don't belong here or something."

"How's your family doing?"

"Mom was really an asshole last night, and I found out this morning that my dad is back in jail. But I went to see Jon this morning, and he's doing a lot better. Way better than the last time I saw him. He looks pretty good and sounds OK. He seemed like he was happy to see me and even joked around a little."

"That's great Caitlin."

"Yeah, it was really cool. It was a relief to see him looking almost normal again."

"How's your grandmother?"

"Oh she's doing great. She was really happy to see me and my uncle yesterday and thanked us both a million times for coming down for her birthday. It's been really good to see her and see my grandfather and Eileen."

We chatted the rest of the way to the park, and I forgot, for a moment, that Charlie was in the car with us. I told Jason about signing up for the baby sitting class, and he talked about school.

The semester was coming to an end, and Jason was worried that he wouldn't be able to finish all his projects and reports before school ended.

"Yikes. Will they flunk you if you don't finish everything?"

"No, they'll give me incompletes, and I'll have to stay here for part of the summer to finish up."

"Bummer."

"Yeah, no shit. I want to get back to Salem and get a job so I can save up some money for next year."

We parked above the bench lands next to the river and got out of the car. Jason opened the back door for Charlie, who jumped out and ran towards the levee. He got halfway across the field, then turned around and sprinted back to us. Jason pulled an orange Frisbee out from under the seat and flung it towards the dog. Charlie leaped up, caught it in the air and raced back to Jason. Charlie dropped the Frisbee at Jason's feet, took a step back, then barked twice.

"OK, buddy, OK. Here we go."

Jason picked up the Frisbee and tossed it again. Charlie raced after it, while we walked behind him on the grass. We walked and talked while Jason and Charlie played fetch.

Despite my indifference to dogs, I found myself laughing at Charlie's acrobatics and enthusiasm. He would drop the Frisbee at Jason's feet, then spin around in circles until Jason picked it up. Then he'd watch Jason's hand intently, not moving his feet until the Frisbee took flight.

"How did you get so far behind in your schoolwork?" I asked.

"I've been too busy doing my homework," Jason replied.

"Huh?"

"I took your advice. I've been going to the library to research bipolar disorder and have been reading a lot of stuff about it."

"Really? What did you find out?"

"I'm still reading, but I found out a lot about what they say Alex has already. Some of it makes sense, and some of it doesn't. And some of it makes me feel better about his chances, and some of it makes me feel worse."

"What makes sense?"

"Well, apparently bipolar disorder causes extreme mood changes, from high highs to low lows. That sort of fits Alex. Remember how I told you that last summer he was so jacked up about coming to CCC that he drove me crazy?"

"Yeah."

"Well, that was probably the high high. And after he got to school and started majorly slacking was probably the start of the low lows. He was probably really depressed. They used to call it manic depression, which I think is a more accurate way to describe it, 'cause last summer, Alex was manic, and during the school year, he was depressed. So depressed that he tried to kill himself. Most of the stuff I've read said some bipolar people get so depressed they turn suicidal."

"Wow, that's heavy. Is there anything the doctors can do to help him?"

"Apparently, from what his folks have told me and my folks, they're giving Alex some antidepressants and some mood stabilizers to try to get him evened out, but it hasn't been helping much. They've switched his meds a couple of times."

"What's up with that? Don't they know what they're doing?"

"I don't know. The books I've looked at all say that lots of people have to try different medications before they find the right one or ones to help them."

"Gee, that sounds like psych meds. My mom and dad have been on all kinds of different drugs over the years."

"Yeah, I bet. There's no blood test they can do for mental illness, or any other kind of diagnostic test, so it's kind of hard for the doctors to figure out what to do."

"That sucks. So you mean they have to keep playing around with his meds and hope he gets better?"

"Yeah, sort of."

"What took them so long to figure out Alex was bipolar?"

"I don't know. Supposedly it's hard to diagnose, especially when a patient isn't very cooperative."

"Oh. Do they know how Alex got it?"

"No, it's not like a virus or anything. It's not contagious and they don't know what causes it exactly, but some people think it's brought on by a chemical imbalance in the brain. It's supposed to run in families, but as far as I know nobody in Alex's family has it."

"So for Alex, it was probably just bad fuckin' luck."

"Yeah, I guess so, really bad fucking luck."

We walked in silence for a while.

"It kind of sounds like nobody really knows all that much about bipolarism," I said.

"Yeah, that's the tough thing. I keep reading more and more articles and more and more books, and I don't really learn anything. But I feel so helpless, that I keep reading and trying to find something that makes sense."

"How many books have you read?"

"Oh, God, at least six. Right now I'm reading one by a woman who's bipolar herself."

"No wonder you're behind in your school work."

"Yeah. I wish I could get college credit for studying bipolar disease, and the effect it has on a patient's best friend."

Chapter 29

Jon was in a good mood when Granddad and I visited him the next morning. So was I. Mom had refrained from annoying me the night before, although she did insist on being driven home immediately after dinner because, "I can't eat cake you know, because of my diabetes."

Jon was talking rapidly and had a hard time staying still. He had a small rubber ball in his hand, like the ones I used to use to play Jacks with when I was in grade school and kept bouncing it on the floor. His hands shook, slightly, and his right leg twitched. But his mind seemed clear, and I could follow his conversation even though he jumped from one subject to another.

"I'm getting better," he declared at one point. "I'll be out of here soon. You just wait and see. I'll be out of here before you know it."

Jon had big plans for the future.

"I'm going to go to medical school. How much money do I have in my college account, Granddad? I'm going to be a psychiatrist. After I get my degree I'm going to come back here and run this place."

Jon chattered on for most of the visit. He kept talking when Granddad and I got up to leave after the aide announced it was time for Jon's morning therapy session. I could hear his voice as we went out the door saying,"Mark my words, I'll be running this place one day."

"He seems better today," I said to Granddad as we walked through the parking lot.

Granddad just shook his head. "I don't know honey. I hope you're right."

Granddad dropped me off at Nana's house. I thought Uncle George would be busy with repairs, but he was sitting in the center of the couch playing his guitar when I came in.

"How's Jon?"

"Good. Amped. He looked pretty good. He talked a lot and was talking really fast. He was kind of jittery, like he'd been drinking too many double cappuccinos."

"Hmmm."

"Hmmm what?"

I felt a twinge of worry course through me and changed the subject in an attempt to ignore it.

"Where's Nana?"

"She's out in the back 40."

"Oh. What are we working on today?"

"Actually, nothing. Jamie got almost everything done yesterday, and he promised to come back this afternoon and finish up."

"Cool. Wanna go skateboarding?"

"Actually, Mom and I were thinking about picking up your mom and going to the gallery to check out her paintings. We were just waiting for you to come by to see if you want to go with us."

Marianne was alone in the gallery when we arrived and came out from behind the desk to give Mom a hug. "Lisa, it's so good to see you! You're not going to believe this, but I just sold one of your paintings."

Mom beamed and chatted with Marianne while the three of us wandered around. Five of Mom's paintings were hanging on the rear wall, and there was an empty space on the wall where the sixth had been. I recognized Mom's style, even though I hadn't seen those particular works. She was still using watercolors, as she had been doing for the past three years, and was still painting garden scenes. Her technique had changed, however, and these new paintings looked almost three-dimensional.

I lifted my hand to touch the front of one to see if the trees really did stick out from the canvas, but dropped it sheepishly when I realized the painting was behind glass.

"These are really good," Uncle George said, walking up to me. "Her work has really evolved. These are incredible. Look at this one. It makes me feel like I'm walking through a gate into another world."

"They're amazing," I agreed.

Nana nodded. "She's taken her work to a whole new level. It's wonderful to see it."

I glanced back at Mom, who was engrossed in conversation with Marianne. It was hard to believe these peaceful and serene works were created by someone whose life was so chaotic and troubled.

Mom saw me looking her way and smiled.

"Do you like them Ava?"

"I sure do Mom, they're beautiful."

"Better than your Nana's?"

My jaw dropped, and I, for once, didn't know what to say. Uncle George came to my rescue.

"That's like comparing apples to oranges, Lisa. Both of you are creating wonderful artworks these days, but your mediums are so different there's no way to compare them."

I walked out of the gallery and headed toward the parking lot. I was leaning against Uncle George's minivan, muttering curse words when Nana walked up.

"Why does she have to do that? Why does she have to ruin everything?"

"Your mother is just insecure. She just needs constant reassurance that she's OK."

"She's not OK. She's nuts. She's mean. She's always trying to put someone down or create a scene. I can't stand it."

Uncle George went with Granddad and me to visit Jon the next morning. Jon was in a bad mood when we got there, and our presence didn't help. In fact, I think it made things worse. Jon started getting agitated, and an aide rushed over and told us he thought that Jon was getting overwhelmed by having so many visitors.

Since George and I were leaving for Portland later in the day, Granddad suggested we stay with Jon since he could always visit him later.

Jon calmed down a little after Granddad left, but seemed more nervous than he had the day before. His right leg was bouncing up and down so rapidly that his voice was actually warbling. He kept rubbing the palms of his hands together and speaking quickly. After a couple of minutes, Uncle George said good-bye to Jon and told me he'd wait for me in the lobby.

"What's the matter?" I asked Jon.

"What's the matter? What do you think is the matter? I'm locked up in a nuthouse, and the doctors won't let me go. They're afraid I'll tell everyone how fucked up this place is."

148

"What's so fucked up about it?"

"What isn't? I'm incarcerated here, and I didn't commit a crime, and I haven't had a trial. I'm locked up with a bunch of crazy people, and the doctors who run this place are crazier than the patients."

Jon's voice got louder as he spoke, prompting me to wince, and the aide who had suggested Jon wasn't up for multiple visitors looked over at us.

"It'll be OK, Jon. It's a hospital, not a prison. You're only here so the doctors can help you get better."

"You don't understand!" Jon shouted. "You just don't get it!"

The aide rushed over to Jon and put his hand on Jon's arm. Jon jumped up angrily, breaking the contact. The aide grabbed Jon's arm again, and yelled "Stanley, I need help over here."

Another aide, who I hadn't noticed before, rushed over and grabbed Jon's other arm. Jon started screaming for them to let him go. I started crying as the two aides began walking Jon away from me.

"Don't worry, miss, we've got it under control," one of the aides said.

The other added, "You'd better leave now."

I nodded and walked to the door.

When someone from behind a counter buzzed me out, I stumbled into the hall and fled to the lobby where Uncle George was waiting.

I had stopped crying by the time we got to Nana's but started weeping again when I told her about Jon. "He's never going to get better," I said. "He's just getting worse and worse."

"No he's not, Ava," Nana said. "This is just a little setback. I've been visiting Jon regularly, and with him, it's been two steps forward, one step back. This is just a little step back."

"You didn't see him. You didn't hear him. It was awful."

"I'm sure it was, honey, I'm sure it was. But try not to let it upset you. Jon's just having a bad morning. He'll keep getting better."

I didn't believe her, but didn't see any point in arguing. If Nana wanted to believe Jon was getting better, who was I to put a damper on her hopes. Besides, I was suddenly drained from my visit with Jon. I just didn't have the energy to continue the conversation.

Chapter 30

I was glad to get back to Portland, well, more accurately, I was glad to get out of Cumberland. I've heard the expression that you never have another chance to make a first impression, which implies that the first impression someone has of you sticks with them forever. In my case, it was the last impression that I couldn't forget; my last impression of my brother was disturbing, and I couldn't shake it. My last impression of Mom wasn't ideal either, although it wasn't horrible, but the fact that my father was back in jail made me feel sick to my stomach.

George and I had swung by Mom's house to say good-bye on our way out of town. We had planned to stay for just a few minutes, but Mom seemed particularly needy, and we spent at least an hour in her company before hitting the road.

I had said good-bye to Eileen after breakfast and had planned to say good-bye to Granddad after we had visited Jon together. Since he left the hospital before I did, I asked Uncle George if we could stop by the hardware store on our way out of town.

I gave Granddad a hug, while George sought out Jamie to thank him again for all his help at Nana's house. As we were walking towards the door, Granddad called me back and offered to let me pick out a candy bar from the rack near the cash register, like he used to when I was little.

I grabbed a Snickers for old times sake, and he tossed a second one to Uncle George so we could "share" in the treat.

I gobbled down my candy bar as soon as we got back in the mini-van. George stuck his in his shirt pocket and started the motor.

"Are you gonna eat that?"

"Why? You want another one?"

"Uh huh."

"OK, but don't blame me when your teeth fall out." George pulled the candy bar out of his pocket and handed it to me. I unwrapped it and ate it slowly, trying to let the sweet candy chase away my sour thoughts. It didn't work, but the candy did taste pretty good.

"I'm glad that's over," I said.

"The candy bar?" George said with a smile.

"No, the visit."

"Yeah, it was kind of a brutal morning."

"Brutal morning, it was a brutal trip. Jon's never going to get better, Mom was totally annoying, and my father's in jail. It sucked. I never want to see Cumberland again."

"But other than that, Mrs. Lincoln, how did you like the play?"

"Huh? What are you talking about?"

"Don't you know your US history? President Lincoln was shot in Ford's theater while he and his wife were watching a play. So when someone had a really shitty experience, you ask them…"

"Yeah, yeah, I get it," I interrupted. "The play sucked, too." I paused and thought for a minute.

"Well, actually it was good seeing Nana and Granddad and Eileen."

"What about Jason?"

"That was OK," I said, as my cheeks suddenly grew warm.

Uncle George glanced at me and smiled. "Just OK?"

"Well, maybe better than OK. Jason's, he's, um, pretty cool."

"He seems like a good guy."

I didn't answer, because I realized, in a flash, how much I liked Jason. I was afraid to admit it, afraid that George would tease me about him. After a moment or two, I spoke again, changing the subject.

"Do you think Nana liked the presents we got her?"

"Oh yeah, definitely. She was out in the yard this morning using her new shears to trim her roses and trying to decide where to plant her new rose bush. She was really pleased, because she didn't have that variety.

"But to tell the truth, I think she would have been thrilled even if we didn't get her any presents. She must have told me 15 different times how happy she was that we came down to visit for her birthday."

"Do you think she misses us when we're in Portland?"

"Of course she does. But I think she's glad that we're leading our own lives. And she's glad you're getting a break from your parents."

"But she loves Mom."

"Sure she does. But my mom is pretty realistic. She knows how tough it is for you to be around your folks, how tough it is for anyone to spend much time with them. And she knows it's even harder now with Jon in the hospital and all, and she really doesn't like the way Lisa manipulates you into taking care of her and your Dad."

"But Mom and Dad need me."

"They need more help than anyone can give them. And you need to stop feeling guilty about leaving them and start taking care of yourself for a change."

"I thought taking care of me was your job."

"You know what I mean."

"Yeah, I do. It's just hard to not feel bad about leaving them on their own."

"I know."

"Do you think Jon will ever get better?"

"I don't know Ava, I mean Caitlin. I hope so, but I just don't know."

Chapter 31

In the aftermath of the trip I had forgotten all about the Red Cross babysitting course. I remembered just in time, but would have been late if Uncle George hadn't been able to drive me there.

When I got there I discovered I was the oldest kid in the baby sitting class, which came as a surprise. I had gotten used to being the youngest student at the adult ed school.

I felt self-conscious in a room full of 11 and 12 year olds and slouched down in my seat trying to appear shorter than I was.

The instructor, however, didn't act like it was weird for an almost 16-year-old to want to learn how to be a baby sitter and asked me to help some of the other students who were having trouble putting diapers and clothes on the plastic baby-sized dolls and wrapping bandages around each other.

We learned how to supervise kids, when to call 911, how to fix simple meals, what not to feed kids and not to let your friends come over while you were baby sitting.

I got worried when the instructor taught us how to perform CPR on babies and young kids, wondering how often those skills would be needed. The teacher must have sensed my concern, because she made a point of telling us several times as we practiced on plastic dummies that none of the students she'd ever taught had actually had to do CPR, but that it was an important thing to know just in case. Besides, it was required for anyone who wanted to earn a Red Cross Babysitting Certificate, she pointed out, which was a good enough reason for us to practice it. When Uncle George picked me up at the Red Cross office on Sunday afternoon, I had my newly minted certificate in one hand and an official Red Cross First Aid kit in the other.

Uncle George thought I'd rush out and tell the neighbors who'd been asking me to babysit that I was certified and available. I didn't, in fact I started taking different routes to and from our house to avoid the families with young kids that I knew.

After a week, George asked me what was up.

"I'm scared," I admitted. "I've never babysat anyone before, and I'm scared I'll screw up."

"What are you afraid of?"

"I'm worried the kids won't behave, and they'll get hurt. I'm worried that I won't know what to do, and that I'll blow it, and nobody will ever want me to babysit again."

"Well, you're not babysitting now, so how much worse could it be if that happened?"

"I'd be humiliated. Who fails at babysitting?"

"No one who passed the Red Cross Babysitting class, I would imagine. Why don't you give it a try? Maybe start with someone who only has one kid, or someone who has kids who like you. Weren't you teaching the two kids across the street how to skateboard?"

"Yeah, so?"

"So they look up to you. They'll listen to you and do what you say. Especially if you play with them."

"I don't know. I'll think about it."

At my uncle's urging, I finally called Nana and asked her for advice. Like my uncle, she was convinced I could handle taking care of a kid or two.

"Start small," she advised. "Sit with someone for an hour or two and see how it goes."

Even after our conversation, I wasn't confident enough to go out and look for work. But work came looking for me. A couple of days after Nana's pep talk Samantha, who lived across the street, asked me to look after her 6-year-old daughter for a couple of hours the next afternoon.

When I said I would, Brianna, who had come to the door with her mother clapped her hands with excitement and said, "Oh goody!"

When I showed up at Samantha's the next day, she had a list of phone numbers and instructions for me.

She had written out the number for her doctor's office, where she'd be, the number for her husband Mitch, at work, and the number for her mother, just in case of an emergency.

She had written down that Brianna could have a snack at 4 p.m., either a piece of fruit or some toast only after she washed her hands, but no cookies of any kind. Brianna could watch TV, but only the cartoon channel and nothing else, and that she was not allowed to play out front, even with me there.

Samantha showed me where she kept the Band-Aids, where the phone was and told me I was welcome to have a snack, too.

While she was giving me instructions, Brianna was tugging at my hand, asking me if I would play Barbies with her. When Samantha finally left, Brianna led me to her bedroom and pulled her dolls out of her toy chest. We sat on the floor and invented a whole new life for Barbie that involved riding in her car, going to school, being on television, going to a dance and going shopping.

Before I knew it, Samantha was back, and I had survived my first afternoon as a baby sitter.

After that, I started babysitting regularly, working four or five days a week and bringing in more money than I had working at the coffee shop.

Between working, studying, going to school and skateboarding with my uncle my days were pretty full, leaving me less time to worry about Jon and my parents.

Chapter 32

In late May, I received a phone call from Grandmom Jensen, who lived in Idaho. She was planning her annual trip to Oregon and Washington and asked if I wanted to go to visit Aunt Beth's family with her.

I was thrilled. I hadn't seen Aunt Beth or my cousins since that wonderful summer three years ago, although Julie and Katie and I sent letters back and forth regularly, and Aunt Beth called on my birthday and most holidays.

Billy was in college on the East Coast and was planning to join some of his baseball teammates playing summer ball in a wooden bat league in Maine, so he wouldn't be there. But Julie and Katie would both be at home, and I was looking forward to seeing them again.

Two days after my last class, Grandmom came to Portland.

I was afraid to ask her about Dad and Jon, but when we got back to the house she told me she had seen them both, and that she had good news and some not-so-good news.

The not-so-good news was that Dad was still in jail, although he was in the hospital wing and receiving treatment.

She said he was depressed but responding to his medication. The drugs, or the depression, or both made him docile and lethargic.

Jon was doing much, much better, Grandmom said. The doctors were planning to release him to a halfway house—the same one Dad had lived in—as soon as a bed opened up there.

Jon was chatty, she reported, and cheerful. He was looking forward to getting out of the hospital. I was glad to hear Jon was apparently improving, but sorry to hear about Dad.

I asked if she knew when he was going to be released and tears came to her eyes. "I don't know Ava. He still has to go back before a judge, once he's deemed well enough."

Grandmom and I drove up to Aunt Beth's the next day. I was a little nervous about spending so much time alone in the car with her before we set off.

Until the night before, I couldn't remember ever spending time with Grandmom unless someone else was there. She had divorced Granddad and moved to Idaho before I was born, so I had only seen her when she'd come to Cumberland to visit. Sometimes her husband, my step-grandfather, came with her and sometimes she came alone. Even when she came by herself, Jon had always been with me when I saw her and sometimes Dad as well.

I was afraid we'd run out of things to talk about, or I would say something about Dad or Jon that would make her upset. I was worried she'd ask me questions about why I was living in Portland and would try to talk me into returning to Mom's.

Once again though, for the umpteenth time, I had worried about something that didn't happen.

Grandmom was in a good mood during the drive and looking forward to spending time with Aunt Beth, Julie, Katie and Ben. We chatted about them, and she told me stories about how smart and popular Aunt Beth had been growing up.

"She was always surrounded by a group of friends. Beth was the one who organized all the activities and games. She put on plays in the garage when she was a little girl and would recruit all the kids in the neighborhood to act in them. When she was in high school, her classmates voted her the girl who was most likely to succeed."

Grandmom didn't say anything about Dad's childhood, and I didn't ask, even though I was curious about what he was like as a boy. Dad had been sick my entire life, and I wondered what he had been like before the disease took over.

Before I knew it, we were getting off the highway, and Grandmom asked me to pull the map out of the glove compartment and direct her to Beth's. I didn't know how she expected me to find the way until I unfolded the map and saw she had highlighted the route with a yellow magic marker. I navigated, getting more and more excited as we got closer.

"There it is," I said, pointing at the house after we turned on the block.

"I see it. We're here."

Unlike my previous visit, nobody ran out of the house to greet us. We made our way onto the porch and rang the bell.

After a moment, Katie flung open the door. Aunt Beth, who was drying her hands on a kitchen towel was walking up behind her.

"You're here!" Katie said.

"Welcome," Aunt Beth said. "Come on in. We weren't expecting you so soon. You must have made good time on the road."

Chapter 33

Katie chattered excitedly while Aunt Beth got Grandmom settled in the guest room, and I dropped my skateboard and my duffel bag off in Billy's room. Julie was at softball practice, she said, and wouldn't be home until 3 p.m. Dad's at work, she added, and won't be home until dinnertime. You're staying in Billy's room, because he's playing baseball Back East

this summer. Before I could digest Katie's information she launched into a new topic.

"Guess what? We got a boat."

"A fishing boat?" I asked, since I knew Uncle Ben liked to fish.

"No a sailboat. It's beautiful. It's 27 feet long, and it's white and blue and has two sails. Dad and I took sailing lessons last summer, and he bought it last month from a guy at the marina. I can wait to go sailing with you, you'll love it."

My cousin Julie gave me a big hug when she got home from practice. Her auburn hair was long, much longer than it had been three summers ago, and streaked with blond highlights. I felt dowdy beside her, with my mousy brown hair pulled back into a ponytail.

"Ava! I'm so glad you're here. Sorry I wasn't here when you got here. We're playing in a tournament next week, so I couldn't skip practice."

"That's OK," I said. "I'll be here for two weeks, so we'll have lots of time together."

As it turned out, we didn't get to see each other as much as I would have liked. Julie was busy most of the time, I was disappointed, but the vacation was still a lot of fun. A couple of days after I arrived Uncle Ben took us sailing. After just one trip across the lake I was hooked,

I was tired by the time we got back to the house, and my face felt raw and red from the sun and the wind. My hair was completely tangled, and the ground felt like it was moving up and down beneath my legs. I helped hose off the boat before Uncle Ben backed it into the garage and helped Katie lug the picnic basket and cooler into the kitchen.

I lay down on the couch to read Katie's instructional sailing book and fell asleep before I finished a page. I was dreaming about skateboarding across the water, carving big wide turns on the lake, when Aunt Beth woke me up for dinner.

We went sailing again on Sunday, and Julie left with her softball team for a week long tournament in southern Washington the following day. I started missing her as soon as we dropped her off at the rec center, where a bus was waiting to take the squad on the road.

Between softball, Justin and fundraising for the trip, Julie had been so busy that I hadn't had much of an opportunity to spend time with her. I was disappointed, but between Katie, Aunt Beth, Grandmom and Uncle Ben, I had plenty of company. We went sailing again on Wednesday afternoon and twice the following weekend. All too soon, it was time to head south and say good-bye.

Both Katie and Aunt Beth invited me to stay for the rest of the summer, and I was tempted, especially when Uncle Ben said he'd teach me how to sail. In the end, however, I decided to go back to Portland to earn some more money for college and take a couple more classes. I needed to complete three more classes to finish my sophomore year, and I was determined to finish them by fall.

Despite my decision, I couldn't help but cry when it came time to leave.

Chapter 34

I quickly settled into a routine when I got back to Portland. I went to classes at the adult ed school three times a week and lined up as many babysitting jobs as I could. I liked working evenings best, because I could do my schoolwork after the kids went to bed. Besides, Uncle George was gone most evenings, and after spending two weeks in a house full of relatives, I didn't relish the idea of being home alone.

It was a lot more fun to hang out with my uncle and his buddies and go skateboarding with them. Nana called about four days after I got back to Portland to say that Jon was finally out of the hospital and living at the halfway house that Dad had lived in years before.

The day after that Jon called and told me he was having group therapy every day in the same room we had been in when we were in the children of schizophrenics support group.

"It's really weird," he said. "I keep expecting that geeky guy to come in and tell us 'it's OK to be sad when mommy and daddy are sick and can't take care of you.'"

Jon gave me the phone number in his wing and told me he could receive calls between 7 and 9 p.m. I promised to call him every evening that I wasn't babysitting, but warned him I worked most nights.

"You can call on weekends, too," he said. "Sunday morning is a good time to call, 'cause a lot of people here are in church then, and the phone is free."

Granddad called too, to find out how my trip went and to tell me he'd seen Jon. I told him all about Uncle Ben's sailboat, and how he and Katie had started teaching me how to sail.

I told him about Aunt Beth's vegetable garden, and how it was even bigger than the one she'd had during my last visit, and how Julie wasn't around much because of her softball tournament.

"I didn't see Billy 'cause he's playing baseball with wooden bats Back East, but I stayed in his room. It smelled like a guy, like dirty socks and old cheese. I had to sleep with the windows open every night."

Two weeks later, I took the bus down to Cumberland to see Jon. I left on Friday, right after class and planned to come back on Sunday evening so I'd be able to go to school on Monday. I called ahead to let Jason know I was coming, and he offered to pick me up at the bus station. He was still in Cumberland, going to summer school.

Like he had feared, he didn't complete the final projects for two of his classes before the semester ended. Instead of getting incompletes, which would have allowed him to turn in the work later to get a grade, both instructors required him to take their classes over to get credits.

Jason was bummed, because he had a job lined up in Salem and most of his friends from CCC had split town for the summer.

It was too late to go visit Jon when I got into town, so Jason drove me to Nana's house and came in with me while I visited with her. After about an hour, he gave me a ride to Granddad's, where I was staying.

"What time are you going to visit your brother tomorrow?" he asked when we got into the car. "I can give you a ride there and back."

"That's OK, Jason. I'm sure Granddad can take me. I don't want to make you wait while I visit Jon."

"I don't mind. I'm taking care of Charlie tomorrow, and there's a big field near the halfway house that I walk him in sometimes. I'll even get paid for driving you there. My dog sitting duties begin the minute I pick up Charlie, and I'm on the clock until I take him home."

"Well, if you insist, and if you promise to share your babysitting money with me I guess that would be OK."

Jason laughed and said he'd call me in the morning around 9 to set up a time.

"Call me at 8 a.m., and I bet Eileen will invite you for breakfast."

"You got it. Will she make her famous waffles for me?"

"Maybe, if I look pathetic enough. Do you have my granddad's phone number?"

"Yeah, you gave it to me the last time you were here."

Eileen did make us waffles the next morning and even made a small one for Charlie, who woofed it down so fast I don't think he even tasted it.

After breakfast, Jason dropped me off at the halfway house and said he'd be back for me in an hour.

I took a deep breath, walked up to the main door and rang the buzzer.

I wasn't sure what to expect, or what condition Jon would be in, especially since our last visit ended so badly. He was in a good mood, however, and gave me a big hug when I walked in.

"It's so good to see you, Ava."

"It's good to see you, too, Jon. Are they treating you OK here?"

"It's not too bad. It's really weird being here though, after all those time we came here to visit Dad. I never thought I'd be a patient here. Then again, I never thought I'd be a patient at the nuthouse either."

"How's the food?"

"Worse than at the hospital, but they give you bigger portions. I'm gaining some weight. My pants are starting to fit again."

I looked at Jon closely. He was still thin but no longer looked anorexic. His skin was no longer pasty, like it had been in the hospital, and his hair was clean and combed.

His eyes, while they weren't sparkling like they used to when he was younger, were no longer dull and glazed.

"Yeah, you look better. How are you feeling?"

"You mean, how psychotic am I? Not very. They've got me on a shitload of meds. It makes it hard to read and kind of hard to think, but I don't hear those horrible voices anymore. I think they might have me on something they used to give Mom, 'cause I'm thirsty all of the time, and my mouth is constantly drying out."

"Uh oh, are they checking you for diabetes?"

"I don't know. But they draw blood from me once a week, so maybe."

"What are you on, I mean what drugs are you taking?"

"I'm not sure. I get a shot once a week, and two blue pills every morning and a yellow and a white pill in the evening. I can't remember what they're called."

My heart sank when I heard that. When he was in elementary school my brother could tell you what medications our parents were on and spell them for you. He could even tell you the dosages. Now he couldn't tell me what he was on, but I gathered it was four different medications, judging by his description. I never remembered either Mom or Dad taking more than two different drugs at a time for schizophrenia.

163

Jon and I talked about my trip to visit the Johnsons on the phone, but I guess he had forgotten, because he asked me about the trip. I told him all about their sailboat and how much fun I had sailing with Katie and Uncle Ben, and that I didn't get to see Julie very much because she has a boyfriend and was playing so much softball.

"She was away at a tournament most of the time I was there," I complained.

"How's Billy doing?"

"I don't know. I didn't get to see him. He stayed Back East after school got out to play baseball with some team. I stayed in his room, though, and it was kinda gross."

"Gross how?"

"Well, it smelled funny. And one night I was looking for something to read, and I found a bunch of gross magazines he had stashed behind the books on his bookshelf."

"What kind of gross?"

"You know. Naked women doing gross things with guys and other naked women."

Jon laughed. "What, were they Playboy and Penthouse magazines?"

"No, they were weird magazines I've never heard of before, with weird names like Sizzling Snatches and stuff like that. A couple of them were in some other language, Spanish, I think."

"Remember that Playboy Magazine we found in the alley that time?"

"The one you brought home and hid under your bed?"

"Yeah. That was so funny when Dad found it when we were moving. He sat down and read it from cover to cover and wouldn't do anything until he finished. Mom was so pissed. Say that reminds me. Will you do me a favor and bring me something when you come back tomorrow?"

"Sure, what do you want? The new Playboy?"

"No, um, condoms."

"Condoms!"

"Yeah, condoms. You know what condoms are don't you?"

"Well, duh. Uncle George buys them by the carton at Wal-Mart. But I didn't know you could use them in here."

"Well, not exactly. But she's a girl, and I guess she's a friend, and she sure likes having sex with me. I just don't want to knock her up or get AIDS or anything. She says she's on the pill, and that she's been tested, but you never know."

I was too embarrassed to go in the drug store and buy Jon condoms, so Jason went in instead.

I shoved the paper bag he came out with in the pocket of my jacket.

"Thanks, Jason. You really are a good friend."

"No problem, Caitlin. It's no big deal."

Jon was pleased when I handed him the bag the next morning.

"Thanks," he said, after peering inside. "I really appreciate this. I don't know how many people Karen has slept with before me, and I don't want to get anybody's cooties. There's a lot of shit going around now that you can't cure with penicillin. Besides, I don't think it's a good idea for two crazy people to start making babies. Having a pair of lunatics for parents didn't work out too well for us."

"Mom and Dad didn't worry about that."

"What, taking care of us, or making babies?"

"Well, both, I guess, but I meant making babies. I mean they had us after all."

"Yeah, but Mom wasn't sick when she had us. At least she hadn't been hospitalized or anything. And they made sure they didn't have any more kids after she was diagnosed."

"I thought they just got lucky, or stopped sleeping together."

"Oh no, they had sex all the time. Don't you remember hearing them go at it?"

"Yuck, no."

"Oh yeah, they could hardly keep their hands off each other. Being crazy must make you really horny. Everyone in here is screwing ever chance they get. But Dad got a vasectomy after Mom got out of the hospital that first time."

"He did? I didn't know that."

"Oh yeah. I remember him coming back from the doctor and whining about how much it hurt. He spent the next week sitting around the house in his boxers with an icepack on his crotch. It was actually kind of funny. But that's why we don't have any little brothers or sisters."

Hearing about my parents' sex life creeped me out, so I changed the subject.

"I'm going back to Portland tonight. I've got school tomorrow."

"School, huh. Maybe I'll finish school one of these days. I don't think I'm gonna go to college though."

"I thought you wanted to be a doctor."

"Naw, I changed my mind. It'll take too long, and I don't have that much time."

"What do you mean?"

"I mean I don't want to spend the next 8 or 10 years going to school. I just want to get out of here and on with my life.

"You can have my college money, by the way," he added. "I'll tell Granddad the next time I see him to get the bank to put it in your account."

"No, don't do that. It's your money, and you're gonna need it when you get out of here."

"We'll see," he said.

We talked for a while longer. I'd be back in Cumberland soon to see him again. I thought he'd be glad to hear that, but he just shook his head and told me I'd be better off in Portland.

"You're the only one in our family who isn't crazy. If I were you, I'd go far, far away and never look back."

166

Chapter 35

My birthday was coming up in early September, and I would be 16. Most of the 15-year-olds I had known at Cumberland High School couldn't wait to turn 16 so they could get their driver's license. Despite Jon's admonition about staying away from our family, I was looking forward to turning 16 so I could visit Dad in jail.

You had to be at least 16 to visit an inmate at the Cumberland County Jail, and unlike the Behavioral Health Unit at the hospital, the jail guards checked your identification before letting you in. I told Jason before I got on the bus to go back to Portland that I'd see him in September if he was still in Cumberland.

"Oh, I'll be here. The fall semester starts Sept. 5."

"Cool. I'll be coming down right after my birthday."

"Right on. Are you coming to celebrate it with your family?"

"Not exactly. More to see my Dad since I'll finally be old enough to visit him."

"Oh that's right. You're turning 16."

"Yeah. Sweet 16 and never been kissed."

"For real?"

"Yeah for real."

"We can take care of that right now."

"What, making me sweet," I said, blushing.

"No the other part."

I blushed some more and said "Well, that would be OK."

Jason leaned towards me and kissed me on the lips. I felt his warm lips on mine and a thrill run down my back. I didn't want the feeling to end. I kissed him back.

Jason called two days after I got back to Portland.

"I just talked to Alex. He called me from Salem and acted like nothing had ever happened, like we'd talked last week or something. It was weird, but it was great. Or great, but it was weird. I don't know, but he must not hate me anymore. It was such a relief to talk to him."

"That's great Jason. I'm glad he called you."

"Me too. He's been my best friend forever, and it was really weird being on his shit list and not being able to talk to him."

"You weren't on his shit list, Jason. You were on his sick list."

"Well, whatever list I was on, now I'm off it. This was a good week for the two of us. You got to see your brother, and I got to talk to Alex."

"Yeah, that's cool," I said, hoping he'd add another reason for it being a good week for the two of us.

"Way cool. I just wanted to tell you about it since you're probably the only one who really understands what this means to me. Anyway, I've gotta go. I was supposed to pick up Charlie about a half-hour ago, but I wanted to call you first."

It was a good thing I was babysitting a lot, because I spent a lot of time over the next month on the phone. When I had a free evening, I'd call Jon, and we'd talk for an hour or more at a time.

Jason called every three or four days, and in between his calls, I'd call him to chat. Uncle George didn't mind me tying up the phone, but he blanched when he saw the phone bill.

I assured him I'd pay for all the calls to Cumberland.

He told me it was OK, and he could cover the phone bill without my help. But I added up my charges and stuck the cash on his dresser without a word.

Despite my original apprehensions about babysitting, I was enjoying my new career. I babysat regularly for four families in the neighborhood and occasionally for half a dozen others. I liked playing with the kids, and the kids I babysat really liked the fact that I would play with them. I rarely had any problems with kids misbehaving. If they started acting bratty, I threatened to send them to their rooms and told them I wouldn't play with them for the rest of the afternoon or evening.

I never had to act on that threat, but they didn't know that.

My schoolwork was also coming along.

I not only kept up with my assignments, but I often moved onto the next section before the class reached it. Both my English and social studies teachers told me I could work independently if I wanted and take the final test for credit whenever I was ready.

168

I really started working hard after I heard that.

I figured if I finished two of my three classes early, I could sort of have a summer vacation, at least not have to work so much, with just my geometry class to worry about. Between schoolwork and babysitting, I kept myself pretty busy, but my life wasn't all work and no play.

Uncle George and I went skateboarding together at least four times a week. I had finally gotten comfortable riding the half pipes and deep bowls at the skate park and wanted to skate there all the time. A couple of times, when my uncle was busy, I rode the bus there and skated by myself, well, with about two dozen other skaters but none that I knew. It wasn't as much fun without George, and I found I was a little timid when he wasn't around to encourage me.

Things were going better for me than they had in a long time, and I was happy. That all changed early one morning while my uncle and I were eating breakfast. There was a knock at the door. Uncle George and I looked at each other.

"Are you expecting anyone?" I asked him, as I stood up and crossed the living room.

"No. At least I don't think so."

"It's probably for me, then. Probably one of the neighbors needs an emergency babysitter."

I opened the door, expecting to see an anxious parent.

Instead, I saw Granddad and Eileen standing on the front porch.

Chapter 36

I knew instantly that something was horribly wrong when I saw my grandfather's face. It looked like gravity was working at double strength, making his cheeks, jaws and mouth sag. His hair was uncombed, and there were bags under his eyes, which were rimmed with red.

There were lines etched under his eyes that I'd never seen before, which made him look 10 years older than he really was.

I looked to Eileen, in hopes of seeing some reassurance in her face. There was none.

Her eyes were bloodshot from crying, and the expression on her face was one of shock and sadness. Someone had died, and the only question was who.

"No. Oh no. No," I screamed.

Uncle George ran up behind me, put both hands on my shoulders and gently pulled me away from the door so that Granddad and Eileen could come in.

"Ava," Grandad said, his voice cracking.

"Who died?" I blurted out.

"I'm so, so sorry," Granddad said. "I've got some terrible news. Your brother killed himself last night."

My legs turned to rubber, and I screamed. The next thing I remember was lying on the floor, with my uncle kneeling on the ground next to me.

"What happened?" I asked. "Where am I?"

I looked up, saw Granddad and Eileen clutching each other, looking down at me with anxiety and grief on their faces and remembered.

I gasped for breath, trying to draw air into my lungs and feeling as if someone had dropped a 50-pound weight on my chest.

I struggled, coughed and then started to cry.

Uncle George helped me up from the floor and gathered me into a hug. I buried my face in his shirt and heard Eileen and Granddad murmur they were so sorry, followed by the sound of first Eileen, then Granddad, then finally Uncle George crying.

I sobbed until my temples ached, stopped crying for a moment, then sobbed some more.

Someone handed me a glass of water.

I swallowed it slowly, feeling the liquid slide down past the huge lump that had formed in my throat. After a while, I'm not sure how much later, I stopped crying long enough to ask what had happened.

"We got a call last night around 8 from the director of the halfway house," Granddad replied.

"He called us, because he couldn't reach your mom. He told us that Jon had committed suicide. One of the staff members had found him in his room. Jon had used his bed sheets to hang himself. I'm so sorry honey."

"Did they call 911?"

"They did, honey, but it was too late. Jon was gone by the time they found him."

I cried some more, then asked "are you sure he killed himself? Maybe another patient or someone else killed him."

"No honey, it was a suicide. Jon left a note."

"What does it say? Did you bring it?"

"The police have it right now, and you can read it once they're finished with their investigation and release it. But the cops read it to me, and essentially, Jon wrote that he couldn't live with schizophrenia any longer."

"Does Mom know?"

"Yes, the police notified her late last night."

"How come she didn't come with you?"

"Well, honey, as you can imagine she's pretty upset. She didn't take the news well, and she's back in the hospital."

I started crying again. Granddad put his arm around my shoulder, and I leaned against him.

"Does Dad know?"

"Not yet. The jail chaplain will break the news to him later today."

"What do we do now?"

"I don't know honey. We grieve, and we miss him, and we try to carry on."

I sleepwalked through the next few days, feeling alternately numb with grief and aching with sorrow.

Granddad and Eileen stayed in Portland for two days, checking into a hotel in the early afternoon when it looked like they were ready to collapse with exhaustion.

Uncle George cancelled all his gigs and called the people I was scheduled to babysit for over the next four days and let them know I was unavailable due to a death in the family.

It sounded so matter of fact, the phrase "a death in the family."

I didn't even come close to conveying the pain and emptiness that wracked through my body and mind.

The phone rang nonstop for hours as the news spread. Nana, Aunt Beth, even Billy called from a pay phone out on Cape Cod. Grandmom Jensen called from Idaho, and several cousins I didn't know even existed called to talk to Uncle George.

I called Jason and began crying almost before I could choke out the words. He called back four times over the next two days to try to console me, then showed up at the door the morning after Granddad and Eileen left to return to Cumberland. He stayed for two days and sat quietly with me for hours while I cried and vented my anger at that horrible disease that had destroyed my brother.

We had to wait until Mom was out of the hospital and Jon's body was released by the coroner to hold his funeral. For some reason I'll never understand, the coroner had to conduct an autopsy on Jon.

Ultimately, he came to the same conclusion everyone else had reached, that Jon was an acute paranoid schizophrenic, had written a suicide note, left it on his bed and hung himself.

Uncle George and I drove down to Cumberland the day Mom was discharged from the hospital.

She was heavily sedated and at least 15 pounds lighter than she'd been the last time I'd seen her, when we arrived. We hugged and cried together in each other's arms.

"Oh Ava," she said, with her voice wavering in pain.

"I know, Mom," I answered. "I can't believe he's gone."

The funeral itself was surreal.

Our family had never belonged to a church, let alone attended one, so the memorial service was held at the funeral home.

I didn't think anyone would come other than Jason and our relatives.

So I was surprised to see the room overflowing with people when Uncle George, Jason and I arrived.

People who worked at the hardware store, Jon's high school soccer coach and some of his former teammates, Mrs. Beachman, our Kindergarten teacher, Tom and Marianne from the art gallery, two people from the Red Cross who had presented Jon with his award for rescuing me from the fire. The Johnsons, even Billy, who had skipped several games to fly in and pay his respects. Former classmates, regular customers from Swarthouts Hardware Store, even a few fellow patients from the hospital were there and dozens of people I didn't recognize or know.

The staff at the funeral home scrambled to set up more chairs as more and more people squeezed into the room.

When the room was packed, and more people were lined up at the door trying to enter, they opened up a partition to expand the room to accommodate Jon's mourners.

"Your brother sure touched a lot of lives," Jason said, as we watched with amazement at the throng of people.

Mom, Nana, Granddad and Eileen were sitting in the front row, to the left of the aisle, and Grandmom and Harold were in the front row to the right. Uncle George sat down next to Mom, and Jason and I sat down next to Grandmom.

A moment later two uniformed policemen brought Dad in, and the three of them sat down at the end of our row.

I jumped up and went to Dad, who stood up and hugged me.

The service, which was scheduled to begin at 2 p.m., was delayed about 45 minutes so that everyone could get in and find a seat.

The funeral director, a tall, stocky man with short gray hair and long bushy eyebrows that partly hid his eyes, welcomed everyone and talked about how we were gathered together to mourn a life that ended too soon. An organist played Amazing Grace, and then Granddad got up to talk about Jon's life.

Jon had been brilliant, Granddad said, an excellent student before he got sick and a wonderful, caring, considerate young man.

"Jon was an old soul," he said.

"He was wise beyond his years and very, very responsible. I was blessed to have him as a grandson, and I'll miss him deeply."

When he was done, Nana went to the front of the room and told everyone how wonderful Jon had been and how devoted he had been to me.

"Jon adored Ava, and he took wonderful care of his little sister. He taught her to read, walked her to school, played with her and kept her safe. He saved her life when their house caught on fire, and he helped provide her with stability when her parents were ill. He taught her to play soccer, to find the joy and humor in life and to persevere when things got tough."

I blushed, imagining I could feel everyone's eyes on me. Jason squeezed my hand, and Grandmom put her arm across my shoulder.

Mom got up and gave a rambling speech about Jondalar living up to his namesake until his purity angered the demons, who caused his death. The joke was on the demons, she said, because Jondalar was one of the Children of the Earth, and his death had returned him to the earth.

People were starting to squirm uncomfortably while Mom spoke, and I closed my eyes and tried to pretend Mom was saying what I wanted her to say instead.

In my mind I heard her say 'Jon was a wonderful son, grandson and brother, a smart, funny, brave, handsome, responsible young man who loved and cared for his family and protected and raised his sister who worshiped him. Jon's life was cruelly cut short by a terrible disease, and we should remember him as he was before he got sick and not how he died. That Jon was.'

Mom's imaginary speech was cut short when Mom started crying so hard she couldn't talk anymore, and Uncle George got up and helped her back into her seat.

There was a reception after the service, and dozens of people came up to me to tell me how sorry they were about my brother.

I followed Uncle George's cues, and thanked people for their kind words and either shook their hands or allowed them to hug me.

I had hoped to spend some time with Dad, but the police escorted him out of the funeral home right after the service and presumably returned him to the jail.

Finally, people started filing out.

I watched them walk out of the building, drive out of the parking lot and thought about how unfair it was that everyone else was going home and getting back on with their lives except for Jon.

Chapter 37

Jason and I walked around the cemetery after Jon's memorial service. I needed to get some fresh air, and I wasn't ready to go back to Grand-dad's house, where the family would be gathering.

We wandered aimlessly, walking up and down the paths that laced through the cemetery.

I knew my father's grandparents and their parents were buried somewhere on the grounds, as well as some of Mom's relatives, but didn't know where. Mom had originally wanted Jon to be buried next to her father, the grandfather who died before I was born. At the last minute, she changed her mind and decided to have Jon's body cremated.

She said she wanted to have Jon's ashes scattered "to the four winds," instead of buried in the earth.

We walked in silence for about 20 minutes. I felt talked out after having spoken to so many mourners after the service. Jason seemed to sense how burnt out I was and walked quietly beside me, leaving me alone with my thoughts.

My emotions were a mixture of grief and anger, both fighting for supremacy in my head. I wanted to cry, scream, shout and rail against the injustice of whatever force had cursed my family with schizophrenia, while at the same time I wanted to sob away the emptiness that filled me, along with the realization that I would no longer have my brother to help me negotiate life's rocky roads. But exhaustion prevented me from doing anything but put one foot in front of the other.

The afternoon sun was beating down on us, and we were both sweating by the time we found a bench underneath the shade of a fir tree. Jason brushed some cones and duff off the seat, and we sat down next to each other, gazing out at the rolling green lawn dotted with tombstones.

"Thanks for hanging with me," I said, finally breaking my silence.

"No problem. This has to be tough for you."

"You got that right. I just can't get over the fact that I'll never see Jon again."

Jason reached for my left hand with his right and squeezed it gently.

"I knew this was going to happen. I knew it the minute I heard that Jon had tried to kill himself last spring. I knew it was going to happen, but I just didn't know when. I've been so scared, so worried about it. I, I, I just wish I'd been wrong."

"I wish you had been, too, Caitlin. I wish you had been, too."

There were cars parked up and down the block on both sides of the street when we got the Granddad's house.

"Do you want to come in?" I asked.

"No, thanks. I figure you might want to spend some time with just your family."

"Yeah, I guess I should. Thanks for coming to the service and all. I hope it wasn't too much of a bummer."

"It wasn't. Well, it really was, especially for you, but it wasn't as bad for me as my sister's funeral was. I'm just really, really sorry about Jon. I just wish he'd never gotten sick and this had never happened."

"That makes two of us."

I climbed out of Jason's car and started up the driveway. I turned back toward the road when I reached the front porch. Jason was sitting behind the wheel, watching me. I waved, and he waved back. I heard him start to drive off when I opened the front door.

The house was jammed with relatives.

Mom, Nana, Uncle George, Grandmom, Harold, the Johnsons and at least a dozen cousins and great aunts and uncles. I slipped into the guest room to change my clothes and found Julie and Katie lying on their stomachs on the bed and talking.

"Hey Caitlin, we're just kickin it," Julie said. "Hope you don't mind us hanging in your room."

"Was that your boyfriend?" Katie asked.

"Who Jason? I don't know. And don't worry Julie, this isn't my room."

"What do you mean you don't know? Is he or isn't he? He's cute."

"Katie shut up. I know it's the guest room, but you're staying here aren't you? At Granddad's?"

"Yeah. There's not enough room at my Nana's house, 'cause my uncle and my mom are staying with her. And yeah, Katie, he is cute."

"He is. I saw him holding your hand. I think he's your boyfriend."

"I don't know what he is. He's a boy, and he's my friend, and, oh I don't know."

"Has he kissed you?"

"Katie!" Julie admonished.

"It's OK. Yeah, but just once."

"I knew it! I knew it! He's your boyfriend."

'I hope you're right,' I thought. "I don't know Katie. I'm gonna go get something to eat."

Everyone cleared out by 8 o'clock, and Eileen slumped back on the couch and gave a sigh of relief and exhaustion. Granddad loosened the belt of his pants, untucked his shirt and moaned.

"I had too much of Cynthia's chocolate cake. I think I'm going to burst."

"I think I had too much of everything," Eileen said. "I can't believe how many people brought us food. I won't have to cook for a week, even after sending more than half of it home with Lisa."

"I'm going to see if there are any more cookies," I said, and headed for the kitchen.

"Help yourself," Eileen said. "The more you eat, the less I will."

Granddad followed me into the kitchen.

"I thought you were full," I said.

"I am. I just wanted to talk to you. The police returned Jon's suicide note to me this morning. Do you want to read it?"

"Yeah, I do."

"I'll go get it."

Granddad returned to the kitchen with a piece of lined notebook paper in his hand.

"Here it is honey. You better sit down to read it."

I pulled out a kitchen chair, and sat down at the table.

Granddad placed the letter on the table in front of me, and I started reading Jon's scrawling printing.

I could see the disease in his handwriting, which had always been neat and precise before he got sick.

I have seen my future, and I want no part of it. My father has been crazy my whole life. My mother has been crazy ever since I was five. I've watched them go in and out of sanity too many times.
I've lived with the chaos of their madness. I know I am much, much sicker than either of them, and I know my madness is getting worse. I hate the way I feel. I hate the voices in my head. I hate the zombie meds they give me. I hate schizophrenia. I hate being crazy. Please don't cry for me anymore.
If you're reading this, I'm finally at peace.

Jon

P.S. Ava, you can have all my college money and all of my stuff.

Chapter 38

Uncle Ben, Billy and Julie left Cumberland the day after Jon's memorial service, and Grandmom and Harold headed home a day later. Aunt Beth and Katie decided to stay for a while.

I offered to move out of the guest room and onto the couch to make room for them at Granddad's so they wouldn't have to stay in the motel. But one of Aunt Beth's old friends from high school invited them to stay at her house, so they camped out there. I wanted to leave the day after the service, and get out of town and pretend everything was OK; that my brother really was at peace. Uncle George, however, wanted to stay to help comfort Mom and Nana.

As much as I wanted to escape, I didn't want to be alone in Portland. So I stayed, too.

"Do you think Jon's really at peace?" I asked Ganddad a couple of days after reading Jon's note.

"I don't know, honey. I wish I did. I just don't know what happens after someone dies. All I know is that Jon was miserable, and that schizophrenia is a cruel, cruel disease."

I asked Aunt Beth the same question after she'd read Jon's suicide letter. She didn't say anything for several minutes, and I was wondering if she was going to answer me at all when she finally spoke.

"I don't know Ava, but I'd like to think he is. Your poor brother was so tormented by his illness. I'd like to think he's at peace now."

"Me too," I said. "But I'm not sure either. I guess I'm just confused and angry."

"Angry that he's gone?"

"Yeah I guess, but mostly angry that he got so sick. It's just so not fair that Jon was schizophrenic. He was so wonderful before he got sick. And he was right, you know, he was so much sicker than Mom and Dad, and they're both so fucked up. What's wrong with my family? Who cursed us and made my father and mother and brother so crazy?"

Aunt Beth shook her head sadly.

"I don't know Ava, I just don't know. There are so many mysteries in life, so many things that just don't make any sense. I'm just so, so sorry. I hate schizophrenia, too. I was just about your age when your dad got sick, and I remember how awful it was and how scary. It felt like my whole world fell apart when my brother got sick."

"At least you still have a brother. And your parents aren't crazy."

"That's true, honey. You do have it much, much worse than I did. But I thought it was the end of the world when your dad got sick. I thought I'd never get over it, especially after my parents got divorced, and Mom moved back to Idaho. But life goes on."

"Was that why Granddad and Grandmom split up? Cause of my dad?"

Aunt Beth nodded.

"The strain of your father's illness was just too much. I think my mother blamed herself for it, and that made things even worse. People didn't know as much about schizophrenia then as they do now, and I think my mother believed Keith got sick because she had done something wrong when he was young."

"That sucks. People don't get schizophrenia because of something their parents did."

"I know, and I'm sure your grandmother knows that too. But she was so upset when your dad got sick that I don't think she was thinking clearly. Everyone was pretty stressed out and confused."

"That sucks."

"Well it did, but that was a long time ago, and this is now. I don't dwell on the past, and besides, both my mother and father have remarried and seem pretty happy."

"Yeah, but my dad's still sick."

"Well, unfortunately you're right about that."

"Do you think my dad is unhappy? Do you think he's tortured like Jon was?"

"I don't know Ava. I certainly hope not."

I didn't ask Mom what she thought, because she was so despondent over Jon's death that Nana, George and I were all worried about her.

Mom had been staying at Nana's ever since she had been released from the hospital, sleeping in the art room on the fold-up chair bed Nana had

181

bought years ago when Jon and I lived with her briefly.

Mom's doctor had put her on some kind of drug, a tranquilizer I suspect, and she was lethargic and quiet. She slept late in the morning, went to bed early and took several naps a day. When she was awake, she'd sit on the couch in a daze, not paying attention to anyone or anything.

For several years Mom had been fanatic about her medication, eating and exercising schedule. Now, Nana had to coax her to take her pills and to try to get her to eat. Uncle George kept trying, unsuccessfully, to get her to go for a walk, or even take a drive with him. I was worried she'd end up back in the hospital.

I think Nana and Uncle George were afraid she might commit suicide, because they made sure someone was with her all the time. I came over to Nana's at least twice a day, but couldn't bring myself to stay very long. Seeing Mom in her near stupor got me too upset.

Dad, on the other hand, seemed to be taking Jon's death much better than Mom or me. Aunt Beth had gone to school with the guy who ran the jail, and she talked him into letting me come with her and Granddad to visit Dad, even though I wasn't 16.

I was glad when Aunt Beth told me I'd be able to visit Dad; Jon's death made seeing Dad even more urgent to me.

I didn't know what to expect, however.

I was hoping Dad would be healthy enough to comfort me.

It was scary and strange the first time I went to visit Dad.

The Cumberland County Jail was a big, ugly one-story cement building on the outskirts of town, surrounded on all sides by an asphalt parking lot. Inside the jail there were armed guards in uniforms everywhere, including the waiting room, the hallways and the visitors' room where we met with Dad.

It was awkward, at first, talking to Dad with a stranger in the room listening to everything we said and watching everything we did. Granddad and Aunt Beth acted like the guard wasn't there.

I couldn't forget that he was in the room, but I tried not to look at him.

Dad was surprised to see me, since I wasn't old enough to visit.

He wrapped his arms around me and held me tight, murmuring "Ava, Ava, Ava." I hugged him back.

"I've missed you so much, Dad," I said, when he let me go.

"I've missed you, too, Ava. That's one of the worst things about being here, is that I haven't been able to see you." He hugged me again, then gave Aunt Beth and Granddad quick hugs. Dad looked over to me and asked, "How are you holding up?" My eyes misted immediately, and my throat tightened.

"Not so good, Dad. I can't believe Jon's dead."

Dad's eyes misted too, and he wrapped his arms around me again.

"I can't believe it either, Ava. It seems like a bad dream. I never thought I'd outlive either of you kids. I almost wish it was me, not Jon who had died."

"Oh Dad," I said, and started crying in earnest. Dad squeezed me, held me tight and started crying, too.

All too soon, visiting hours, or more accurately, visiting minutes were over, and we had to say good-bye as Dad was being led out of the room and back to his cell. Aunt Beth put her arm around my shoulder, and the three of us followed one of the guards back to the waiting room. We signed out and headed to the parking lot.

"Dad was all there," I said.

"I know," said Granddad. "He's been completely coherent for a while now. He does pretty well under controlled conditions where he's required to take his medication."

"How much longer will he be in jail?"

"I don't know. It all depends on his health, and what the judge decides. He'll have to go back to court to face the original charges once the doctors agree he's stabilized. I don't know what's taking them so long. It's pretty obvious to me that he's much better these days, but then again, I'm not a psychiatrist."

Chapter 39

U ncle George and I stayed in Cumberland until Mom started to emerge from her daze about 10 days after the memorial service. The weather turned hot the day after my first visit to the jail, with the temperature soaring into the 90s by 10 each morning, and getting even hotter in the afternoons. Dad was only allowed two 50-minute visits per week, so I only got a chance to go back to the jail to see Dad two more times.

It was cool inside the cement building, so both times it was a shock to walk out of the jail into the heat waves rippling up from the asphalt parking lot.

After visiting Dad with me, Granddad would drop me off at Nana's before heading to the hardware store.

When Mom started to get on my nerves, I'd go back to Granddad's and hang out with Katie and Aunt Beth if they were there.

The heat made me lethargic and grumpy, grumpier than usual, and my visits with Mom grew shorter and shorter. I'd beg Uncle George for a ride back to Granddad's, arguing it was too hot to walk or skateboard the mile or so between their homes.

The heat was getting to Uncle George, too, and he was sweating profusely one afternoon about a week after we'd arrived in Cumberland.

"I don't know how much more of this heat I can take," he complained, as he drove me back to Granddad's. "It's really cooking today. I feel like my brain is boiling."

"Let's go swimming," I suggested.

"That's a great idea. Let's go down to the river."

He turned the car around and went back to Nana's for a pair of shorts to use as a bathing suit. We swung by Mom's house, and I went into what had been my old room and dug around until I found my bathing suit. It was a little snug, but I squeezed into it, and pulled my shorts and T-shirt over my one-piece and went back to the car.

"It's hotter than hell in the house," I commented. "And it's weird being in there. It almost feels like it's been years since I lived there instead of just months."

"I wonder how long it's going to take Lisa to move back in there. It seems like a waste for her to pay rent on it while she's at Mom's."

"Gosh, I hope she doesn't stay at Nana's forever."

"Me too. It'll drive Mom absolutely crazy. It's hard on her taking care of your Mom."

"I bet. I can hardly stand to hang out over there when my Mom's like this."

"Yeah, I've noticed. She can be hard to take even when she's not comatosed with grief."

"You've got that right," I replied. "Where are we going anyway? To the Bixby Ranch?"

"Yeah, that's my favorite swimming spot."

"Mine too."

There were a dozen or more places where you could swim in the Chabot River as it snaked its way through town, but we preferred a spot located about 3 miles south of the city limits. To get there you had to turn off the main road onto a bumpy and narrow dirt road leading to the trailhead that led to the swimming hole.

There had been a hand-painted wooden sign on the dirt road reading "Bixby Ranch Road" when Uncle George first started taking Jon and me there during his summer visits to Nana when I was five or six.

The sign was long gone, but the name stuck.

We bounced down the dirt road for a mile or so, then pulled off to the side at a wide spot and parked under a grove of cottonwood trees. Then we hiked about a quarter of a mile down a narrow, tree-shaded footpath to the river. I could hear the water before we reached the riverbank.

The river took a short but steep drop, which created a six-foot waterfall as it cascaded over the rocks. The water pooled up between the banks, the cliff and a natural, rocky barricade about 80 feet to the south, creating an ideal swimming hole.

You could jump or dive off the rock cliff into a pool of cool water that was at least 15 feet deep, or sit on a rock outcropping below the falls and let the water cascade down your back.

You could sit in the shallows along the banks and feel the sun on your shoulders and let the moving water massage your legs.

You could swim on the surface, or underwater, or float on your back and watch the sunlight dapple through the leaves of the overhanging trees. In short, it was the perfect place to spend a sweltering afternoon.

Uncle George had told me his father had started taking him to the Bixby Ranch when he was about three. His dad, the grandfather I had never met, taught him to swim in the cool waters there.

George was carrying on the family tradition when he taught first Jon, then me, how to swim in the river, nurturing a love of fresh, moving water in me and a disdain for chlorinated pools.

There were four teenagers hanging out on the opposite bank when we arrived and a family with three small kids splashing in the shallow waters near the shore.

We dropped our outer clothing on the bank and jumped in.

I swam underwater, feeling the heat dissipate from my overheated skull, then surfaced and tread water for a few minutes while I gazed around.

A dozen or so dragonflies zipped over the pool, flashing their iridescent wings as they fluttered in and out of the sunlight and shadows.

I flopped over on my back, spread my arms and legs and floated for a while, enjoying the water. My legs kept sinking, so I turned over and swam, dolphining under the water as I made my way towards the base of the waterfall, where my uncle was perched on a rock with the water rushing down on his head and back.

"This is heavenly," I said.

"What?" he asked, leaning his head out of the path of the waterfall.

"This is great."

"It sure is. We should have been coming here all week."

Chapter 40

We swam every afternoon after that, and the cool waters helped make Cumberland more bearable for me. We brought Katie and Jason with us most days, and while they enjoyed the swimming hole, they didn't seem to need it like George and I did.

I craved the water, and I suspect my uncle did too.

Anticipating a swim made it easier for me to go into the jail to see my father, as well as to hang out with my mother and feel more compassion than irritation for her.

The cool water and the exercise helped me sleep better at night, which also made me less grumpy; a fact I'm sure all my relatives appreciated.

Mom's doctor began weaning her off whatever medication he had given her when Jon died, and she began emerging from her stupor.

She cried every day, sometimes four or five times a day, which often made me cry for Jon as well. Our shared grief seemed to pull us closer together than we'd ever been.

Mom started taking control of her medications and her diet again. Once she resumed her rigid schedule, Nana, George and I all breathed sighs of relief. When Mom started talking about returning to her own house, George and I started making plans to head back to Portland.

Aunt Beth and Katie left town four days before we did. Before she left, Aunt Beth asked me if I wanted to go to Washington with her and Katie and live with their family while I finished high school.

"I can help you get back into a regular high school," Aunt Beth said. "You'd be able to go to school with kids your own age again. I think it would be the best thing for you. And we'd love to have you stay with us. Ben and Katie have promised they'll teach you how to sail."

I was taken aback by her offer, and her generosity and concern brought tears to my eyes. I remembered pretending Aunt Beth was my mother during the first summer I stayed with the Johnsons, but had never seriously considered that my wishes would come true. Now that she was essentially offering to be my surrogate mother, I had mixed feelings about it.

Terri Morgan

I had begun building a life for myself in Portland and was on track to finish high school faster than I would have in a conventional setting. I was making money, making friends in the neighborhood and at school, and I loved living with my uncle. After having so much freedom, I wasn't sure I wanted to give that up, even for the chance to be part of a loving family.

"Ah, let me think about it," I said finally. "I'll let you know."

"Give it some thought, honey. We can help you apply for health insurance and other benefits you're entitled to and get you some counseling."

"Counseling? What do I need counseling for?" I asked, bristling at the suggestion.

"You've been through a lot, honey. You've just lost your brother, and you've had a rather unconventional childhood. You might find it helpful to talk to someone about it."

"I'll think about it."

The day before George and I left Cumberland, we went over to Mom's house to help clean up Jon's room. I didn't want to go; I'd only been in the house once since we'd been in town and had avoided my brother's room.

"It would be nice for your mom if we did this before she moved back in," George said. "Besides, your brother left you everything. There might be something you'll want to take back to Portland."

I was skeptical and afraid I wouldn't be able to be inside the room my brother had lived in.

"If it becomes too much for you, we can leave," George said, sensing my unease. "I won't make you go through anything you can't handle."

Once we were inside the house my fears vanished.

The door to Jon's old room was open, and we walked in. It was just a room; there were no ghosts or evil spirits inside waiting to haunt me or snare my soul.

We looked around. The bed was unmade, there were dirty clothes on the floor, an empty glass on the night stand, crumpled papers on the desk, floor and in the wastebasket and a thick layer of dust everywhere.

"I don't think Mom's been in here since Jon tried to kill himself the first time," I said.

"It doesn't look like it. I guess it was just too much for her."

I sneezed. "It's almost too much for me. It's like a hazardous waste zone
in here."

George laughed.

"Yeah, it is. Let's at least get rid of some of the dust."

It took us over an hour to clear up all the clutter. We filled the washing machine with Jon's dirty clothes and bedding and four big plastic trash bags with debris we pulled out from under the bed, behind the furniture and off
the floor.

George got a broom from the kitchen and knocked down all the cobwebs from the ceiling, walls and light fixture while I dragged the trash bags to the curb. I grabbed some rags from the kitchen, filled a bucket with warm water, carried it into the room and started dusting the furniture and windowsills, sneezing violently as I worked.

George took the rag away from me and told me to go find the vacuum cleaner. I looked in several places before I found it in the closet in Mom's room, pushed back behind some boxes.

I dragged it out, and wheeled it to Jon's room. George plugged it in and waved me out of the room.

"Go get yourself something to drink. I'll finish this up."

I was pulling Jon's stuff out of the washer and putting it in the dryer when George came into the kitchen and asked me where the vacuum cleaner went.

"I'll put it away if you get the dryer started," I offered.

George was drinking a glass of water when I returned to the kitchen.

"We should stick around until the clothes are dry and put them away," he said.

"OK, I guess. We should probably remake the bed, too."

While we were waiting, I went into my old room to see if there was anything I wanted to take with me.

Even though I had only been gone a few months, I had outgrown most of the clothes I had left behind.

I found my Teddy bear, the one Granddad and Eileen had given me when I was in the hospital and tucked that under my arm.

I squatted down by my bookshelf and pulled out "East of Eden," "Tom Sawyer" and the old copy of "Wind in the Willows" Nana had owned when she was a girl.

I carted everything into the kitchen and put them in a grocery bag.

The dryer was still humming away, so I went to find my uncle.

He was in Jon's room, looking around.

"Is there anything here you want to take?"

"I don't know. Do we have to do it now?"

"No, but we're here now. This would be a good time to take some stuff."

"Well, I do need some clothes. Most of my old stuff doesn't fit anymore."

I pulled some T-shirts out of Jon's dresser and piled them on the unmade bed. I opened the closet and saw his Seattle Mariners cap hanging on a hook inside the door. I put it on and rifled through the clothes hanging on the rack. I found a couple flannel shirts that I liked, a couple of sweaters that looked like they might fit and tossed them on the bed.

I pulled Jon's skateboard off the shelf and spotted a second skateboard behind it. I reached up and tugged it down. The wheels were worn, the deck was scratched and scraped, and the deck tape was peeling.

"Hey, that's the board I gave Jon for Christmas when he was about 11," George said with surprise. "I can't believe he kept it all these years."

"It must have meant a lot to him. It's pretty trashed, but he hung onto it. We should take it with us."

"Definitely," George said, with a catch in his voice. I looked over at him as he was daubing his eyes.

"Why don't you keep it," I said, handing it to him.

"Thanks. I'd like that."

I went back to the kitchen for some more grocery bags and brought them back to Jon's room. I loaded up the clothes and sat down on the bed.

"I know what else I want," I said, jumping up and going to the dresser. I opened the top drawer, where Jon kept odds and ends along with his socks. I rifled through it and pulled out a tin box.

I opened it and pulled out the Red Cross medal Jon had been given for saving me from the fire.

There was an envelope in the box as well, and I took that out and opened it. Folded up inside was the proclamation he'd received at the same time. I unfolded it and smoothed the thick paper with my hand as tears welled up in my eyes.

"Maybe we can get this framed," I said.

Chapter 41

The morning after Uncle George and I returned to Portland, I discovered my motivation had completely and totally disappeared. I finally decided to turn down Aunt Beth's offer to join the Johnson family, largely because I was in a hurry to finish school and get into college. I had planned to go to school the day after I got home.

The term was winding down, and I wanted to finish the two independent study classes I had been taking and try to catch up in my geometry class.Instead, I slept in 'til past 11, lounged around the house in my jammies, took a late afternoon nap and watched TV all evening.

It took me four days before I began opening up the pile of condolence cards people had pushed through the mail slot in our front door while we were in Cumberland, and I never did return any of the messages from neighbors asking me to call them when I was back and ready to resume babysitting. I didn't feel like talking to anybody, so I let the answering machine take all the calls, even those from Nana, Granddad, Jason and Aunt Beth.

Uncle George, on the other hand, went off with his guitar to meet his band mates at a gig an hour or so after we pulled into the driveway.

He spent the next five days in the studio, recording background music for an independent film one of his friends was making and the next eight evenings playing in clubs and at private parties.

I barely saw him, because I was usually sleeping when he stopped by the house to take a shower and change clothes, listen to his phone messages or grab a bite to eat.

It took him nearly a week to realize I hadn't left the house, answered the phone, or eaten much besides cold cereal since we'd been back home. When he did, he felt terrible.

"Oh God, Caitlin, I'm so sorry. I've been so busy catching up I haven't been spending any time with you."

"That's OK. I haven't been very good company lately."

"Yeah, I'm starting to notice that. Have you been back to school yet?"

"No."

"Have you done any babysitting?"

"Not since we've been back."

"Have you returned any phone messages?"

"No."

"Have you talked to Jason?"

"Not really."

"Houston, we have a problem."

"It's not a big deal. I just haven't felt like doing much lately."

"Much? Or anything?"

"Don't bug me, OK? I'm, I'm, uh, I'm."

"I know you're bummed Ava, I mean Caitlin. But you're starting to trip me out."

To prove to George he didn't have anything to worry about, or at least try to convince him, I took a shower, got dressed and let him take me out for dinner. We went to Danny's Diner, a small, funky restaurant that specialized in inexpensive, all-American cuisine, and sat down in one of the vinyl booths near the back.

George flipped through the miniature jukebox on the table, loaded it with quarters and punched in his selections. Elvis Presley's voice began booming over the speakers hung in two corners of the room, crooning about a blue Hawaii.

"Let's get up and dance to a song that was a hit before your mother was born," George said with a smile.

"Though she was born a long, long time ago," I answered. "Naw, let's order instead."

I hadn't realized I was hungry until our food arrived. I woofed down my cheeseburger, doused my French fries in a puddle of ketchup and got my fingers sticky and red picking them up and shoving them into my mouth. I gulped down a chocolate milkshake, barely breathing while I sucked it up through a wide straw. I set the glass back down on the table, leaned back, burped and sighed.

"Are you feeling any better?" he asked, as we left the restaurant.

"I guess. Thanks for dinner. I'm not hungry anymore."

"But are you feeling any better?"

"I don't know. Maybe. I think I need a nap."

My uncle drove me to the adult school the next morning and went inside with me to talk to my instructors. My English and social studies teachers both said I could continue to work independently and take the final exam for credit whenever I was ready.

My geometry teacher, however, said I had missed so many classes that it would be impossible to catch up. She suggested I drop the class and take it again the next term.

Instead of being disappointed, like I would have been a month or so earlier, I was relieved not to have to worry any more about how I was going to finish the class. That is, I was relieved until I started walking out of the school and realized that dropping the class and taking it over would change my carefully laid plans.

I had mapped out my high school career and counted credits. If I passed three classes each term, I would earn my diploma by the end of next summer. Repeating geometry would delay my dreams of starting college next fall, when my former classmates in Cumberland would be starting their senior years.

I wanted to walk back into the classroom and tell my teacher I was going to stick it out, no matter how far behind I was.

As that thought was going through my head, a wave of anxiety swept through my body. I knew I had missed far too many classes to catch up. If it had been an English class, I could have hustled, done the reading, written the reports and maybe, just maybe, caught up. But math classes are sequential, with each lesson building on the previous lessons. Trying to make up for three weeks of missed geometry classes, out of a 10- week term, wasn't possible. I felt the frustration building, but managed to keep a lid on it until we got back to Uncle George's minivan.

As soon as I sat down in the passenger seat, however, I had a major meltdown. I started crying like a two year old who has her favorite toy snatched out of her hands.

Uncle George looked at me with concern and let me cry for a while, obviously realizing it would not do any good to try to get me to stop before I was ready. When my tears subsided, and I caught my breath, he touched me on the shoulder and asked what was wrong.

"I'll never finish high school," I wailed.

"Sure you will, Caitlin. This just means you'll have to retake one class. You'll sail through it the second time."

"I'm going to have to stay in school for an extra term because of that stupid geometry class and that stupid teacher."

"So you'll have to go one more term. It's no big deal."

"It's no big deal to you, but it's a big deal to me. I wanna go to college before...."

"Before what, Caitlin."

"Before, before, before nothing," I said, afraid to voice my greatest fear, that I'd develop schizophrenia before I could experience college.

"Look, you're on track now to get your diploma in a year from now."

"A year and 10 weeks," I interrupted.

"OK, in a year and 10 weeks. That means you'll graduate eight months earlier than you would have if you'd stayed at Cumberland High School. Besides, you'll only have to take one class during that final term, so it'll be a cakewalk for you."

"So what. I won't be able to start college until the winter semester. I'll lose half a year in college."

"Maybe not. I bet you can start taking classes at a community college while you finish up your last high school class."

"I don't think so."

"Well, we should find out. Let's ask someone who knows."

"I'm not going back in there now to talk to anybody," I sniffed.

"We can come back tomorrow when you're not so upset. Or maybe we can call your Aunt Beth. She's a high school teacher, I bet she'll know."

"She teaches in Washington, not Oregon. She's not gonna know."

"She grew up in Oregon. If she doesn't know, I bet she'll know someone here who can give you some good advice."

Chapter 42

I started taking baby steps back into the world the day after I met with my teachers. Uncle George drove me to the adult school every morning, so I could work in the learning center where there were tutors available to help me when I got stuck on something. Most importantly, however, there were people around to ease the sudden loneliness that threatened to overwhelm me.

I wasn't ready to reach out to anyone, so being with people who were too busy working to interact much with me was ideal. Working at school also had the added advantage of eliminating the temptation to close my books and take a nap.

Even so, it was hard to concentrate.

I kept plugging away at my schoolwork but was making very little progress. It would take me four hours to complete an assignment that used to take maybe an hour.

I just couldn't seem to stay focused for very long.

I kept thinking about Jon, and how much I missed him.

My brother was on my mind constantly. No matter how hard I tried to push the thoughts away, they kept popping back into my brain.

When the ache of the loss got too strong, I'd go into the ladies room and lock myself in one of the stalls where I could cry in privacy. When my tears eased, I'd wash my face and go back to the workroom to attempt to continue my studies until Uncle George came by to pick me up.

We'd go home, eat a late lunch, then go out and have fun. We often went swimming in the river that wound through Portland.

We discovered half a dozen different swimming holes, but none were as deep, wide and nice as the Bixby Ranch. When we didn't go swimming, we'd go hiking, wandering around in the deep shade of the forest.

Occasionally we'd go skateboarding, but the weather was so hot it was uncomfortable being on the asphalt or on the cement, even late in the day. Sometimes one or more of George's friends would come with us, but often it was just the two of us.

George would usually take a nap when we got home, and I'd watch TV or try to read. He'd get up after an hour or so, take a shower, and we'd eat dinner together. Then most night, he'd head off to play a gig somewhere, leaving me alone.

"Do you have a babysitting job tonight?" he'd ask before departing.

"Naw. Not yet. I'll start making some calls tomorrow."

Although I didn't have the energy, or the motivation to rustle up some work, I discovered I hated being alone. Growing up amongst the chaos of my family, I had craved solitude. And for months in Portland I'd been totally comfortable being by myself when George was out.

Suddenly, though, I discovered I'd become anxious when I was alone. I would feel butterflies fluttering in my stomach and chest, and when I was sitting down and raised my heel off the ground my knee would piston up and down violently. I would wander around the small house aimlessly, heading to the living room to watch TV, then deciding to take a shower, or clean the kitchen, or go to my bedroom and look for something to read.

No matter what I did, I felt like I should be doing something else. It was unsettling, and I wished I had someone to talk to. But when the phone would ring, I'd let the answering machine take the call. Even when I could hear the call was for me, I didn't have the energy to pick up the phone and chat.

Sometimes I would find a good movie on TV and watch it long enough to be distracted. On the few days that I planned ahead, I'd ask George to stop at the video store when we were out and would pick up a couple of movies to watch. Most days, however, I didn't think ahead and would be forced to channel surf until I found something that would hold my interest.

After a couple of weeks of torturing myself, I decided I'd better start babysitting in the evenings so I would at least be around someone, even if they were just six or eight years old.

I had planned to start slowly, babysitting just a couple of nights a week, but once again, the demand in our neighborhood for a reliable babysitter was huge.

As soon as word got out that I was back in business, my nights filled up quickly. It turned out to be a good thing.

I liked being around kids and discovered that my charges kept me so

197

busy I could forget about my brother's death for a few hours while I played with them, kept them fed, clean and safe.

I tried to arrange only for short jobs, where the parents would return before the kid or kids went to bed. Without someone to interact with, my anxiety and grief would return. I also developed an annoying tendency to fall asleep after the kids settled down and the house was quiet. I'd turn the TV on or open a book and would suddenly find it hard to keep my eyes open. I would wake up with a start when I heard someone fumbling to put a key in the lock and would try to pretend I had been awake.

I rarely fooled anybody. Even though the parents didn't seem to mind, I was embarrassed when it happened.

The strange thing was that once I got home, I would have a hard time getting back to sleep. I would feel my muscles tighten with tension when I got into bed, and a weird sensation, like a low-grade electrical charge, would course through my body. I would lie in bed for a while, trying to will my muscles and nerves to relax.

Once in a while I was successful and could drop off to sleep.

Most of the time, however, I'd get up and wander around the house until George got home. The later I'd stay up, the later I'd sleep in the next morning. That suited me fine as I didn't like getting up so early.

I preferred it when my uncle woke me up with just enough time to dress and eat a bowl of cereal before heading out the door.

I don't know if it was my unusual sleeping habits, or my grief, but shortly after I started babysitting again I started falling asleep in the minivan, at the movies, or any time I was sitting quietly somewhere.

It only happened during the day, but I quickly noticed a pattern. If I sat in one position for 15 minutes, I'd drop off.

The skateboard park was just 10 minutes away, so I would be able to stay awake while we drove there. Culver Park, one of the places we liked to hike, was a 20-minute drive from the house, and I'd be sound asleep when we pulled into the parking lot. I thought it was a little strange, but the more it happened, the more concerned my uncle became.

"How come you're so tired?" he asked the third time I dozed off on him in the car.

"I don't know. I didn't know I was until I woke up."

198

"Do you feel OK?"

"You mean other than Jon? Yeah, sure, other than that the play was great."

"Don't be a smart ass. Are you sure you're not sick or anything?"

"I'm OK. Just sleepy I guess."

"I'm worried. This isn't normal."

"Don't trip out on me OK? I'm OK."

Chapter 43

A s it turned out, I wasn't OK. Uncle George called Nana, who urged him to take me to a doctor. She went over to Mom's house and dug around until she found my Oregon State health insurance card, then mailed it to us. Since my family was so crazy and my parents could barely work, we were considered destitute by the state and qualified for numerous benefits.

I found that to be humiliating, especially when we had to use food stamps at the grocery store, but the upside was that the state had given us full medical coverage. The downside was that it was difficult to find a doctor who would accept new patients who were covered by the state.

Nana spent a couple of hours making phone calls, then called Uncle George and told him she'd made an appointment for me at a clinic for the following week.

I didn't say anything, but I wasn't planning to keep the appointment.

However, I didn't factor in how persuasive my uncle could be.

When I finally spoke up, about an hour before we were supposed to leave George guilt tripped me.

"Your grandmother went to a lot of trouble to set this up for you. Don't be an asshole and let all her hard work go to waste."

"OK, OK, I'll go. Just don't hassle me."

"Well let's go then."

"I've got to take a shower first."

"Well hurry up. We're going to be late."

We arrived at the clinic 15 minutes after my scheduled appointment and still had to wait over an hour before my name was called.

I wanted to leave after 30 minutes, but my uncle wouldn't budge.

So we sat in the crowded, noisy waiting room and waited.

There was a TV set hanging from the wall in one corner of the room that nobody was watching, but the volume was turned up so high, you couldn't help but listen to it. There were at least a half-dozen harried mothers, each with three or more restless kids.

One of the babies woke up from a nap and started crying, which woke up the three other babies in the room. They all started wailing, too. The noise was starting to give me a headache, and I was irritable when I finally was led to the back of the building, where I was weighed, measured and taken to an exam room. Uncle George followed me in, ignoring my protests that I didn't need him there.

"I'll leave if they make you take off your clothes," he reassured me. "But I want to talk to the doctor. You'll just tell him everything's OK."

We waited about 10 minutes before a nurse came in.

She took my temperature, listened to my pulse, took my blood pressure and jotted everything down on a piece of paper attached to her clipboard. She asked me a number of questions.

Did I ever have asthma, cancer, heart disease, pneumonia and a number of other conditions I'd never heard of. She asked if I'd ever been in the hospital, and if I had all my vaccinations.

I told her about the car accident, and that I'd had all my shots.

Finally she asked what was the reason for my visit.

"I don't know. My uncle thinks I'm sick."

"Caitlin keeps falling asleep almost every time she sits down. She'll be fine, and then I'll look over at her, and she'll be asleep. It happens so much I'm worried she has narcolepsy or something."

The nurse scribbled something down, said hmm, and then "the doctor will be with you shortly."

Shortly turned out to be another 20 minutes, and when the doctor came in, I thought she was another nurse until I noticed the stethoscope looped around her neck.

She introduced herself as Dr. Adams, read the notes the nurse had written on the clipboard, then asked me to sit up on the examination table. She listened to my heart, then my lungs and then looked into my ears, and had me open my mouth so she could look down my throat.

Then she started asking questions.

I let Uncle George answer most of them, feeling suddenly tired when he began describing how I'd drop off to sleep regularly.

I yawned and stretched my arms. The doctor listened to my lungs again, then asked, "When did these spells start?"

I burst into tears.

"After my brother killed himself."

I was mortified by my emotional outburst, but once I started crying I couldn't stop.

Uncle George took over again, filling in the doctor on the date and circumstances of my brother's suicide and my family's sad history of mental illness. They talked for a while, and I finally stopped crying and was able to respond to some questions on my own.

The doctor jotted down something on the clipboard, then spoke.

"I think we can rule out narcolepsy," she said. "I don't think there's anything physically wrong with you, Caitlin. But I do think you're suffering from a major depression."

I started crying again. I didn't know nearly as much about mental illness then as I do now, but I knew enough to know I'd just been told I was crazy and one of my biggest fears had been realized.

"No," I wailed. "I can't be depressed. There's nothing wrong with my brain."

The doctor wanted to run a few tests to eliminate any other illnesses or conditions before treating me for depression.

The nurse who had taken my temperature and asked all those questions came back in the room shortly after the doctor left and drew two vials of blood out of my arm.

After she put a bandage over the little hole inside the crook of my elbow, she picked up a plastic cup, wrote my name on it, then handed it to me and told me I needed to provide them with a urine sample.

I spaced out while she was giving me instructions, then went into the bathroom and peed into the cup, capped it, and left it on the shelf that held four other urine samples from other patients.

I washed my hands and went out to the waiting room.

My uncle was at the check-in window making a follow up visit for the following Monday, Sept. 7, my 16th birthday, so we could obtain my test results. I sat down and stared out the window, not really looking at anything until he had an appointment card in his hand, and we were ready to leave.

I started crying again as soon as we got into the van.

George looked in the glove box for some tissues, but didn't find any. He rummaged around in the back and handed me a damp beach towel.

I wiped my eyes and face and blew my nose, then cried some more.

He waited patiently until I stopped crying.

"It'll be all right, Ava. You'll be OK."

"I'm crazy. I'll never be OK."

"You're not crazy. You're just depressed. And anyone who's been through what you've been through over the past few months would be depressed. I'd actually be worried about you if you weren't depressed."

"That doctor just told me I'm mentally ill. That's crazy, just like the rest of my family."

"No that's not what she meant."

"Yes it is. I might as well just kill myself now, like Jon did, and get it over with."

"Oh Ava, I mean Caitlin, I know you're upset, but you're not crazy. You're depressed; you're not schizophrenic. There's a huge difference between the two conditions."

"Not much difference. I'm always gonna be depressed. I'm always gonna be crazy."

"No you won't. The doctor said you mostly likely have situational depression, which means you're temporarily depressed due to recent circumstances and events. That kind of depression is very treatable, and it doesn't last very long."

"How long does it last?"

"I don't know, she didn't say. But I know it's a temporary condition, not a chronic one like schizophrenia."

"How do you know?"

"I listened to what the doctor said. And besides, you're not the only one in this family who knows a lot about mental illnesses. I know an awful lot about schizophrenia, and I know that's not what you've got.

"I'm sorry, though," he added. "That you have to go back to the doctor on your birthday. That was the only day they had available for an appointment next week."

"That's OK. I don't mind. It gives me a good excuse not to have to go to Cumberland and celebrate it with Mom."

Chapter 44

My uncle tried to cheer me up on the way home. He stopped at an ice cream parlor and offered to buy me a sundae. "I don't want to go in. I don't look so good."

"That's OK. I'll get it to go."

He hopped out of the minivan and disappeared into the store. He came out a short time later with a cup of coffee in one hand and a banana split in the other. He handed me the gooey treat through my open window, then went around the van and climbed into the driver's seat. He put his coffee down in the cup holder, dug through his shirt pocket and handed me a small sheaf of paper napkins and a plastic spoon.

"Thanks."

"You're welcome. Dig in. I want to sit here for a minute and drink my coffee."

He sipped his coffee while I spooned chocolate, vanilla and strawberry ice cream that was melting under a big dollop of hot fudge sauce into my mouth. I finished three quarters of the ice cream, all of the whipped cream and half of the banana, then got too full to finish. My uncle took a couple of spoonfuls, then jumped out to drop the rest into the trash, along with his empty coffee cup.

"Thanks," I said. "That was good."

I lay down and took a nap when we got home, after asking my uncle to wake me up at five because I had to babysit that evening. After a brief, dreamless sleep, I got up, took a shower and washed my orange and brown two-tone hair.

George had dinner on the table by the time I finished getting dressed. We ate a quick supper together, then I went off and played with 5-year-old Noah while his parents went out for dinner. I earned some money and actually stayed awake until his parents returned.

I didn't feel like going to school the next day, so George let me go back to sleep. Later that afternoon, we went for a swim.

The following morning, he dropped me off at the Learning Center. I didn't get much done, however. Reading my schoolbooks made me sleepy, and I had to get up several times and walk around the building to stay awake.

"How'd it go today?" my uncle asked when he came to pick me up.

"Well, I read the first paragraph at least six times, but I still don't remember what it said."

"Not good then."

"No, not good. But I'll do some work later at home. I don't have a job lined up tonight."

My books, however, remained in my backpack until the next day, when I pulled them out at the Learning Center. I found it still hard to concentrate and to stay awake.

Instead of getting up and walking around when reading made me tired, I put my head down on my arms and napped.

The inability to read without falling asleep was not only distressing, but it was annoying. It removed one of my primary sources of entertainment. I was not only unable to stay awake long enough to do any schoolwork; I couldn't even keep my eyes open long enough to read for pleasure.

That left a big gap in my days, and I filled it largely by letting my mind wander. After a few days, I noticed an uncomfortable trend. No matter what launched my thought process, it seemed like inevitably my thoughts would link back to old hurts, anger and embarrassments.

A conversation with my uncle about hearing the Rolling Stones on the radio for the first time got him so excited about music that he started playing the guitar. It got me ruminating about the Beatles, who were my all-time favorite band. That led to how I couldn't afford to buy their CDs, which led to how we couldn't always afford to buy food, especially after Mom and Dad used our food stamps to get cigarettes.

You couldn't buy cigarettes with food stamps, but Mom and Dad figured out a way to use them to finance their smoking habits. If you purchased something, say a $1.35 can of soup with a $5 food stamp, the clerks would give you three $1 food stamps in change, and 65 cents in coins.

Mom and Dad would buy stuff that we didn't need if it would net them 95 cents back in change. Then they'd go back in the store and do it over and over until they had enough cash for their smokes.

That memory, and the memory of our often-empty refrigerator, led to remembering how Jon and I, when we were really hungry, would dive into the dumpster behind a fast food restaurant in Cumberland.

We started doing that when I was about eight, after we discovered the staff discarded unsold hamburgers after they'd spent 20 minutes under the heat lamp. That led to me remembering how mortified I was when I was crouched in the dumpster one afternoon, gathering bags of warm food, when I was hit in the head by a big bag of French fries tossed in by a teenage counter boy.

I yelled in surprise and anger and jumped to my feet, raising my head above the rim of the dumpster. The boy jumped back, then found his voice and started yelling at me to get the hell out of the trash. Jon helped pull me out of the bin, and we ran off with the pimply faced food slinger yelling insults after us. At least once a day, my mind would take me back to an unpleasant childhood memory, and I'd spend the rest of the day fretting about the past, unable to remove the thoughts from my mind.

Uncle George filled Nana in on my preliminary diagnosis and my other symptoms. She wanted to come up to Portland to help in some way. I squirmed when George told me that, and asked him, begged him, not to let her come.

"What's she gonna do, watch me fall asleep every time I open a book? The only time I'm awake is when I'm babysitting or we're swimming or hiking or skateboarding. She's not into skateboarding, and I'm not supposed to have anyone come over when I'm babysitting."

Granddad was also concerned when he called to talk to me.

I was babysitting when he called, so Uncle George talked to him and told him what was going on with me. He, too, wanted to help in someway, and asked George to tell me to call him.

I didn't have the energy, however, to make any calls, so Granddad did the next best thing.

He called Aunt Beth, and she called me.

Chapter 45

I lied to my aunt on the phone, and told her I was fine, and that everyone was exaggerating about my so-called health problems. She pretended to believe me, but after having taught school for over 12 years, she had a finely honed bullshit detector.

When she detected not only that I wasn't being truthful with her about how I was doing, but that Uncle George was extremely worried, she decided to come down to Portland. If I'd known she was coming, I probably would have hidden out somewhere.

But Aunt Beth showed up unannounced the following Monday, wished me a happy birthday and took both George and myself out to lunch.

After we finished eating, she dropped George back off at the house, then drove me to the clinic.

She was so efficient that we arrived at the clinic 10 minutes before my appointment was scheduled. That meant we had to spend over an hour and a half in the waiting room for my name to be called.

It was just as crowded as the week before, and if anything, even noisier.

I had such a hard time hearing Aunt Beth over the din that she finally pulled a notepad out of her purse and jotted down a note.

"Do you have to work tonight?" she wrote.

I shook my head.

"Do you want to go out for a birthday dinner?"

I shrugged.

"How about we stop on the way home and get a cake and some ice cream?"

I shrugged again.

She raised her eyebrows.

I felt like a jerk and nodded. I reached over, took the pad and pencil out of her hand and wrote,

"Thanks, that would be nice."

She smiled.

I drew a hangman's gallows on the next page and six short lines underneath it, then passed the pad back. We played hangman's bluff until a man, likely a medical assistant, came and ushered me into an exam room.

"It's nice and quiet in here," Aunt Beth said, while we waited for the nurse. "My ears are still ringing from sitting in the waiting room."

"Mine, too. That was even worse than last week."

My aunt introduced herself to the doctor, when she finally arrived, and they shook hands.

"How are you feeling Caitlin?" the doctor asked.

I shrugged. "I don't know. About the same as last week I guess."

"Are you still having problems staying awake?"

"Yeah, and now I fall asleep whenever I try to read, too."

"Well, I've got your test results here, and your blood work looks great. The tests on your urine were negative for any infection or other problems. So it looks like my original diagnosis was correct. You're suffering from a major depression."

My eyes started to well up with tears.

The doctor put her hand on my shoulder briefly and said, "Don't worry honey. You've got a very treatable condition."

"What do you recommend?" Aunt Beth asked.

"I'd like to put Caitlin on an anti-depressant medication, and I'd like for her to see a therapist for at least the time being. I'll write you a prescription and a referral for a youth counselor. Then I'd like to see Caitlin back here again in two weeks to monitor how she's doing."

Just like the week before, I zoned out and let the adults talk.

Aunt Beth asked a lot of questions, scribbled a lot of notes down on her pad and waited with me while the doctor left the room and returned with a handful of pamphlets. Then she thanked the doctor for her time, and we got up to leave.

The doctor reached over, shook my hand and said, "Good luck, Caitlin. I'll see you in two weeks," then walked out of the room.

There were four messages for me on the answering machine when we got back to Uncle George's house. Mom, Granddad, Nana and Jason had all called to wish me a happy birthday.

I was playing them back when the phone rang.

I hit the stop button on the machine and picked it up.

"Hello?"

"Happy birthday to you, happy birthday to you, happy birthday dear Caitlin, happy birthday to you," Julie and Katie sang.

Katie started giggling before I could speak.

I heard Julie telling her to keep quiet so she could talk to me.

We chatted for a couple of minutes, then I handed the phone to Aunt Beth.

She walked out onto the front porch with the cordless phone to talk to her daughters, and I finished playing back my birthday greetings.

"Nothing from Dad," I said to Uncle George who was sitting on the couch.

"He must not be able to make any phone calls," George replied.

"I can't imagine him forgetting your birthday."

When Aunt Beth came back in and hung up the phone, I picked it up and took it into my room to call Jason back.

"Thanks for calling," I said to his answering machine. "I'm sorry I haven't called you back in so long. I'm kind of sick; the doctor says I'm depressed, and I'm gonna have to take some pills and see a therapist. I think the whole thing sucks. My aunt is here, and she's making me a birthday dinner to celebrate my sad 16. Talk to you later."

I took a nap while Aunt Beth made dinner.

It was ready when I woke up.

George hadn't scheduled any gigs that night, because he said he wanted to stay home with me in honor of my birthday.

The three of us ate together, took a break to go for a walk around the block, then came back for chocolate cake and ice cream. They both sang happy birthday while I blew out the candles.

After we finished the dessert, they brought out some wrapped packages.

George gave me a brand new skateboard, wrapped awkwardly in the Sunday comics. I laughed when I saw the package, because it was obvious what was hidden under the paper.

Aunt Beth gave me a small package wrapped in shiny silver paper.

I opened it up and found a silver necklace with a silver sailboat charm hanging on it.

209

George brought out the cards that had come in the mail for me over the past few days, cards he had stashed away.

Grandmom and Harold had sent me a card and a check for $200.

There was a letter from Dad, with the words "Jail Generated Mail" stamped on the front in red ink, a card from Granddad and Eileen, with a $100 bill in it, a card from Julie and Katie and a homemade card from Mom promising to give me her gift when she saw me next.

There was also a card from Jason, signed *Love, Jason and Charlie.*

Chapter 46

I thought Aunt Beth would go back to Washington the next day, but when she returned to our house in the morning after spending the night in a motel nearby, she told me she had planned to stay in Oregon for a couple more days. Classes at the school she taught at didn't start until the 21st, she said, so she didn't have any reason to rush back home.

She had stopped at the drug store before coming over and had picked up my prescription.

"The instructions say to take one tablet every evening before you go to bed," she said, as she handed me the pill container. "It's always best if you take medication at the same time each day."

"OK."

"Don't forget."

"I won't. But if it makes me feel really weird or anything, I'm going to stop taking it."

"It can be dangerous to stop taking medication suddenly. If the pills make you feel strange, you should definitely talk to your doctor about it before you make any changes."

"If the meds are dangerous, maybe I shouldn't take them."

"They aren't dangerous. I just meant you should discuss any side effects or decisions with your doctor before making any changes."

"What if they are dangerous? What if they screw my head up like Jon's meds did to him? That's one of the reasons Jon killed himself, because he hated the way his medications made him feel."

"Jon was on anti-psychotic medications, as well as some powerful tranquilizers. You've been prescribed anti-depressants. They're completely different medications. They have completely different purposes."

"But they're both for the brain. What if they do mess me up? My mom got fat and then got diabetes from one of her schizophrenia drugs. And my dad acts like a zombie when he's on some of his meds. What if something like that happens to me?"

"It won't happen."

"How can you be so sure?"

"Because anti-depressants don't work like anti-psychotic drugs. They don't change your personality or behavior. They just work with your natural brain chemistry to get it back into the correct balance."

"I don't know. I'm not so sure I want to take anything."

"Well, Ava, that's up to you. But tell me something, are you happy with the way you feel these days?"

"Not really."

"Don't you want to get better?"

"Well, yeah."

"Let me ask you something else. Would you rather be around your mother or father when they're on their medication, or when they're not?"

"What are you saying? Does that mean nobody wants to hang around me 'cause I'm depressed?"

"That's not what I'm saying at all. What I'm getting at is that prescription drugs can be very effective for some people with certain conditions."

"But what if something goes wrong?"

"Then you call your doctor."

"But what if I don't realize something's going wrong?"

"Don't worry Ava," George, who had been listening to our conversation, said. "I'll keep a close eye on you. If I notice anything wrong I'll help you take care of it."

"I guess if anything goes wrong, Aunt Beth will be here to see it, too."

"Not necessarily," Aunt Beth said. "It takes some time for anti-depressants to begin working."

"How much time?"

"You should start to feel a little better in a week or two, but generally it takes about six weeks for them to become fully effective."

My aunt stayed at our house to make some phone calls while George drove me to school. I tried to work, but got very little done. Along with being depressed, I was agitated; anxious about the medication I was supposed to start.

Despite what Aunt Beth had said, I was still apprehensive about taking anti-depressants. Although I was loath to admit it, Aunt Beth had made some very good points.

Especially when she pointed out I was pretty miserable the way I was. I guess I knew logically that the medication would probably do me some good, but emotionally, I wasn't so sure. And I had been running primarily on emotion since my brother's death.

Despite being depressed, I had, well not exactly fun, but a nice time with Aunt Beth. She took me shopping and bought me two pairs of shorts, three pairs of jeans, four tops, new underwear and some sandals. We went to the zoo one afternoon and came home with a stuffed monkey for me and a T-shirt for Uncle George. Aunt Beth bought a postcard with a picture of a lion on it to send to Ben, Julie and Katie, so I bought one with a picture of two monkeys to send to Jason. When we got back to the house, she wrote:

Dear Family,

Having a wonderful time; wish you were here. It was quieter at the zoo than at home.

Love Mom

There was a little room below her message, so I wrote,
The zoo rocked! Love Caitlin

I took the postcard I had bought for Jason out of the flat little bag it had been put in and wrote:

Dear Jason,

Can you believe it? This is the first time I've ever been to the zoo. My aunt took me there. It was cool. Didn't see any dogs, tho. Say hi to Charlie.

Caitlin

Aunt Beth suggested we walk down to the Post Office, which was about five blocks away, to get stamps and mail our cards. I didn't have Jason's address, however.

"Call him," she suggested.

"Why do you want my address?" Jason asked when I reached him.

"I'm sending you something."

"What is it?"

"A surprise."

He recited his address, then asked me for mine.

"Why?" I wanted to know.

"Just in case I want to send you something back."

"Like what?"

"That depends on what you're sending me. I might want to send you a thank you note or something."

I laughed.

"You're so fuckin' polite."

"Hey, I can't help it. My mom ground it into me. I think it's in my DNA by now."

Beth took me to the aquarium the next day, and I bought another postcard for Jason.

Dear Jason,

I'm never swimming in the ocean. There are sharks that can eat you, sea urchins with spikes that can stab you, jellyfish that can sting you and really ugly things that crawl around on the bottom.

Love, Caitlin

After school the following day, we went to the Natural History Museum. We wandered around looking at all the exhibits. Before we left, we stopped in the gift shop. Aunt Beth bought a book on West Coast birds for Katie and a sweatshirt for Julie.

She bought a guide book to the museum and gave it to me.

"Aren't you going to get anything for Uncle Ben?"

"He doesn't need anything."

"Won't he feel left out?"

"He'll be so glad I'm back and cooking dinner for him again that he won't even notice I'm not bringing him something."

I picked up another postcard for Jason. Later I wrote:

Dear Jason,

There is a whole room here filled with stuffed birds. It's creepy. They should call this place the museum of dead animals. Don't tell Charlie about it.

Love, Caitlin

I was grateful to Aunt Beth for taking me on the outings.

Like the zoo, I'd never been to the museum or aquarium before. It was interesting enough seeing things for the first time that it would actually penetrate my funk for a few minutes at a time.

Best of all, though, was the time we spent together in the car.

For some reason, probably because we weren't looking at each other, I felt most comfortable talking to my aunt when we were riding around. We talked about a lot of things, including what I could expect from the counseling sessions that were due to start in a week, my dad, life with Mom and, of course, Jon.

I was apprehensive about going to counseling and didn't know what to expect. I was also apprehensive about talking to a stranger about my life and how I felt.

"Counseling is completely confidential," Aunt Beth said. "The counselors don't talk to anyone about what you've told them."

"Yeah, but I don't like talking to strangers. Especially about our family. It's too weird, they'll think I'm a freak."

215

"Therapists have seen and heard it all. I don't think there's anything you could tell a counselor that would make them think that you're a freak. Besides, they're there to help you, not to make judgments."

"I don't know. Why can't I just talk to you, or Uncle George, or Jason?"

"Well honey, you're always welcome to talk to me. You can call me anytime. But therapists are specially trained to help people get to the roots of their problems and help them heal."

"I know all about my problems. If it wasn't for schizophrenia, I wouldn't be depressed."

"I know, but believe me, a good counselor can help you cope much better than a good friend or a family member. They're trained to help. Just give it a try."

"I don't know."

"If you won't do it for yourself, will you do it for me? And for Granddad and Eileen and your uncle and your Nana? And for Jason and for all the kids you baby-sit that look up to you? And for your mother and father?"

"OK, OK, just don't guilt trip me about it."

"I'm not trying to guilt trip you. I just want to remind you how important you are to so many people who want the best for you."

We also talked a lot about school. Aunt Beth knew I was in a hurry to get to college, and she told me she thought I could achieve my goals faster if I returned to a regular high school.

"How's that gonna work? I'm on track now to get my diploma eight months earlier than I would have if I stayed at Cumberland High School. If I go back to high school, it's gonna slow me down."

"Not necessarily honey. You can start taking college classes at a community college while you're finishing your senior year in high school. And you can also take AP classes in high school and earn college credits. Julie took a lot of AP classes in high school and earned so many college credits that she's on track to graduate in three years, not four."

"There are other advantages to going back to a regular school. You can take some electives, some interesting classes. You'll get a much more rounded education at a high school than at the adult ed school."

"Yeah, I guess so."

"And I know it must be hard to stay motivated since you have to do so much work on your own."

"I didn't have any problems staying motivated until Jon killed himself."

"But what about now?"

"Well, this is different."

"I understand. I just think it would be better for you to go to a regular high school and be around kids your own age. Aren't you lonely?"

"Not really. I hang out with Uncle George a lot, and I baby-sit all the time."

"Wouldn't it be nice to hang out with some friends your own age?"

"I don't know. Other than Jason, I haven't really had too many friends. I was always the freak with the psycho parents."

"Well, nobody at a new school has to know your parents are mentally ill. You could make a fresh start and enjoy being a kid for a while. You're only a kid for a little while, but you'll be an adult for a long, long time."

"Hmm."

"Give it some thought, honey. I think going to a regular high school will be good for you."

The day after Aunt Beth left, I received a postcard in the mail from Jason. It had a picture of the Cumberland Memorial for World War I soldiers on it. He had written:

Dear Caitlin,

Cumberland is so hysterically historical. Miss you, but I know you're glad you're not here. Charlie says woof.

Love, Jason.

I walked down to the drug store and picked out a postcard for Jason. Mine had a picture of a statue of a horse on it. I wrote:

Dear Jason,

Portland is hysterical too. I wish you and Charlie were here. He could chase the horse.

Love, Caitlin.

Chapter 47

The school term was winding down, and I still hadn't made much progress in my classes. I figured I'd just keep plugging away at them during the break, as I was taking them both independently.

My teachers, however, suggested I take the final exam.

"It won't hurt to try," my social studies teacher said. "You don't have anything to lose. If you pass it, you'll get your credits this term. If you don't, well, you'll be able to keep working and take the final later on."

I said "OK" and took both my English and social studies exams with the rest of my classmates.

I struggled with some of the questions in social studies and had trouble with two of the four essays I had to write during my English final. I was worried I had done so poorly that I'd flunk both classes. So I was surprised when I got my test results back on the last day of school and discovered I had passed, albeit just barely, both exams.

I squeaked by with a C minus on my English exam and a D on my social studies test. Combined with my other test and essay scores, I had enough points to earn credits in both classes. I received Cs, though, the first Cs of my high school career, which was a bit disappointing.

But I passed, which was the most important thing, and earned five more high school credits.

I met with my counselor for the first time the day after my English final. Uncle George and I got lost trying to find the Youth Services building where my counselor's office was. He had looked on the map before leaving the house for Swift Street, but didn't realize that Swift and several of the streets near it were one-way.

We drove around, trying to negotiate the maze of streets until George got frustrated, and we found a public parking lot that he reckoned was near our destination.

He parked the minivan, we got out and walked the rest of the way. It was a hot afternoon, and we were both sweating by the time we found the building, which was an old, three-story Victorian house that had been converted into a set of offices.

It was cool inside the building, which prevented me from having a meltdown when we couldn't find the Youth Services offices. George stopped a woman walking down the hall of the second floor, and she pointed the way.

We were nearly 15 minutes late for my appointment when we finally arrived in the right place. A petite, dark-haired woman who was wearing glasses and looked to be in her early 20s was waiting in the reception area when we walked in.

"Are you Caitlin?" she asked.

"Uh huh," I said, surprised because I had assumed she was waiting for an appointment.

"Oh good. I'm Clarissa, and I'm scheduled to meet with you. I hope you didn't have too much trouble getting here. Those one-way streets throw a lot of people off."

"Yeah, we got lost," George said.

"A lot of people do. Well, let's get started. We have some paperwork to fill out first. I've got the forms in my office, so why don't both of you come back there with me, and we can get it out of the way while we're getting to know each other."

"You want me to come too?" George asked.

"Yes, if Caitlin doesn't mind. I was hoping you could help Caitlin fill me in as to why she's here."

"That's easy," I said, as we followed Clarissa out of the waiting room and into a hallway. "My doctor told me I needed to get counseling."

Clarissa led us into a sunny room with a couch and two overstuffed armchairs. There were six colorful posters of wild animals on the walls.

"Have a seat," Clarissa said.

I sat down on one of the chairs, and George said down on the end of the couch.

She handed him a clipboard, with several sheets of paper on it and a pen tucked behind the clip.

"Why don't you work on this while I get to know Caitlin."

"Sure," he said to her, then turned to me. "Give me your insurance card. I'm sure that's the most important piece of information they're asking for."

"Well Caitlin, while he's working on the forms, let me tell you a little bit about myself. I'm a certified family and marriage counselor, which means I have earned my master's degree and have been trained to work as a therapist. I'm 29 and just got married two months ago. I've been working with teenagers here at Youth Services for nearly three years now, and I absolutely love my job.

"What we'll be doing here is talking, mainly about whatever is bugging you. Today is just a consultation to get your history and find out a little bit more about why you're here. That's why I asked your father to join us today."

"He's my uncle," I interrupted.

"Excuse me, your uncle. That's right, I saw in the chart your doctor sent over that you live with him. Is that correct?"

"Yeah."

"I want you to know a little bit about how counseling works. Everything you say in here is confidential. I have a professional obligation not to disclose anything you tell me, unless you threaten to harm anyone, harm yourself, or report that you've been abused. I'm a mandated reporter, which means if I discover anyone is hurting you, I must contact the authorities. Do you understand?"

"Yeah."

"Do you have any questions?"

"No."

"Do you want to tell me a little about yourself?"

"Not really."

"Do you want to talk about why you're here?"

"I told you, my doctor told me to come."

"I understand. What I meant was do you want to talk about why your doctor referred you for counseling?"

"Not really."

"OK. I see by your chart that Dr. Adams recently prescribed an anti-depressant for you."

"Uh huh."

"Have you started taking them yet?"

"Uh huh."

"How do they make you feel?"

"I don't know. I can't really tell."

"She's just been on them for the last 10 days," George said.

Clarissa nodded. "OK. Caitlin, are you a Mariner's fan?"

"They're OK, why?"

"I noticed you're wearing a Mariner's hat, so I thought you might be a fan."

"Oh, it was my brother's. I'm just wearing it 'cause my hair looks like shit."

"I guess it's good that you've got a hat then. Do you want to talk about why you're so depressed? What's going on with you these days?"

I was getting annoyed with all her questions.

"You really wanna know?" I snapped. "I'm depressed because my parents are crazy, and my brother killed himself last month."

"Oh Caitlin, I'm so sorry. That must have been horrible for you."

"Yeah, it fuckin' sucked. It still fuckin' sucks. My parents are still crazy, and my brother is dead. I, I, I fuckin' hate it."

I started crying.

Clarissa handed me a box of tissues and repeated how sorry she was. I nodded, unable to speak. "Do you mind if I ask your uncle some questions?"

I shook my head, blew my nose and tossed the used tissue into the trash can next to my chair. I picked up another tissue, wiped my eyes and cried some more. I listened as my uncle filled Clarissa in on my whole sad family history of schizophrenia.

"My goodness, Caitlin, you've really had a rough go of things, haven't you," Clarissa said. I nodded.

"You've been through a lot, and I know it must have been difficult. But I think I can help you. Would you like to work with me?"

"Huh?"

"Would you like to continue counseling with me?"

"I didn't know I had a choice."

"You always have a choice. Would you like to let me try to help you work through your depression?"

I nodded.

"Good, because I'd like to work with you. What would you like to get out of our sessions?"

"Huh?"

"Do you have any goals regarding counseling?"

"I just wanna stop feeling so shitty all the time."

Chapter 48

The mailman was just pulling up to our box when George and I were coming out the door to go to my doctor's appointment. The mailman waved and gestured for one of us to come over. I walked to the curb, and he handed me a stack of mail.

"Special delivery," he said with a smile.

"Uh, thanks."

I got into the minivan, secured my seat belt and started sorting through the stack while George started driving. There were two catalogs, a phone bill, a blue envelope proclaiming it was full of value coupons and a postcard with a picture of the Cumberland bridge on it.

I flipped over the card and started reading.

Dear Caitlin,

Two more days, and I'm through with summer school and heading back to Salem. I'll miss Charlie, but it will be great to be home.

Love, Jason

I smiled and put the postcard on the dashboard, and the rest of the mail on the floor.

"Was that from Jason?"

"Yeah. He's almost out of school."

"Cool."

The waiting room was only half full when we walked in, and I only had to wait 20 minutes before my name was called. I stood up and asked, "Are you coming with me?"

"Do you want me to?"

"Naw, I can handle this by myself."

"I'll keep reading this fascinating article about making Halloween decorations then."

The same nurse who was there two weeks earlier took my blood pressure, pulse and temperature. She breezed out of the room after jotting the results down, and I stared at the poster on the wall.

The words "Building A Rainbow" were printed on the top, and the artwork depicted a crew of tiny little people hanging from wires who were piecing small, colorful curved strips together to make the different bands of colors. I started counting how many workers were illustrated and had just reached 17 when the doctor knocked on the door, then opened it and walked in.

"Hi Caitlin," she said, while looking at my chart. "How are you feeling today?"

I was surprised to realize I was starting to feel a little better.

Until she had voiced that question, I hadn't given any thought to my state of mind.

"It's weird. I'm still pretty bummed about Jon, but I don't feel as shitty as I did two weeks ago. It feels almost like the black cloud that is surrounding me is fading just a little. I'm still really bummed about my brother, and I think about him all the time, but I don't feel like crying so much any more."

"That's good. That means the medication is starting to help. Have you been taking your antidepressants regularly?"

"Every night, just before I go to bed."

"Good. Have you noticed any side effects?"

"Like what?"

"Oh, like any change in your moods. Have you been feeling irritable, or restless? Or talking a lot more than usual?"

"No, I don't think so. Maybe not as pissed off as I usually am, but that's a good thing I think."

"That's definitely a good thing. Any trouble sleeping? Or oversleeping?"

"No."

"Good. It sounds like the medication is starting to work without any adverse reactions. I'd like you to keep taking your anti-depressants and come back and see me again in another two weeks. You should continue to improve. It generally takes about six weeks for anti-depressants to be fully effective.

"Have you started seeing a counselor yet?"

"Yeah, I saw her on Monday."

"Good. How often are you going to see her?"

"She had me make appointments to see her every Monday for the next seven weeks."

"That's good. Do you have any questions?"

"I don't think so."

"OK. Keep up the good work, and I'll see you again in two weeks. Don't forget to make an appointment on your way out."

After we got home, I walked down to the drugstore to pick out a postcard for Jason. When I got back to the house, I wrote:

Dear Jason,

I think I'm starting to climb out of the pit. Still got a long way to go, but I can see the sky again from here.

Love, Caitlin

I started to address the card, then realized Jason might already be back in Salem, and I didn't have his parents address.

I propped it up on the windowsill in my room so I'd be able to find it and send it after I spoke to him next.

Jason called two days later. I had started answering the phone again, so I picked it up and said hello before the answering machine kicked in.

"Hey Caitlin, I was expecting the machine."

"I can hang up, and you can call back and talk to it."

"No way. I'm glad you're home. I've been getting your postcards, but I keep missing you by phone."

"Yeah, sorry about that. I haven't been feeling much like talking lately."

"Yeah, I bet. I understand depression can do that to a person."

"Really? How do you know?"

"I've been doing my homework. I've been reading about it since you got sick."

"Really?"

"Yeah, really. I wanted to understand what you're going through."

"Wow, that's really nice of you."

"Well, I was kind of bored and sick of school so I didn't have much else to do."

"Are you back at your folks' house now?"

"Yeah, I got here yesterday. It's great to be back. I was getting so lonely in Cumberland. Everyone I knew was gone for the summer except for Charlie. He's a great dog and all, but you can't discuss politics or anything with him. He doesn't even know who Calvin Coolidge was."

I chuckled.

"Lucky dog. So what have you been doing since you got home?"

"Sleeping and laundry mostly. I only went to the Laundromat once this summer, so just about everything I own was dirty. I was hoping my mom would wash everything for me, but she just laughed at me and told me I was on my own. I've been washing clothes all day, well, all afternoon, since I slept 'til 11, and I've still got about four loads to go. I might be washing clothes until the fall semester starts. How are you doing?"

"Not too bad. I've been babysitting a lot since school ended and going swimming a lot with my uncle, but not much else. It's been too hot to skateboard, except for just before dark, and I'm usually working then."

"How are you feeling these days?"

"Not great, but a lot better than I was. I'm not falling asleep all the time like I was, and I'm getting my head shrunk once a week by a counselor. I'd tell you about it, except I can't cause counseling's confidential. How are you doing?"

"Better now that I'm out of school. I was really getting tired of it. I've never gone to summer school before, so this was the first time I didn't get a summer vacation. Goin' to school year-round sucks. I think I might have strained my brain."

"You got any plans?"

"You mean besides laundry?"

"Yeah, and besides sleeping in."

"Look for a job. I'm gonna go over to Alex's tonight and hang out, then start looking for work tomorrow."

We talked for another 20 minutes or so. Before I hung up, I asked Jason for his parent's address. He gave it to me, then asked if I was going to send him some more postcards.

"Yeah, at least one. I've got it all written out."

"Cool. I like getting your cards."

Chapter 49

Slowly, but surely, I started feeling better and better. I could almost feel the changes daily. My energy began to return, and I no longer wanted to sleep all day. I started asking my uncle if he wanted to go skateboarding, swimming, or hiking, rather than the other way around. And if he was busy, I would often pick up my skateboard and go ride around the neighborhood by myself. I stopped ruminating about ancient hurts and slights.

Then one day, about five weeks after I started taking the antidepressants, my uncle and I were talking about the Bixby Ranch.

I smiled and was stunned to feel a little jolt of pleasure surge through my face and chest.

I had been depressed for so long that I had forgotten how good it was to smile. A few mornings later, I realized I had been awake for at least 15 minutes before I thought about Jon's death.

While my brother was often on my mind, the waves of grief that had been washing over me for weeks seemed to be smaller and further apart.

My anxiety levels also dropped, albeit slowly, as the black cloud that had been surrounding me continued to diminish. I no longer dreaded being alone and rarely felt my body trembling for no reason.

Despite the improvements, my life was far from perfect.

I had stopped dodging phone calls, but talking to my mother still got me frustrated and upset.

She would call every few days and try to make me feel sorry for her.

"I'm too sad to paint" or "I miss Jon" were two of her favorite themes.

I heard "when are you coming home" and "your father is still incarcerated, and I don't know what I'm going to do without him" often, along with complaints about "my diabetes."

I would either get angry, and we'd end up arguing, or I would make up an excuse to get off the phone. My counseling sessions with Clarissa continued to make me uncomfortable, mainly because she would ask me about painful memories, about my brother and my parents.

I talked to Aunt Beth and Nana regularly, and they got me to realize that facing the past, however unpleasant it may be, would ultimately help me come to terms with my life.

Each week, I'd go to my therapist planning to open up to her about everything to try to speed the healing process along. Inevitably, however, I'd get overwhelmed by whatever we were discussing and would start clamming up when her questions brought up memories that were too painful to delve into.

Clarissa was adept at reading me and would back off a topic and change the subject when I started holding back.

"We don't have to talk about that now," she'd say unnecessarily, because by that point I had either started crying, or had stubbornly dug in my heels and refused to continue the conversation.

Then later, I'd regret not opening up, because, often, whatever subject we had been addressing that had gotten me so upset would remain on my mind. I'd grind on the thoughts by myself for hours, sometimes days, without the benefit of her counsel.

Although I can't say my counseling sessions were fun, I liked Clarissa and sensed that she liked and truly cared about me. I also liked the fact that Clarissa never told me what do to.

Instead, she'd make suggestions, like suggesting I keep a journal and write in it about my past and the present. When I gave her a blank look, she said she was only suggesting it, because writing in a journal had helped her make sense of things during a difficult time in her life.

"When I was 17, my boyfriend suddenly decided he didn't want anything to do with me," she told me. "We'd been together for nearly two years and had planned to get married after we graduated. But one day, he told me he was breaking up with me, and after that, he wouldn't even talk to me. I was devastated, and I poured out my heart in my journal."

"How did that help?"

"It helped me, because I could be totally honest with how I felt because nobody was going to read what I said. So I could write about how hurt I was and how it made me feel and my fear that nobody would ever love me again, or that I would be too afraid to fall in love like that again. Then I wrote about him and our relationship and what I liked and disliked about it. By the time I put everything down on paper, I had decided he was a jerk, and I was better off without him. A couple of years later I met Tom, who is the love of my life. If I'd still been with Robbie, that jerk from high school, I never would have fallen in love with Tom."

Clarissa also suggested I consider going back to a regular high school, especially after I admitted I was bored at the adult ed school.

"I had a lot of fun in high school," she told me. "I joined the drama club and the choir and made a lot of nice friends who I had a lot in common with. The extra curricular activities gave me something to look forward to almost every day after school, which made it a lot easier to get up at 6:30 every morning to get to school on time."

When I mentioned that my aunt, as well as my grandfather and Nana all were encouraging me to go to a regular school she nodded. "Great minds think alike. Maybe you should give it some thought."

"Yeah, maybe. My aunt said I could take some special classes and get college credit for them."

"I guess you're right, but it would slow me down. I can't wait to get into college. Though I'm still pissed I have to retake geometry. Unless I take four classes one term, I'll have to wait another semester to start college."

"Why are you in such a hurry to get to college?"

"Why not? I want to get a degree so I can get a good job and support myself. And I get along better with adults than I do with teenagers."

"Hmm. Have you thought about going to City College to finish your high school work there? They have a high school diploma program that allows people to earn college credits while they're completing their requirements for a high school diploma."

"Really? That sounds awesome."

"You might want to look into it. It's too late to enroll in the fall semester, but if you're really interested, I suggest you go to the school and talk to a counselor or adviser. They'll be able to tell you all about the program and what you'd need to do to enroll."

"I'll ask my uncle to take me there on the way home."

Chapter 50

Janson called to tell me he had bad new. "I found out today that I can't go back to Cumberland this year to go to school."

"What? Why not?"

"My parents are pissed that I had to go to summer school and didn't get a job. So they're not gonna help pay my rent or anything next year. And I don't have any money, so I can't afford to do it myself."

"That bites. What are you gonna do?"

"The only thing I can do, I guess. Stay home, go to Capitol, get a job and work at the same time and save up for my junior year."

"Well, at least you can still go to school."

"Yeah, but I've got to live with my folks. It's hard being back home after living on my own. They've got all these annoying rules, and they treat me like I'm five years old or something. My mom always wants to know where I'm going, who I'm going with and when I'll be back. My dad acts like I'm his slave or something, and he's always ordering me to mow the lawn or take out the trash or clean the garage. He's got something he wants me to do for him just about every day. And if I complain about it, he yells at me, and says I need to work for my room and board."

"Geeze, that sucks."

"Yeah, they're driving me crazy. And the evil twins have been giving me shit about it, too."

"What's their problem?"

"I don't know. They're just evil."

"What are they giving you shit about?"

"They keep telling me I'm a loser and a slacker, and I'm too lame to make it on my own. And I'm gonna be mooching off Mommy and Daddy forever."

"Nice sisters."

"Yeah, real nice. And it's real nice that there's two of them ganging up on me."

"Yeah, that sucks. At least you can go to school."

"Yeah, but it sucks going to the local community college. It's like an extension of high school, and I had enough of high school. And they don't have any solar energy classes. But you're right. At least I'll be able to go to school. I guess it could be worse."

For a week or so, I kept alternating between feeling sorry for Jason and missing Jon. I felt vulnerable, and when Clarissa asked me how I was feeling at my next appointment, I dropped my natural reserve and told her how I felt.

"I miss my brother so much that I can hardly stand it. I just wish I could talk to him one more time."

"Why don't you?"

"How? He's gone."

"My grandfather died when I was 12, and I talk to him all the time."

"How do you do that? Do you go to the cemetery or something?"

"No, I talk to him in the sky. After he died, my mother told me to pick out a star and imagine that's where my grandfather is. So I chose the North star, because it's always in the sky at night. Whenever I feel the need, I go outside and talk to my grandfather."

"Don't people think that's kind of weird?"

"I don't think so, and I don't really care one way or the other what people think. I find it very comforting. I imagine I'm talking to him, and sometimes I can almost hear him talk to me. I find it very reassuring to know I can talk to him anytime I want to."

"What if you want to talk to him during the day? What do you do then?"

"The stars are still out during the day. We just can't see them because the sunlight is so bright. So I look to where the North star should be and talk to my grandfather. He doesn't seem to mind it if I'm not looking straight at him."

I thought about what Clarissa had said later that evening.

I thought it was a little goofy, talking to a star and pretending it was someone you loved who had died.

I wasn't sure I wanted to do it but walked outside anyway and looked up at the stars.

There were hundreds of them visible in the sky, maybe more. They all looked the same to me. I scanned the sky, trying to find the brightest one. I'd never really looked at the night sky before and had no idea how you could tell one star apart from another.

My neck started to hurt from tipping my head back so far. So I gave up and walked back into the house.

I kept thinking about what she'd said and went back outside an hour or so later. The moon was a thin crescent hanging above the treetops across the street.

"Hey Jon," I said quietly. "Are you the man in the moon now? I sure hope so, cause I need to talk to you. I miss you. I wish you hadn't gotten sick. I wish you were healthy and here and helping me out. It's scary not having you in the world anymore."

Chapter 51

It was too late to enroll in the fall semester at City College, so I started another term at the adult ed school. But I discovered that if I wanted to enroll in the college's adult high school diploma program, I would have to jump through a couple of hoops.

It turns out that I needed to take several college placement exams to prove that I could read, write and do some math. I also needed to meet with an academic adviser, a school counselor and the financial aid department.

That was a surprise.

I was also surprised, well, actually shocked, to see how expensive it was to take college classes.

Combined with school fees, it would cost me about $450 to take a full load of classes to earn 15 credits each semester. My aunt told me I'd need to spend between $100 and $200 every semester on books. At that rate, I'd burn through my college fund pretty quickly.

I knew Jon had left me his college money, but I had no idea how much was in his account, or what I needed to do to get the bank to transfer the funds to me. Aunt Beth assured me that I qualified for financial aid and urged me to make an appointment with an adviser as soon as possible.

"It can take a long time to get the ball rolling, so the sooner you start applying for financial aid the better."

I was nervous about making an appointment and asked my uncle to call the school and set things up for me.

He refused.

"If you're ready for college, you're ready to handle these responsibilities by yourself. Besides, you're competent and capable. I know you can do this."

"I don't know where to start."

"Look in the catalog under Financial Aid for the number. Then call it and ask to make an appointment."

I found the number and dialed it.

I was surprised to have a friendly sounding man answer the phone.

I told him why I was calling, and two minutes later I had an appointment set up.

"This is exciting," I said, after hanging up the phone.

"I'm gonna go to college."

"I knew you could do it. To achieve, you must first attempt. Half of someone's success in life comes from taking the first step. At least that's what I've heard."

Buoyed by success, I called the number for the academic advisers.

It was busy.

"Shit!"

"Keep trying," George said. "Use the redial key."

"Lemme try the counseling office."

I dialed, the phone rang four times, then an answering machine clicked on.

"Shit!" I said hanging up.

"Call back and leave a message."

"I don't know what to say."

"How about telling them your name, your phone number and ask them to call you back so you can make an appointment?"

"OK."

I hit redial, waited for the machine, then waited for the beep. I left an awkward, stuttering message and hung up.

"Good." George said. "Now write down the number, and if you don't hear back from them today, call tomorrow and leave another message."

"OK."

I picked up the phone again and called the number for the academic adviser. It was still busy.

"Just keep trying," my uncle said. "That's why they invented the redial button."

It took seven more tries, but eventually I reached a real person and made an appointment.

"Two out of three ain't bad," I said.

"Not bad at all. I'd say you're ready for college."

A week or so later, Granddad called to tell me that Dad was going to be released from jail soon.

236

"That's great, Granddad. When is he getting out?"

"I'm not sure yet. The judge ordered him to live in a group home for mentally ill adults, and we're waiting for an opening. Once a bed is available, he'll move from the jail to the home."

"Where's the home? Is it in Cumberland?"

"Well, there are actually four different homes in the county. It all depends on which one has an opening for him. Two of the homes are in town, and the other two are outside the city limits, but nearby. I think all of them are along the bus line, so your dad will be able to get around."

"That's great. How long will he be in the group home?"

"That I don't know. I would imagine until he can demonstrate he's able to take care of himself and keep his illness in check."

"Oh. So he could be there forever."

"I just don't know, honey. Your father always does better when he's living under controlled circumstances. This may just be the best thing for him."

"Maybe, but it sounds kinda sucky. Sort of like he'll be back in jail or the mental hospital or something."

"No, it shouldn't be that bad. He won't be locked up, so he'll be able to come and go freely. So he'll be able to work and see your mother and the rest of the family. And he'll have people at the home that can take care of him and make sure he takes his medications."

"Nobody's ever been able to get him to take his meds for very long unless he's locked up."

"Well, hopefully the people at the group home will have more success with that. They're trained professionals, and I'm sure they work with non-compliant patients all the time."

"Well, I guess it's better than jail. Will I be able to call him when he's in the group home?"

"Of course. Any time you want to. And you'll be able to visit any time you want to as well."

"Well, that's good. Let me know when he's out of jail."

"I certainly will, honey. And I'm sure your dad will call you as soon as he can."

I thought the news about Dad was pretty good, as I hated the thought of him being in jail. My mother, however, who called me shortly after I spoke to Granddad, had another opinion.

"This is absolutely horrible," she said.

"The judge has taken my husband away from me. First your brother, now your father. I just don't know what I'm going to do."

"Mom, nobody's taking Dad away from you. Granddad said we can see him anytime we want at the group home, and he can come and go as he pleases."

"Don't tell me you're believing their lies now, too. That's just something they're telling us to keep us from knowing the truth. Your father is lost to me now, and I need your help in getting him back."

"Calm down, Mom. I think you're over-reacting."

"Don't tell me to calm down! This is a crisis." Mom started crying, wailing actually. I held the phone away from my ear and could still hear her.

"Mom?"

The wailing continued.

"Mom?'

She continued to sob.

"Mom, I can't talk to you when you're like this. I gotta go." I hung up the phone. My hand was shaking so hard that it took me three attempts to return the handset to the cradle. I was still shaken and upset when my uncle came home about 15 minutes later.

"What's wrong?" he asked just as the phone rang.

"Don't answer that!" I yelled.

He jumped back, startled. "OK, OK. What's going on?"

"Just listen," I said. "I think it's my mom."

We heard our outgoing message, a beep, then my mother's voice.

"Ayla, how dare you hang up on me. Pick up the phone. I'm your mother. Pick up the phone right now, you ungrateful brat. This is a crisis, and I need your help. They've taken away Jondalar, and now they're taking away your father. I need you. Pick up the phone and talk to me."

George looked at me with wide eyes.

"What the hell's going on?"

"She's crazy. And she's trying to suck me back into her craziness.

Whatever you do, don't pick up the phone."

"I won't, I won't, just tell me what's going on."

Mom's screeching monologue showed no signs of slowing down, so I gestured to George that we go outside.

We stood on the front porch while I filled him in on Dad's status, and Mom's take on it.

"Oh, God, Caitlin. She's really over-reacting. I'm sorry she's taking it out on you."

"Yeah, that makes two of us."

"I guess we'd better screen calls for a day or two. I don't want to try to talk to her until she starts calming down."

"Yeah, me neither. Actually, I'm not sure I ever want to talk to her again," I said, half seriously.

It took Mom about two weeks to calm down and accept the fact that Dad was going to be living in a group home and not with her.

Then a second crisis occurred when it became apparent she couldn't afford to continue to rent our old, three-bedroom home without Dad's disability income.

While she was panicking, sure she'd be homeless before Thanksgiving, Nana was calling Mom's social worker and begging her to help. After I moved out, following Jon's psychotic breakdown, Nana had gotten Mom placed on the waiting list for subsidized housing for disabled adults.

Mom had slowly been moving towards the top of the list.

With the latest crisis, the social worker pulled some strings and got Mom placed on an emergency list, which meant she'd be eligible for the next available apartment.

All we could do was to hope was that one would become available before Mom ran out of money or the landlord evicted her.

"Hopefully she'll sell some paintings before she goes broke," I said.

"Yeah, but she can't sell too many. If she makes too much money, she won't be eligible for subsidized housing," George said.

"Geeze, she's screwed either way."

"Well, let's just hope for the best."

"Hey, maybe we can see if Joan is still around, and if Mom can borrow *The Dinosaur* again."

"I think *The Dinosaur* died after you guys moved out. As I recall, it was in pretty bad shape before you moved in. And three people in a 24-foot trailer can really do some damage."

"Yeah, especially if one of them's Mom."

Chapter 52

I had been so focused for so long on getting into college that I hadn't given much thought to what I wanted to study once I got there. I knew I wanted to prepare for a career that would allow me to support myself, but beyond that I didn't really have any idea what I wanted to be when I grew up. I didn't know what to say to my assessment adviser when we met for my appointment, and he asked me what my educational goals were.

"Uh, um, uh, I don't know," I said, sure he was going to laugh or tell me I

I thought for a while, then remembered how much I had admired the nurses who took care of me in the hospital. I also remembered how much I liked nursing Dad's woodworking wounds.

"I think I want to be a nurse," I said.

"Nursing is a great field. It's rewarding, pays well, and nurses are always in demand. But it's challenging. You have to be comfortable being around people who are sick or injured and work well under pressure. You also have to be strong enough to move patients in and out of wheelchairs and beds. And you can't be squeamish. Nurses work with patients that are bleeding, throwing up, incontinent and in pain. You should take some time and think it over. Maybe volunteer at a hospital for a while as a candy striper."

"No. I know what nurses do. I was in the hospital for a real long time when I was a kid, and I want to help people get better, like the nurses helped me."

"It's your decision. You can always change your mind later if you find out some of the classes make you uncomfortable."

"Why would they? Are they hard classes?"

"The nursing program is challenging. And it includes several courses in anatomy, which require students to dissect human bodies."

"I can do that. I dissected frogs, cats and salamanders in biology. A lot of kids were grossed out, but I liked it, except for the smell. It was really interesting."

Later, I met with a counselor who helped me plot out my classes. At his advice, I signed up for the college survival and success class. The class was offered once a month, so I enrolled in the November course. It was scheduled to meet four Saturdays in a row, and although I hated the idea of give up half my weekends, I knew it would be time well spent.

I told Jason about my career plans, and he told me he was thinking about changing his major.

"I'm taking this class on green sustainable architecture right now. I signed up for it because it's the closest thing they have at school to solar design. And it's really cool. We're learning how to design environmentally sound homes. You know, with passive solar, green insulation, recycled materials and non-toxic building supplies. It's all about blending the building into the site. I'm taking the lab class, too, and it's really fun. We're designing homes, drawing up plans and building miniature models. It's a blast. I'm having a lot of fun, and I'm actually really good at it. I think I'm going to switch my major to architecture. I think I'll be able to have a much bigger impact that way, 'cause I can incorporate solar power into energy-efficient homes."

"Sounds like you're pretty excited about it."

"Yeah, I am. It's definitely my favorite class. Which is a good thing, cause with the lab and all, it takes up a lot of time."

Dad was released from jail in late October.

Uncle George and I went down to Cumberland on the last weekend of the month to see him. We left Portland early Saturday morning and went straight to Dad's group home when we reached Cumberland.

Dad was sitting in the living room, smoking a cigarette when we arrived.

He stubbed it out in a big, overflowing ashtray and rose to greet me with a hug.

"Oh, Dad, it's so good to see you. I've missed you so much."

"Oh, honey, it's wonderful to see you. Thanks for coming to visit. I've missed you, too."

We talked for a while, then Dad showed us his room, which he shared with another man. "I'd introduce you to my roommate, but he's at work today."

"That's OK. I'll meet him another time."

Dad showed us the rest of the house, and the yard, then George took the three of us out to lunch. After the meal, George dropped Dad and me off at the hardware store to see Granddad.

"I'm going to start working at the store again next week," Dad said. "I'll be working part-time in the stock room."

The next morning, Granddad dropped me off at Nana's on his way to the store. George and I had planned to take Dad out for lunch again before heading back to Portland. I had been looking forward to seeing Nana.

Although I had told her all about my college plans on the phone, I was so excited about starting at City College in January, I wanted to see her face-to-face to share my enthusiasm. I was looking forward to having a good visit with her, but it was not to be.

Somehow, Mom had gotten wind of the fact that George and I were in town, and she was waiting at Nana's for me. She started in on me as soon as I walked in the door. Mom was angry that I hadn't planned to spend time with her and berated me until I started crying.

"Now you know why I didn't want to see you," I said. "You're too intense. I can't handle it anymore."

Chapter 53

M y encounter with Mom left me angry, confused, upset and depressed. Everyone I vented to, George, Nana, Granddad, Jason
and Clarissa, agreed I had a reason to be upset and to avoid
Mom, at least for a while.

Clarissa and I spent several sessions talking about Mom and how her
recent behavior was affecting me. Clarissa suggested I write Mom a letter
explaining how her ranting and rages made me feel, and that we needed
to take a break from communicating with each other until she was able to
calm down.

"That'll just piss her off," I said. "And make her call me to tell me how
much it pissed her off."

"Well, then maybe you need to come up with a strategy to protect
yourself when she calls."

"How about if I just don't write her, or talk to her, or visit her."

"You can certainly do just that. But cutting off all communication
won't solve anything. It would be nice if you could maintain some kind of
relationship with her without letting her get to you."

"I'm not sure that's possible."

"Anything's possible. If you'd like to try I can work with you and help
you figure out how you can keep the lines of communication open while
not letting her verbally abuse you."

"I'll think about it."

"That's a good idea. If you decide later you want some help, just let me
know. In the meantime, what do you plan to do if she calls?"

"I'm not answering the phone these days. We've got a machine, so I'm
screening all the calls."

"Isn't that a hassle?"

"Kind of. But I'd rather do that than talk to her. She's been calling a
couple of times a week, leaving messages and stuff."

"What does she say?"

"Oh, different stuff, depending I guess on her moods. Sometimes she tries to sound cheerful, and that she just wants to chat and see how I'm doing. Other times she's kind of angry and wants to know why I'm not calling. And some times she tries to lay a guilt trip on me and make me feel sorry for her."

"It must be hard to hear some of her messages."

"Not really. I just delete all her messages. And if I'm home when she calls, I just turn the sound down on the machine and delete her message when she finally hangs up."

By mid-December, when I finished the fall term at the adult ed school and racked up seven and a half more high school credits, I was ready and eager for January to roll around so I could become a full-time college student. Everyone, Granddad, Nana, Dad and Mom wanted me to come down to Cumberland for Christmas.

I said "No way."

Uncle George wanted to go to Cumberland, too, as he usually spent the holidays with Nana. I told him to go ahead and not worry about me.

He insisted that he didn't want me to be home alone on Christmas, so I called Aunt Beth and asked her if I could come up and spend the holidays with her family.

"Absolutely," she said. "We'd love to have you."

So I took the bus to Washington, and George drove down to Cumberland by himself.

I was excited, but nervous when the first day of school finally arrived. It was drizzling, but I rode my skateboard to the bus stop, and got to school about an hour before my first class was scheduled to begin.

I wandered around the campus with my skateboard under my arm, trying to get oriented with the layout of the school and locate all the classrooms my courses would be held in. I was looking for the science building when I heard someone call out my name.

I turned and saw a guy skateboarding towards me.

"Travis!" I said with surprise, recognizing one of the guys I had gotten to know at the skate park. "What are you doing here?"

"Goin' to school. What about you? I thought you were in high school."

"I was, I mean I am. I'm starting the high school diploma program. This is my first day."

"Cool. How do you like it so far?"

"I don't know. My first class doesn't start 'til 10. I was just cruising around try to figure out where all my classes are gonna be."

"That's a good idea. What are you taking? Let me see your schedule."

I pulled my schedule out of my back pocket and handed it to Travis.

He examined it and offered to show me around the campus.

We skated around, dodging students, until it was nearly time for my class to start. We rode over to the classroom, said good-bye, and I walked in.

'I'm a college student.'I said to myself. 'I hope I can handle this.'

Chapter 54

There were at least a dozen computers available for use in the school library and more than two dozen in the independent study center. Very fewstudents could afford computers in those days and I needed to use a computer to type up my English composition assignments.

Very few people had even heard about e-mail, let alone had accounts at the time, so I thought I was very sophisticated. I quickly discovered it was a very fun way to communicate, especially after Jason started using e-mail as well. We started exchanging messages two, sometimes three or more times a day during the week.

I got into the habit of doing as much of my homework as possible on one of the school computers, checking my messages after I turned the computer on, and again before I turned it off.

Often, there'd be a message from Jason; a one-line joke or observation about someone or something that had happened during his day.

Surprisingly, even though we "talked" online several times a day, we still found a lot to talk about on the phone. And our phone calls increased after we started e-mailing each other, especially on weekends, when neither of us had access to a computer. Getting involved in each other's daily lives made us closer than ever. And while e-mail was quick and often amusing, it wasn't a substitute for a good conversation.

So I wasn't surprised to hear the phone ring early one Sunday morning, and hear Jason's voice coming out of the answering machine. But I was surprised to hear what he had to say when I picked up the phone and said "Hey."

"I'm so bummed I can't believe it. I think I'm more mad than bummed though. Anyway, something happened last night that really fucking sucked."

"What happened?"

"Well, my parents and I went out for dinner last night. My folks had a couple of cocktails before we left, and a couple of more at the restaurant. I was afraid my dad had had too much to drink, so I asked him if I could drive home. He got pissed off and told me to get in the back and not to be such a smart ass."

"Uh oh, this doesn't sound good."

"It isn't. So we're driving home, and my dad is still pissed, and he's yelling at me, and my mom is yelling at him to shut up and watch the road, and he's telling her not to tell him how to drive, and I'm in the back seat wishing I'd stayed home. Anyway, he's so busy arguing with my mom that he wasn't paying much attention to the road, and when the car in front of us stopped at a red light, we just plowed right into the back of it."

"Oh shit! Are you OK?"

"Yeah, I'm OK, my folks are OK, the air bags in the front went off. And the people we hit were OK. But both cars were smashed up pretty bad, and the cops came and everything."

"Uh oh, what happened then?"

"They figured out right away that my dad was drunk and arrested him. My mom got all hysterical, and I wanted to like crawl under the car and hide, but I had to deal with her and the tow truck guy and exchange information with the people whose car my dad rammed and try to keep my mom from losing her mind."

"Man, that's horrible."

"Yeah, it was. My mom was pretty drunk, too, and really, really upset."

"I bet she was upset. You must have been pretty upset, too."

"Yeah, I was. I still am. But somebody had to take care of everything, and my dad was in handcuffs in the back of a squad car, and my mom was freaking out, so I had to deal with it all."

"How'd you get home?"

"I had to have the cops call a cab."

"Wow. How's your mom this morning?"

"She's still asleep."

"How's your dad?"

"Hell if I know. He's still in jail. It's Sunday, and I don't know if he can get bailed out today. Or if I even want him to get bailed out."

"How bad's the car?"

"I think it's totaled. The radiator was smashed in and wrapped around the engine block, and the hood was completely buckled. The front fenders were bent so bad the wheels wouldn't turn, and the tow truck guy had to go back and get another truck and winch it up onto a flatbed to get it out of there."

"Damn."

"Damn is right. I hate it when my folks drink. Especially when they get that drunk."

"Do they drink a lot?"

"Way more than I'd like to see. They usually have a couple of cocktails before dinner, then polish off a bottle of wine while they're eating. Then sometimes they have a couple of more cocktails after dinner. I hate it."

"I didn't know they drank that much. I know you mentioned they were drinking more than usual after Alex tried to commit suicide, but I assumed it wasn't a big deal. No wonder you were so bummed about having to stay at home this year."

"Yeah, well, it's not something I like to talk about too much."

"I can understand why. It must suck."

"It does."

Chapter 55

Alow-income apartment opened up in Cumberland at the end of
February. I still wasn't talking to Mom, but she left several messages
about it, and my uncle called her back to find out the details. She
could start moving in March 1, and she wanted Uncle George, because he
had a minivan that could hold a lot of stuff, as well as a strong back to come
down and help her. And me to come down too, because she wanted me to
clear out all the stuff from my room and take the rest of the things I wanted
from Jon's.

When George relayed her request, I told him *"No way."*

"Can't say that I blame you. But why don't you reconsider. It would be
your last chance to get the rest of your belongings and Jon's."

"I don't care. I've got most of my stuff anyway, and it's not worth
dealing with my mom to get the rest."

"Let me know if you change your mind. It would be a good
opportunity to visit your grandparents and your dad."

"Yeah I know, but it ain't gonna happen."

"Well, if you don't change your mind, do you want me to bring you
back anything from the house?"

"I don't know. I've got most of the stuff I wanted out of my room,
except for maybe my books."

"I'll pack 'em up and bring 'em home for you."

"Thanks. That'd be cool. If you find any pictures can you bring them
back, too?"

"Sure, I'll look around. If I see anything else I think you might want,
I'll call you. Do you want anything from your brother's room? He left you
all his stuff."

"Maybe his books, too, and any pictures you find in there as well. Oh,
and his CDs. Not that he has all that many, but it would be nice to have 'em."

I talked to Clarissa about Mom's impending move at our next session.
I was bothered by the fact that my mother was still expecting me to drop
everything and come down and help her out. I was also upset about the fact

that she was moving. I'd lived in the house she was moving out of longer than any other place. And even though I'd left home and had no intention really of coming back, I still thought of the house as home base and a place I could always go back to.

Now that wouldn't be an option any longer.

Even more troubling to me was the fact Mom was moving into a one-bedroom apartment. Even if I wanted to come home, there wouldn't be any room for me. It was unsettling to feel fully adrift, even though I was the one who had set that course in motion.

"I think that's a natural reaction to a situation like this," Clarissa said. "Change of any type is hard, and a change like this brings up a lot of issues for you. It's one more loss, and you've already endured quite a few losses. It must seem like a final turning point to you, that there's no going back. But a house is just a building. It doesn't mean your relationships with your family are over just because you can't go back to the house you used to live in."

"Yeah, I know, but it still feels weird. It's especially weird to feel that way, because I can't imagine going back to Cumberland and living with my mother ever again. I don't even want to talk to her. I just don't get why this bugs me so much."

My uncle left early on the 26th to help pack up the old house. He called me that evening from Nana's house to tell me he'd found a journal that Jon had kept while packing up his books for me and asked me if I wanted it.

"Absolutely," I said. "If you find anything else like that be sure to grab it for me."

"I will. We haven't finished going through Jon's room, so I'll let you know what else we uncover."

"How's it going?"

"Slow. Your mom is helping me, and she having a hard time going through your brother's stuff. It's been tough for her."

"Yeah, I bet."

"Your father came over for a while this afternoon to help, and that slowed things down even more. He's pretty sentimental about a lot of things in the house. I think he'd keep everything if he had a place to store it."

"Is he still at the house?"

"No, I drove him back to his place after we quit for the day. Why?"

"Just wondering. What's his mental state like?"

"Pretty good, actually. He's obviously taking his medication. It makes him a little sluggish, but mentally he's all there."

After I hung up I decided to call Dad.

He was happy to hear from me and asked me if I had any room to store a couple of boxes of stuff. When I told him I didn't, he asked me to call Granddad and ask him to let us store some stuff in his garage.

"Why don't you ask him?"

"I already did, and he said no."

"I don't think he's going to change his mind then, Dad."

"He might for you. You're his granddaughter. I think he likes you better than he likes me."

"Who doesn't?" I joked.

We were both chuckling when I heard a woman's voice in the background say, "oh there you are."

"Hi, honey," I heard Dad say. My heart sunk, because I knew he was talking to Mom.

"Who are you talking to?"

"Ava."

"Ava? That ungrateful little brat. Give me the phone."

"Thanks a lot for coming down to help," Mom said to me.

"Hi, Mom."

"Don't hi Mom me. You're no daughter of mine. How dare you avoid me all these months, and then I come over here and find you chatting away with Dad. Don't you know how that makes me feel? You knew I was coming over here, and you called him just to spite me didn't you."

"No, Mom, I didn't."

"Don't lie to me. You're always lying to me. Don't think I don't know. I'm smarter than you think. And I've had it with you. You always hated me, didn't you? You always thought you were too good for me. Not like your brother. He loved me. I wish he was still here. He never would have treated me like this."

"Mom, Mom, stop it."

"Don't tell me what to do."

"Mom, if you don't stop, I'm going to hang up."

"Go ahead, see if I care. I wish you had been the one who killed themselves, not Jon. I wish...."

I hurtled the phone across the room.

It smashed into the wall, knocking a picture onto the floor and bounced halfway back towards me. I could hear my mother's angry voice still yelling.

I took two steps forward and kicked the phone as hard as I could. It hit the wall, and the back of the handset fell off.

I jumped on the rest of the phone and felt it crumple beneath my feet.

Chapter 56

I woke up with a start when I heard the sound of a key being fitted into a lock. I wracked my brain trying to figure out who's house I was baby-sitting at. When the door opened, and my Uncle George walked in, I realized I had fallen asleep on the couch of our house.

"Caitlin? Are you OK?"

I struggled to unwrap myself from the blanket I had cocooned myself in, and realized I was clutching my old Teddy bear.

"Not really. What time is it? What are you doing home so soon?"

"It's about 3:30 in the afternoon. I came back early, because I was worried about you. I heard what happened last night and kept getting a busy signal whenever I tried to call you. So I figured I'd let your Mom finish moving herself and come home and check up on you."

"Oh, yeah," I sat, sitting up. "I think the phone is broken."

George looked over at the table where the phone cradle was kept. "Where is it?"

I pointed to the floor, where the plastic and electronic remnants of my ire were scattered.

"Oh. I guess that explains why I couldn't reach you. Oh well, I never liked that phone anyway. Are you OK?"

"What do you mean, did I hurt myself when I smashed the phone? Naw, I'm fine. But I'm like so fucking pissed," I said, as tears began welling up in my eyes.

George sat down on the couch next to me and put his arm around my shoulders. "I'm so sorry, Caitlin. Your mother should never have said those horrible things to you."

"But she did," I said, starting to cry in earnest. "She hates me. And I never want to see or talk to her again."

I leaned my head against my uncle and sobbed. He just held me and let me cry. When I was finally cried out, George got up and went into the kitchen to make me some tea.

"I brought back some of your stuff. When you're ready, we can bring it in."

254

"Um, OK," I said, remembering the temper tantrum I had had after smashing the phone.

Hot white anger had taken over, and I'd trashed my room, hurtling clothes, books, shoes, whatever I could grab across the room in a rage.

When I'd thrown everything I could get my hands on, I'd pulled a poster off the wall toossed it on the pile of rubble I'd created. "Um, I need to clean my room first."

George looked at me with surprise, as my room was always clean and orderly.

"Sure, whenever you're ready. Everything's in the minivan, and it's not going anywhere."

"I, um, I kind of lost it last night," I confessed sheepishly.

"Lost it how?"

"I guess I had kind of a temper tantrum and took it out on my room."

"Did you break anything?"

"I'm not sure."

"Do you want me to check?"

"No, I'll do it. It's my mess, and I'll deal with it."

"I'd be really angry, too, if my mom had said something like that to me."

"You mean, if she told you she wished you were dead?"

"That was a horrible thing for your mother to say. I don't blame you for being upset and angry."

"I'm not sure upset and angry really describes how I feel."

"What does?"

"Huh?"

"What does describe how you feel?"

"I don't know. I don't know if there are any words that can describe it. I guess the closest thing would be totally fucking enraged and maybe completely devastated and rejected. And I think I totally fucking hate my mom. But other than that, the play was OK."

"I'm so, so sorry this happened. If it's any consolation, Lisa was frantic to get a hold of you to apologize. She wanted to come here with me, so she could tell you how sorry she is."

"I would have killed you if you brought her home with you."

"I figured as much. That's why I didn't."

255

"She'd better fucking not show up here anytime soon. I'm so pissed I don't know what I'd do if I saw her. But I'm sure it would be pretty ugly."

George started digging around looking for his old telephone. He eventually found it out in the garage and carried it inside. He blew the dust off the phone, plugged in the cord and plugged it into the wall. He picked up the receiver, held it to his ear and said, "Ah ha. Got a dial tone. This old baby may be primitive, but it still works. I've got to call my mom. She's really worried about you."

"My mom!" I shrieked.

"No mine. Your grandmother."

"Oh, sorry."

"That's OK. Do you want to talk to her?"

"Maybe later. I'm kind of talked out. I don't really feel much like talking to anybody else right now."

"Fair enough. Do you mind if I call your father and let him know how you're doing? He was really upset and worried about you, too."

"Yeah, I guess, but I don't want to talk to him right now either."

I went in my room to try to restore it to normal while my uncle was on the phone. I could hear him murmuring, but couldn't quite make out what he was saying.

I closed the door and got to work.

My uncle was sitting on the couch, strumming a guitar when I emerged from my restoration project.

"How's it going in there?"

"Pretty good. I got everything picked up and put away. Nothing was broken except for a coffee cup, although there's kind of a dent in one of the walls."

"How big of a dent?"

"About the size of a silver dollar."

"Oh, well it should just add character to the room then."

"How's my dad?"

"Relieved you're OK, but still very upset with your mother. Your mom caused quite a bit of drama last night."

"I guess. Telling your only surviving child you wished she was dead is pretty dramatic."

"Yeah, but that was just the first part of her wild evening."

"Why? What happened after that?"

"Apparently what happened after that was she and your father had a huge argument. Your father, understandably, thought she was completely out of line and had no business even grabbing the phone away from him, let alone saying what she did to you. And your mother, of course, has never responded well to criticism. She lost her temper and was ranting and raving so loudly that the supervisor at your dad's place told her to leave. When she refused, he called the cops, and they came and took her away."

"Did they take her to jail?"

"No, they took her to Mom's house and warned her that if she didn't behave herself they'd come back and arrest her."

"What happened then?"

"Your grandmother tried to calm her down and find out what happened. We knew she'd had a fight with your dad, cause the police told us where they'd picked her up. Once we realized she had been talking to you, I called your father and found out what she had done. Then I started trying to call you. When I still couldn't get through this morning, I decided to come home and see how you were doing."

"Thanks for coming home. I, I, it's really nice not to be alone right now. I mean I'm really glad you're here."

Chapter 57

When I first started counseling, I felt like I'd been sentenced to a series of torture sessions that would consist of being forced to talk to a stranger who would try to get me to relive my childhood and spill out my guts. I counted down the weeks, after each session, looking forward to a time when I wouldn't have to give up one afternoon a week being counseled. Something strange happened, though.

By the sixth session I realized I was comfortable talking to Clarissa, and by the eighth session, I was disappointed that my 10 weeks of therapy were coming to an end.

So when Clarissa asked me if I wanted to continue counseling, I said sure. It took a couple of weeks to get the additional sessions approved, something Clarissa, Dr. Adams and Aunt Beth took care of.

I was glad when our sessions resumed, especially after Mom's latest flip out. I hadn't talked to Mom since that horrible night and had no plans to do so. Dad, Nana, even Granddad and Eileen told me Mom felt terrible about what she had said, and that she said those awful words because she was hurt that I had been avoiding her.

When people are hurt they often get angry, everyone told me.

My response was always "Well, duh" especially with a new telephone and a new poster covering the dent in the wall of my room reminding me how badly I'd lost it that night.

Mom had written me a letter, which I mailed back unopened after scrawling "leave me alone" on the back of the envelope.

I knew my actions further validated the hurt leads to anger theory, but I just didn't want to have anything to do with Mom.

For me, the latest hurt inflicted on me by my mother was the last straw.

I had endured so much angst, frustration, embarrassment, guilt and anger over the years, that it probably wouldn't have taken much for me to finally snap and decide I needed to protect myself from her emotional turmoil.

Clarissa didn't try to change my mind, or make me feel bad about rejecting a mother who had severely wounded and rejected me. She did, however, after hearing me talk about Mom and my childhood for several weeks, remind me that my mother had some serious flaws.

"Well, duh. She's schizophrenic."

"I understand that. And it sounds like she also very insecure and self-centered."

"Oh she's self-centered all right. She thinks everyone should worship her like she's a queen or something. She totally hates it when anyone else gets attention for something good. And she's always trying to make people think she's so much better than everyone else by putting other people down."

"That's very common among people who are insecure. They feel like they have to drag people down to elevate their own sense of self-esteem. People who are insecure are also very vulnerable to slights and wounds. A comment or criticism that most people would shrug off, for example, can make them feel like they've been attacked."

"That's not my fault."

"No one says it is. I'm just addressing some of the tendencies insecure people have."

"I'm not so sure Mom's insecure. She's got a huge ego. She thinks the world revolves around her, and that everyone should constantly admire her greatness. She also thinks she's so special that everyone should take care of her when something goes wrong. She conned my brother into taking care of her and the rest of us when we were kids, and once he was gone, she kept trying to con me into taking care of her."

"She's a difficult woman, and she certainly has her problems."

"Yeah, and I'm trying to keep her problems away from me so they won't become my problems."

My relationship with Mom remained non-existent, but my relationship with Dad was good.

Since he had access to a phone, we talked regularly, although I sometimes found his conversations confusing. Dad would occasionally launch into a monologue involving people I didn't know and suspected may not exist, or jabber about situations that likely existed only in his mind.

If I had time, I'd let him ramble for a few minutes before hanging up the phone.

Most of the time, however, Dad was coherent, at least to people who knew him well and could follow his train of thought. The supervisors at the group home made sure he took his medications as prescribed, which helped and allowed him to hold down a job.

He was working at the hardware store again and would frequently tell me about the customers who still asked about me, then ask me about school, even if we had talked the day before.

He was proud of the fact I was in college, especially at such a young age. "I wish I'd gone to college," he said several times. "Maybe I should start taking some classes down here, too."

Chapter 58

Jason and I both decided to go to summer school, even though we were both longing for a break from our studies. We were both in a hurry, however, to get through school. We both were anxious to launch our careers and start earning enough money to support ourselves. Jason had the added incentive of finishing community college so he could move away from his folks' house.

We both had two weeks off between the end of the spring semester and the start of summer school. When Jason asked if he could come up and visit for a couple of days, I was thrilled.

Jason arrived at our house in the early afternoon, and we planned to go hiking later, after catching up.

We started talking, and the next thing I knew, we both were getting hungry. After dinner, we walked to the video store to rent a movie, then stayed up late talking some more and never even took the movie out of the box.

"We should make some plans for tomorrow so we can actually get out of the house and have some fun," I said before going to bed.

"I am having fun."

"Me too, but still."

"I know what you mean."

Over the next few days, we went hiking, swimming, to the movies and to the zoo. We drove around Portland and went sightseeing. We went to hear my uncle's band play at a private party. I showed Jason around the City College campus. We checked out some of the universities in town, because Jason was trying to decide where to transfer after he finished up at Capitol.

"I thought you were planning to go to Oregon State," I said.

"Plans can change. I'm thinking it would be nice to finish up in Portland."

Before I knew it, Jason said it was time for him to head back to Salem.

"I've been here for five days, and I was only planning to stay for three or four."

"Plans can change. Why don't you stick around and go for double digits."

"You mean stay for 10 days?"

"Yeah, why not?"

"I don't know. I'm all out of clean underwear."

"We've got a washer and dryer. My uncle is real civilized and all."

"Well, if you insist."

I had to baby-sit three of the evenings while Jason was in town and go to my final two counseling sessions, but other than that, we spent all our time together. Clarissa and I both agreed that I although I had benefited from counseling, that it was time for me to take a break.

Our therapy sessions left me drained, and I felt like I needed some time to absorb some of the insights Clarissa had helped me uncover.

"You can resume counseling anytime you feel the need,"she told me. "Just call my office anytime you want to talk, and we'll set up an appointment."

Jason, who insisted on driving me to my appointments, took me out for lunch after my final session with Clarissa to celebrate. The celebration was bittersweet, because Jason would be leaving the next morning to get ready for summer school.

"You know he's in love with you, don't you?" my uncle said after Jason left for Salem.

"What do you mean?"

"I've seen the way he looks at you. He's got such love in his eyes for you. He adores you."

"Really?"

"Absolutely."

"Well, that's cool, 'cause I think I'm in love with him, too."

"So what's stopping the two of you from hooking up?"

"Well, I'm scared. He's my best friend, and I'm afraid that if he becomes my boyfriend and something goes wrong, it'll ruin our friendship. Besides, he hasn't said anything."

"I think he's scared, too."

"You do?"

"Yeah, I do. You should let him know that it's OK for him to make a move on you. That is if you want him to."

262

"I think I do, but I'm scared. What if we break up?"

"How can you break up if you haven't started going together? And while you're worried about breaking up, why don't you worry about a meteorite hitting the earth and wiping everyone out? I think you should stop worrying about things that probably aren't going to happen and start living. You guys have been good friends for awhile now, and obviously care a lot about each other. You've helped each other through some pretty tough experiences, which has made you two even tighter. The best relationships are built on good friendships. I think you two would be really good together."

"Yeah, but..."

"But what?"

"I'm also scared about something else."

"What are you afraid of?"

"Getting sick. I'm afraid of getting sick and having Jason go through with me what I've been through with my family. He's such a good guy, I'd hate to put him through that."

"But what if you don't get sick?"

"How do I know if I'm going to get sick or not?"

"That's my point. You don't know. Nobody knows. You just have to take chances and live your life."

"But what if I do get sick? You know that schizophrenia has a tendency to run in families. That means I've got a much better chance of getting it than Jason does."

"Why don't you cross that bridge if you get to it? And why don't you give Jason a little credit. He knows all about your parents and brother. For Christ's sake, you met each other in the waiting room of a mental hospital."

"Behavioral Health Unit."

"What?"

"That's what they call it. A Behavioral Health Unit. They don't call it a mental hospital anymore."

"Whatever they call it, if Jason hasn't been scared off by now, he's never going to be. If he loves you as much as I think he does, he'll be willing to take that gamble."

I thought about what my uncle had said, and when I went to school on the first day of the summer term, I sent Jason an e-mail.

Dear Jason,

I don't want to freak you out or anything, but I'm in love with you. For real.

Caitlin

I went back to the computer center every hour to check my messages, worried I'd made a big mistake, and hopeful that I hadn't. At 3 p.m., just before I was ready to leave campus for the day, I checked my messages one more time and found one from Jason. Nervously, I clicked it open.

Dear Caitlin.

Getting your message was the best thing that has ever happened to me. It was even better than when my high school soccer team won state. I've been in love with you for months and months, but was afraid I'd freak you out if I said anything. I wish I could see you tonight, but I'll have to settle for calling you on the phone.

Jason started coming up every other weekend through the summer term, sleeping on the couch in the living room until we finally made love in mid-August. My uncle must have sensed the change in our relationship, because when Jason came back to Portland two weeks later, George told him to just put his bag in my room.

264

Chapter 59

W e'd been ringing up large phone bills for some time now, but the bills got larger over the next 12 months as we started talking on the phone almost daily. Jason continued to come up to Portland every other weekend, during the breaks between semesters and spring vacation. We e-mailed each other several times a day on school days, so often it felt like we were having ongoing conversations.

Still, I missed him terribly when he was down in Salem and was thrilled when we both finished the end of our spring semesters at our respective schools.

Jason moved up to Portland the following June, after he graduated from Capitol Community College with an Associates of Arts degree in architecture. He rented a tiny studio apartment near Oregon College and found a summer job as a surveyor for the county.

While he was sweating it out in the hot summer sun under his hardhat and reflective vest, I worked part-time in an air conditioned rest home and part-time as a counselor at a summer day camp for kids held at Jade Street Park by the City Recreation Department.

The kids I helped entertain in the afternoon were between the ages of 6 to 8, while the minimum age of the people I helped care for at the Chanticleer House was about 68, a fact that I thought was ironic.

I couldn't decide which job I enjoyed the most.

I loved leading the kids through games and activities, but the work wasn't necessarily very challenging.

Working in the nursing home was far more challenging, although it included a lot of drudgery and unpleasant tasks, like emptying bedpans, making beds and mopping floors.

Jason and I spent almost every night together, either in his one-room apartment or at my uncle's house. I barely saw my uncle, as he was usually still asleep when I left for work in the morning and out playing music, or squiring some sweet young thing out on the town when I got home.

In addition to playing with his bands, my uncle got hired to score another film and was putting in long hours in the recording studio. We went through nearly an entire 1-subject college notebook leaving messages back and forth to each other about our whereabouts, plans, who George was dating and important and not so important news and thoughts.

By late July, the same name, Trish, was the only female name showing up in George's notes, as in "Trish and I are going to dinner, and I'm probably going to stay overnight at Trish's place."

I finally met Trish near the end of the summer, ironically the same weekend that I met Jason's parents for the first time.

I had been curious about this mysterious woman who had seemed to capture my uncle's heart, but, given George's hook up history, thought she'd probably be out of his life sooner or later so it never occurred to me to ask to meet her.

I figured if they continued hanging out, I'd meet her eventually, and that's what happened. George and Trish came home one morning while I was still at the house. He introduced us, and that was that.

I think Trish was nervous about meeting me, but I had met so many of my uncle's previous girlfriends I didn't think it was a big deal.

Meeting Jason's parents, on the other hand, was a big, nerve-wracking deal for me.

Mitchell and Renee Kane didn't look at all like I pictured them.

Jason was above average in height, about 6' 2" and slender, with blonde hair and blue eyes.

His beard, when he had one, was dirty blonde.

I had imagined his father would look like an older version of Jason, with graying hair and glasses.

After talking to his mother a couple of times on the phone, when she called Jason while I was there, I had pictured her as a tall, middle-aged woman with straight blonde hair.

So I was surprised when Jason and I walked into the restaurant where we were meeting them for lunch and he said, "There they are" and pointed to a heavy-set couple.

"Mom, Dad, this is Caitlin. Caitlin, these are my parents."

"Hello Mr. and Mrs. Kane, it's really nice to meet you," I said, words that I'd been practicing in my mind since Jason asked me to come with him to meet his folks. "Thanks for inviting me to join you for lunch."

"It's nice to meet you too," said his mother, who had curly brown hair streaked with gray. "We've heard a lot about you from Jason."

"It's nice to meet the young lady who my son is spending so much time with," said Mitchell, standing up to shake my hand.

He was a good six inches shorter than Jason and about 80 pounds heavier.

His eyes were brown, like Renee's, and the little bit of hair he had left on his head was gray.

His face was ruddy, and his nose was laced with broken blood vessels. Neither of Jason's parents wore glasses, although Jason later told me his mom wore contact lenses, and his dad used glasses to read.

I had been nervous about meeting Jason's folks because I wanted to make a good impression on them but tried not to show it. Jason, however, knew I was uncomfortable and held my hand under the table. Before his parents could start asking me questions, Jason started talking.

"Caitlin's in the nursing program at City College. She's planning on transferring to Oregon College in January to finish her degree."

"That's nice," Renee said, turning to me.

"She's gotten straight As in all her nursing classes," Jason bragged. I looked at him in surprise, wondering if he'd forgotten I'd gotten mostly Bs and Cs my first semester. When he smiled at me, I realized he was exaggerating on my behalf, and I decided not to correct him.

"That's wonderful," Renee said.

"Thank you."

"That's impressive," Mitchell said. "Maybe you could tutor my son. I seem to recall he had to repeat a couple of classes his first year in school."

Jason ignored the jibe and told them I was working at a nursing home this summer. The way he made it sound, I was heading the medical department and was personally responsible for keeping half a dozen terminally ill people alive.

I thought he was starting to overdo it, so I interrupted and asked his parents how long they were planning to be in Portland.

"We're heading back home after lunch," Renee said. "We just came up here to see Jay Jay. He's been so busy with work, that he hasn't been down to see us for a while, so we thought we'd come up here to see our baby."

We chatted for a while, and I was starting to relax when, inevitably, Renee wanted to know where I had grown up and what my parents did.

"I was born and raised in Cumberland. That's where Jason and I met."

"Is your family still there?"

"Oh, yes. My grandparents live there as well, both my mom's mom and my dad's father and stepmother."

"What do your parents do?"

Jason and I had anticipated that question and had prepared for it.

"My mother's an artist. She paints watercolors and sells them out of several galleries in Cumberland. And my father works with my grandfather at the family hardware store. My great-grandfather opened the store after the Great Depression. Working there is a real family tradition. I worked there part-time when I was in high school. Jason tells me you own your own business as well."

"That's right," Mitchell said. "I've got an accounting firm with four employees working for me."

Mitchell talked about his company, and his disappointment that none of his children were interested in accounting and taking over the business when he retired. Renee said she was glad Jason and his sisters had their own interests and wouldn't be spending their working lives balancing spreadsheets and crunching numbers.

Mitchell frowned at her, but before he could retort, Jason volunteered that his mother worked for the March of Dimes.

"She's the executive director of the Salem office," he said.

"That's really cool," I said. "That must be a rewarding career."

"Oh, it is," Renee said. It gives me an opportunity to make a difference in so many lives."

I got through lunch without spilling anything or attracting any undue attention. Although his parents were pleasant, I was relieved when the meal was over, and it was time to go our separate ways.

Jason's mother shook my hand when we said good-bye, then wrapped Jason in a bear hug.

"It's so good to see you again, honey. I just love you so much," Renee said.

She hung onto him long enough for me to wonder if she would ever let him go.

Finally, she released him, and we headed out to Jason's car before she could grab him again.

Chapter 60

In the fall, I returned to City College for my fifth and final semester, and Jason started his junior year at Oregon College. I had already been awarded my high school diploma the previous year, but would earn my Associates of Art degree in December. There was a graduation ceremony planned at the end of the semester, but I figured I'd skip it and just have my degree mailed to me. When Nana found out, she was disappointed and told me she had been looking forward to coming to my graduation.

"It's no big deal," I told her. "It's just an AA degree. It just means I'm ready to transfer to a four-year college."

It turned out it was a big deal, at least to Nana, especially since neither Mom nor George had gone to college.

She called Dad and Granddad, who both called me to say they wanted to see me graduate.

One of them called Aunt Beth, who called me as well.

Everyone, it seemed, was anxious to see me put on a cap and gown and walk across the stage of the campus auditorium. I gave in to the pressure and agreed to go through the ceremony, only if everyone promised that Mom would not come within 100 miles of Portland.

The ceremony was on the 21st. I thought it was kind of boring.

After listening to too many speeches, we had to wait onstage in our heavy maroon robes in the overheated auditorium while the school president handed out awards to several dozen people who had achieved things like writing the best essay in the English department, captaining the football team, and having their art work displayed in the cafeteria.

Finally, they started handing out diplomas.

It took a while to get to mine, as they went in alphabetical order.

I had hoped that I'd be able to get my diploma and walk off stage.

Instead, we had to go back to our seats after shaking the president's hand and wait for Ralph Zimmerman to get his diploma before we could file out while the loudspeakers in the auditorium pumped out "Pomp and Circumstance."

I met Jason, Uncle George, Trish, Dad, Granddad, Nana, Eileen, Aunt Beth, Katie and Julie outside on the lawn after the ceremony.

Aunt Beth, Granddad and Nana all had cameras; I had to pose for picture after picture until everyone ran out of film.

Then Granddad took us all out to lunch at Bangkok West, a Thai restaurant that Jason and I had discovered recently. Once we had sat down, Katie sidled up to me and whispered, "I knew he was your boyfriend."

I just laughed and smiled.

Everyone told me how proud they were of me, and I kept blushing and saying "thank you."

When our food arrived, Granddad stood up with his water glass in his hand and said he wanted to make a toast.

"To Ava, for working so hard in school and completing high school and her first two years in college."

"Thanks," I said, blushing again. I stood up, held up my water glass and said I'd like to make a toast, too.

"To all of you here today. I couldn't have done it without your support. I hope you'll all come back, and we can do this again in two years when I graduate with my nursing degree."

Chapter 61

J ason started putting together his resume a year later, just before his final semester of college began. We weren't officially living together, although we spent almost every night together, and both had clothes, toothbrushes, books, and CDs at each other's place.

We hadn't really discussed our post college plans, beyond vague references about finding jobs. Now that he was close to graduating we started discussing our options. Jason wanted to stay in Portland until I graduated, then start looking for work in his field.

I told him I didn't think he should wait.

My teachers had been telling me and my fellow nursing students that there was a huge demand for nurses throughout the country ever since I started at City College. I knew I wouldn't have any trouble finding a job as long as I kept my grades up and got my former manager at the nursing home to write me a positive recommendation.

The outlook for new architects wasn't as bright, and Jason was worried he'd have trouble finding work.

I told him I'd be willing to follow him to wherever he found a job, because there were hospitals everywhere that probably needed nurses.

"Would you mind if I looked for a job in Washington State?" Jason asked.

"Washington? That would be great. I'd love to be closer to my aunt and uncle and my cousins and farther away from my mom."

"I'd like to be farther away from my folks, too, and from the evil twins."

Annette had moved to Portland recently, which gave Renee and Mitchell even more reason to visit.

Lately, they'd been coming up at least twice a month and insisting we all get together. Andrea, who was living in Salem with her fiance, often came with her parents to Portland.

Jason's sisters still liked to pick on him and the teasing got much more intense when the two were together.

We both dreaded visits that involved the entire family and lately had been uncomfortable even when we only saw Mitchell and Renee.

The closer Jason got to graduation, the clingier his mother had become. She obviously dreaded having her youngest child become a full-fledged adult.

It took Jason four months and six trips to Washington State for interviews before he was offered a job as a junior architect at a medium-sized firm outside of Seattle. They wanted him to start in mid-May, nearly a month before I was set to graduate. Jason wanted to wait until I was finished school, but I urged him not to ask for a later start date.

"I don't know," Jason said. "I should at least ask if I could delay starting."

"I don't think that's a good idea. You don't want to start off by having them think you're not eager to work for them."

"I am eager, just not eager to move up there without you."

"I'll be up there before you know it. And Seattle's not that far away, we can see each other on weekends. Besides, we've lived apart before. We can survive another temporary separation."

"Yeah, I know we can, but I don't want to."

"I don't really want to either. But there aren't a lot of entry-level architectural jobs out there. I don't think you should let this opportunity pass."

Chapter 62

Jason accepted the job, and we drove up to Buskirk, where the firm was located, to look for an apartment on the last weekend in April. Jason did the footwork, driving around town looking at rentals while I stayed in the hotel and studied. On Sunday, he took me to see his two top choices. We picked the newer one, because it seemed cleaner, and signed the lease.

Jason was quiet on the drive back to Portland. I assumed he was thinking about the move and our impending separation, so I kept quiet too and let him ruminate.

Finally, just before we reached the Columbia River, which separates Oregon from Washington, he spoke up.

"I know we've talked about this a lot before and decided to wait. But I don't want to wait any more. I really want us to get married. I love you, Caitlin, and I want to spend the rest of my life with you."

"I love you too, Jason, but I think we should think about this some more."

"What's to think about? We've had this discussion so many times before. Are you having second thoughts because of my student loans?"

"Of course not." I said. While I'd benefited from scholarships, Jon's college fund, my savings and some help from Granddad to pay my tuition and supplement my savings, as well as my uncle's generosity for supporting me, Jason had had to borrow $20,000 to cover his final two years in school.

"I'm not worried about your loans. It's just..."

"You're worried about your health," he finished.

"You know schizophrenia runs in my family. I could get sick at any time. I just don't want to saddle you with that kind of hell."

"I love you, Caitlin. That doesn't matter to me. If we get married, it will be in sickness and in health. If you get sick, I'll take care of you, just like you'd take care of me if I get sick."

"You just don't understand. It's not as easy as you think. You haven't lived with a schizophrenic before. You have no idea how hard it is. And how heartbreaking."

"I'm willing to take that chance. Besides, there's no guarantee you will get sick. We might be worrying about something that may never happen."

"But it could."

"And pigs could fly. Look, if you do get sick, we'll deal with it together. There are new drugs available now that weren't available when you were a kid. If you do get sick, you'll have a much better chance of keeping the disease controlled than either of your parents did."

"What if I get as sick as my brother did?"

"What if I get in a car wreck tomorrow? What if I'm paralyzed? Would it make you stop loving me?"

"Of course not."

"Well, then give me some credit. Nothing could ever make me stop loving you. I want to marry you, Caitlin. What do I have to do to convince you to say yes?"

"I don't know, honey. I don't know."

I moved all the things I'd left at Jason's studio back to my uncle's house and helped Jason pack. We cleaned out the studio together, but his landlord still refused to give Jason back his deposit. I was angry, but Jason just shrugged it off.

"It's only money, and I've got a real job now," he said. "The only thing that really matters to me is you."

We spent Jason's last night in Portland at my uncle's house.

Jason had planned to leave for Buskirk early in the morning, but his parents insisted on coming up to take us out to dinner. They got stuck in traffic on the way up, so they didn't arrive at George's house to pick us up until 8 o'clock. We had missed our reservation and had to wait for a table to open up. Renee was maudlin over dinner, saying over and over how much she would miss Jason when he was up in Washington.

"You can always come visit me, Mom. It's not like I'm moving all the way across the country or to Europe or anything."

"I know, honey, but it won't be the same. Your father and I won't be able to drive up for lunch or dinner whenever we want to see you."

I breathed a sigh of relief when she said that but tried not to let my feelings show because Renee was so sad. She had been on the verge of tears all night and finally broke down and cried when she was hugging Jason good-bye.

"I can't believe my baby is leaving," she wept.

"Don't make a scene Renee," Mitchell said. "It's not like he's going to disappear out of our lives. We can talk to him on the phone whenever you'd like."

"I know, but this is a big step. My baby is all grown up, through with college and starting a real career. He doesn't need me anymore."

"Oh Mom, I'll always need you," Jason said. "You'll always be my mom, no matter what."

It was my turn to cry the next morning, when I watched Jason drive off. I was still wiping my eyes when I walked back into the house. George was drinking coffee and watched me come in.

"Oh, Caitlin, don't cry. You'll be back together in a few weeks."

"I know. It's just that I'm gonna miss him until then. I already miss him."

"Time goes fast. You'll be through with school before you know it, and I'll be crying watching you leave."

"Or celebrating."

"Well, maybe both. Crying because I'll miss you, and celebrating because you'll have achieved the goals you've worked so hard for and will be starting a new life in a new city with the man you love.

"Speaking of the man you love, when is Jason going to make an honest woman out of you?"

"Funny you should ask. We've been talking about getting married lately, but I'm not sure I want to."

"Why not? Is there something about Jason I don't know about?"

"No, of course not. It's more that I don't want to saddle him with a lunatic."

"What are you talking about? You're not a lunatic."

"Not yet, but I could be. You know as well as I do that my chances of contracting the family disease are really high."

"So?"

"So I don't want Jason to end up married to a crazy woman."

"Now that's crazy."

"What do you mean that's crazy?"

"I mean that you shouldn't let something that may never happen stop you from doing something you know is right. That's like punishing yourself for a crime you haven't committed."

"But what if I do get sick?"

"Well, then you'd be a bigger fool for not fully embracing life and marrying the man you love while you were healthy and had a chance to."

Chapter 63

J ason and I got married at Portland's City Hall the day before I graduated from Oregon College. Julie came down from Washington to be my
maid of honor, and Alex drove up from Salem to be Jason's best man.
They were our only guests and witnesses.

We decided to get married in Portland so my relatives, who were
coming to town for my graduation, could celebrate with us.

I called Granddad, Nana, Dad, Aunt Beth and Grandmom to let them
know our plans and threatened to disown anyone who told Mom about it.

Everyone wanted to come to the wedding, but when I explained we
were just having a very small civil ceremony, they said they'd be happy to
come to a reception party for us the day after graduation to wish us well.

Jason's family didn't take the news as well as mine did.

His mother was upset that she couldn't watch him walk down the
aisle, even though he explained over and over again that there wasn't an
aisle in the city clerk's chambers to walk down.

His father was angry that Jason had upset his mother.

His sister Annette said she didn't care one way or the other, but
Jason told me later that Andrea had left a snide message on his answering
machine saying something to the effect we must have planned a quickie
wedding because he'd knocked me up.

Jason didn't bother to call her back to tell her she did not have a niece
or nephew on the way.

Alex's parents, on the other hand, said they understood when Jason
expla

It was a whirlwind week.

I finished my last final on Tuesday, and Jason came down Wednesday.

We bought our wedding rings, plain gold bands, on Thursday
morning, got married Thursday afternoon, and I graduated from college
with my nursing degree Friday with my new husband sitting with my
father, two grandfathers, three grandmothers, two uncles, three cousins
and an aunt.

We all went out to dinner that night to celebrate my graduation, then Jason and I went back to Uncle George's to spend the night.

We were up early Saturday preparing for our reception.

That afternoon, my family and Jason's crowded into my uncle's small house to toast our wedding and watch us cut our wedding cake.

We spent Saturday evening cleaning up and finishing my packing, then left for Buskirk on Sunday morning after having breakfast with Uncle George and Trish.

I was delighted to be in Washington, because it put me further away from Cumberland. I had made the mistake of opening a birthday card my mother sent me in September, instead of returning it as I had in the past.

I didn't think it was such a big deal, but Mom did.

She took that as a sign I was ready to reconcile with her and had started calling regularly. I went back to screening calls when I was at Uncle George's and threatened anyone who might give her Jason's number with being staked down on a red ant hill if they ratted me out.

Once in a while, I'd pick up the phone and talk to her, but only if she sounded calm and coherent when she was leaving a message.

I had little patience for her, however.

If I detected any anger or self-pity in anything she said, I was quick to get off the phone. I also quickly rejected any requests to visit her or have her visit me. Knowing my mom, however, I was always worried she'd just show up on Uncle George's doorstep unannounced.

Moving to Washington would significantly decrease that threat.

Although leaving Oregon took me further away from my uncle, Nana, Granddad and Eileen, which wasn't so good, it brought me closer to Aunt Beth and her family.

Billy had settled in Seattle after graduating from college and was working as a high school teacher.

Julie was living with her boyfriend in Tacoma and student teaching while she completed her teaching credential.

Katie was going to school in Idaho, which was close enough to her parents' home that she came back for all her school vacations.

The one-bedroom apartment Jason had rented was close to his office and near four separate hospitals that were located along the bus lines.

279

Although my uncle and Jason had offered to teach me how to drive, I had never taken either of them up on the offer and still didn't have a driver's license.

I applied at all four facilities, got called in for three interviews and was offered two different jobs. After weighing out the pros and cons, I took the job at Western Medical because their opening was in the pediatric department, and I wanted to work with children.

"You love kids, don't you?" Jason asked me while I was trying to decide which job to accept.

"Yeah, I really do. I don't know if it was all that babysitting I did, but I really relate to them. They're fun."

"Maybe we should think about having some kids of our own."

"No way."

"Why not? You'd be a great mother, and I love kids, too."

"It's not a good idea, with my family's medical history. I don't think it's a good idea for me to have kids because they'd have a good chance of coming down with schizophrenia. Besides, I could get sick myself. Then what would you do?"

"If that happened, I'd take care of you and our kids."

"Maybe you'd better spend a week with my mom before you decide. It might change your mind."

"If that's a prerequisite, maybe we could get a dog instead."

Chapter 64

My job was challenging. I felt overwhelmed the first day, sure I'd never find my way around the hospital, remember my co-workers names, or successfully care for a patient. My manager had me spend the first week following her around as she worked, job shadowing she called it, to learn all the protocols.

The second week, she followed me around, making sure I did everything correctly. It was nerve wracking to have someone watching my every move, and I made a lot of mistakes the first day that I probably wouldn't have made if I hadn't been under scrutiny.

I came home exhausted, frustrated and convinced I'd made the wrong career choice.

I managed to keep from crying until I walked into the door, but as soon as I entered our apartment, where Jason was in the kitchen cooking dinner, I broke down.

He turned off the burners, put down his knife and held me while I cried out my doubts. Then he told me that I may have had concerns about my abilities, but he didn't.

He reminded me of how well I'd done in school, how my manager at the nursing home had written me a glowing recommendation and how much faith he had in me.

Then he started singing "Mama told me I'd have days like these," until I started laughing.

"Starting a new job is always tough. I was sweating bullets my first month. Remember? I'd call you up every day after work and tell you how scared I was. Things will get better. You're competent and capable, and you'll be kicking ass by the end of the week."

I wasn't exactly setting the world on fire, but by the time I completed my two-week training period I felt much more sure of myself. Still, it took a month or so before I started feeling like a real nurse. I knew I still had a lot more to learn, but I no longer felt like I had a neon sign hovering over my head saying "newbie."

Jason was working long hours, trying to impress his new boss. He was excited about his job, though, and talked eagerly about the projects the firm was working on.

When the first house he helped draft the plans for was under construction, he'd go by the job site almost every day on his way home from work to watch the progress. I was pleased he was so happy about his career and would go with him to the construction site on my days off.

As one of the newest nurses on staff, I had to work at least one weekend day every week.

I hated working when Jason was home and was lonely when I was off during the week and he was at work.

I talked to my cousins and my aunt regularly, and we got together as often as our schedules allowed, but nobody had time off during the week like I did.

To pass the time, I started exploring the area.

If it was drizzling or raining I'd go out on foot, but if it was dry I'd ride around on my skateboard. I discovered the library, about six blocks away, and got a library card.

I explored the local shopping districts and coffee shops.

I found several video stores, still called video stores although they mostly rented out DVDs.

One day, as I was riding my skateboard past a church, the doors to the building's annex opened and women began streaming out. I stopped to let them pass and saw they were all flushed, smiling and happy.

"That was a great workout today," I heard one of them say, and I looked up and saw a banner above the door advertising Jazzercize classes.

On a whim, I walked inside and asked a woman wearing a leotard who was closing the windows in the auditorium about the classes. We chatted for a while; she invited me to try a class for free and handed me a flyer. There were classes at all hours, and the prices were reasonable.

I decided to give it a try, because I could go before or after work, as well as on my days off.

Before I knew it, I had gotten adjusted to living in Washington and being married. Jason and I weren't exactly living happily every after, like in the fairy tales, but life was good.

We had our squabbles, like any couple, but they never escalated into heated arguments like the ones my parents used to have. Jason found some good trails near our apartment and went running four or five days a week.

I went to Jazzercise classes three or four times a week, and although I thought the music was kind of corny, I loved the workouts. Most of our other recreational activities we did together.

We both enjoyed exploring the area, going for long drives when we both had the same day off and finding places to hike and enjoy the scenery.

There were dozens of parks in and around Buskirk and Seattle and dozens and dozens of places to hike. We drove out to Mount Rainer, the Olympic Peninsula and Mount Saint Helens.

We went whale watching, bought bicycles and used them to explore the numerous historical sites, botanical gardens, cultural venues, museums, art galleries and the waterfront.

We visited Aunt Beth and Uncle Ben frequently, and Ben took us sailing. My cousin Billy took us kayaking on Puget Sound, giving us a brief lesson on shore, then helping us climb in the double kayak he'd bought when he was living with his girlfriend.

Billy was an avid kayaker and was excited to introduce us to the sport, telling us he hoped we'd love it as much as he did.

For me, it wasn't as thrilling as sailing, but it was thoroughly enjoyable. It took more than a few awkward strokes to get the hang of the paddles, and a little longer for Jason and I to coordinate our efforts so we didn't smash our paddles into each other's.

Once we got somewhat comfortable with the paddles, we started to relax a little more.

Billy pointed out the different birds that were diving into the water, flying above it, or bobbing on the surface, as well as the seals and sea lions we saw swimming around and beneath our boats and resting on the rocky shoreline.

As well as taking advantage of all the recreational activities in the area, we were both working hard and making good money for the first time in our lives.

After having been so broke for so long, we weren't used to spending money. So we were paying down Jason's loans rapidly, saving for the down payment on a house and still living what we felt was an extravagant lifestyle.

By that I mean we could eat out a couple of times a week and go to the movies whenever we wanted without having to subsist on rice and beans until the next payday.

Best of all, we both enjoyed the freedom of having our parents in another state. For the first time in years, I stopped worrying about my folks.

Dad was settled in the group home and doing fairly well. He was still working 20 hours a week at Granddad's store.

Dad and I talked on the phone regularly, and he seemed fairly content most of the time. It was unlikely Dad would ever be able to live independently again, or work anywhere other than the hardware store where Granddad kept a close eye on him and had him work largely in the stockroom to make sure he didn't get stressed by the job.

Granddad also helped Dad manage his money, giving him his pay in small, daily cash allowances to keep him in cigarettes and coffee, but not enough money to buy drugs or squander, or be taken advantage of by other residents of the group home. It still saddened me to realize Dad would never live a rich, full, independent life.

But for a man who had been in and out of the hospital, halfway houses and jail for most of my life, he was doing as well as could be hoped for.

My mother was also doing fairly well.

I still wasn't comfortable talking to Mom on the phone, and rarely called her, preferring to communicate by mail. Mom called periodically, and I was always wary when we spoke, so our conversations were usually fairly short and superficial.

I was quick to cut her off if she sounded like she was going to start in on me, or try to manipulate me.

I had learned to interrupt, say I had to go and hang up before Mom could continue without feeling guilty. Our conversations were far from ideal, since I was always on my guard when we spoke, but Nana kept me filled in on Mom's life, and I assume she kept Mom updated on mine.

I no longer felt that my parents were my responsibility, and it was refreshing not to worry about them or feel guilty for moving away.

Jason talked to his parents on the phone a couple of times a week and to his sisters rarely.

"I love my folks, but it sure is nice not to have them coming up to see me all the time like they did when we were in Portland," he said. "My dad has never forgiven me for any of the mistakes I made growing up, and he loves to keep reminding me of them. And my mother has never really accepted the fact that I have grown up."

Jason's mother and I got along well, although we didn't talk to each other much when she called.

I knew she wanted to talk to Jason, so after making pleasant chit-chat for a few minutes, I'd hand the phone over to him. I sensed she was reserved with people she didn't know well, much like I was, so I didn't mind that she didn't try to mother me and draw me out.

Still, I didn't really understand why Jason was so relieved to be a state away from his folks until the phone rang one evening when Jason was still at work.

"Hello?"

"Oh hi, Caitlin, it's Renee. Is Jason there?"

Jason's mom sounded funny, like she was choking back tears.

"No, I'm sorry, he's not here. He's working late tonight. He and his boss are out on a site visit, looking at some land where they'll be designing an office complex. Do you want me to have him call you?"

"Please," she said, with her voice wavering.

"Renee? Are you all right? You sound a little upset."

"Oh, I'm just having a rough day. Today's the 20th anniversary of Kayla's death, and it's hitting me harder than usual this year."

"Oh, I'm so sorry, Renee."

"Every year I try to forget I lost my baby girl on April 20, and every year the day rolls around, and it feels like I lost her yesterday. Mitchell doesn't understand why I get so upset. He just gets drunk and tells me to stop sniveling. It just makes me so sad. Kayla would be 25 now if she'd lived. I keep wondering what her life would have been like."

"I'm so sorry, Renee. It must be so hard for you."

"It is. When you're a mother, you never stop grieving for the child you lost."

285

"I'm so, so sorry, Renee."

We talked, or rather she talked and cried, and I mostly listened, for about 20 minutes. I just kept murmuring, "I'm so sorry, Renee." Her grief was so strong, it made me want to weep. I wondered if my mother still grieved that painfully for Jon and felt a stab of guilt for not being more sensitive to Mom.

Eventually, Renee was talked out and thanked me for listening.

"Your welcome, Renee. I'm glad I was here when you called. I'll tell Jason to call you when he gets home."

"Thank you, honey."

Chapter 65

We'd been saving our money and after four years finally had enough for a down payment on a place of our own. We didn't have enough to put down on a house, but we could afford either a condominium or a townhouse.

"We're looking for a starter home," Jason told the realtor. "Something we can afford now, so we can start building up some equity."

We spent the next four weekends going to open houses and checking out what seemed like every condo or townhouse on the market in the state of Washington. We wanted something that would be convenient for both our jobs.

Even though I had finally learned to drive, neither of us wanted to commute very far to work. Jason also knew, through his work, what neighborhoods were good and what areas to avoid.

Although we had given our realtor our criteria, she was determined to ignore it and show us every property in our price range that was on the market. Finally, when we were giving up hope that we'd find something we liked enough to buy, a two-bedroom, two-bath townhouse in a small complex came on the market. Sure our realtor was sending us on another wild goose chase, I didn't want to go see it.

So Jason went to meet the realtor by himself.

Twenty minutes later he called me from his cell phone, giddy with excitement.

"This place is perfect, Caitlin. It's just what we've been looking for and more. It's an end unit with a real back yard, not just a postage stamp sized one, that's fenced in and plenty big enough for a dog. It's got a two-car garage. It's at the end of a cul de sac, in a small complex with just 12, excuse me what was that? oh, just nine units in three buildings. There are big grassy areas between the buildings and lots of parking. The place is cool. It's two-stories, and the kitchen and master bedroom are really big. In fact the whole place is big. It's like 1,200 square feet. There's a fireplace in the living room, and oh, Caitlin, you've just got to come see it."

I liked the unit as much as Jason did, maybe even more after I discovered the unit had a laundry room and found out that all the appliances were gas and were included in the sale price. We had a builder Jason knew inspect it, and after crawling under the building, climbing into the attic space and examining the unit inside and out, Randy said if we didn't buy it he would.

We made an offer and waited nervously for five days until it was accepted. Thirty stressful days later, after we had signed numerous documents, had dealt with unexpected hitches and nearly emptied our bank account, we moved in. The furniture from our old one-bedroom apartment made the rooms look cavernous. I didn't care.

I was so excited that we had our own home that I would have lived there happily without furniture.

About nine months after we moved in, Jason came home from work and said one of his coworkers had a chocolate Labrador that was pregnant.

"If we commit to one of the puppies now, we could have the pick of the litter."

I wasn't excited about the idea of having a dog, but I knew Jason had been yearning for one ever since his old dog died when he was a junior in high school.

"It'll be fun, Caitlin, having a dog. Just like when I used to take care of Charlie for my neighbor in Cumberland. Remember?"

What went unspoken was my determination not to have children.

Jason hadn't brought up his desire for kids for several years, and I knew it would be unfair to deny him a pet.

"You're going to have to take care of it, honey. I don't know anything about dogs."

A month and a half later, two weeks after the puppies were born, we went to Kyle and Amanda's house to check out the litter.

The puppies all looked about the same to me, small, brown, furry creatures squirming around in a heap on the kitchen floor.

Jason sat down on the floor by them and inspected them closely.

I wandered into the living room, where Kyle was watching TV and sat down on the couch while Jason and Amanda discussed each pup's characteristics and personality.

Finally, Jason came in cradling a squirming puppy and put it on my lap.

"Meet your new son, Caitlin. Roscoe, this is your new Mom. Caitlin, this is our new baby."

"Hello, Roscoe. That's a good name. I was afraid you were going to name him Calvin."

"Calvin Coolidge Kane? I thought about it, but decided to save that name for our first son."

"If that's your plan, we are like so not having children."

Jason laughed, and Amanda and Kyle looked at us quizzically.

"It's an old joke between us," Jason said. "It would take too long to explain, and you guys probably wouldn't even think it was funny."

Jason was beaming when we got into the car.

"What do you think honey?"

"About Roscoe? He's cute. But remember, I don't know anything about dogs. You'll have to do all the work and feed him and train him and all. I'm gonna be the hands-off parent."

"Of course. But you'll fall in love with him too. Labs are very friendly dogs that just want to please. And fetch. And play. And cuddle. And swim. We can take him out in the kayak; he'll love it. You'll see. I bet that within two weeks after we bring Roscoe home, you'll be so in love with him you'll want to take care of him, too."

"Maybe. He sure is cute. Roscoe is a cool name. Is that why you picked it?"

"Sort of. I thought about Bosco, 'cause he's a chocolate lab, but that was too obvious. I thought about Rascal, 'cause he's the liveliest pup in the litter. So I just combined the two and came up with Roscoe."

"I like it. It fits him much better than Calvin."

Chapter 66

I woke up feeling queasy, but tried to shake it off and get ready for work. I went into the kitchen to start the coffee and noticed Roscoe's water bowl was nearly empty. I picked it up, filled it at the sink and was just bending down to put it back on the floor when the nausea hit me.

I dropped the bowl, ran to the sink and got there just in time.

Jason came in just as I was rinsing out the sink and wiping my watery eyes.

"What's wrong honey? Are you sick?"

"I think I might be coming down with the flu. I just threw up."

"Oh, no. Maybe you should stay home from work. Do you want me to make you some tea? Why don't you go lay down for a while?"

"I think I'm OK. I'm starting to feel better."

"I'll make you some toast and tea. If you start to get nauseous again, you should call in sick today."

I felt better by the time I'd finished showering.

I put on my scrubs, ate the toast Jason had made me, drank some herb tea and poured myself a cup of coffee. I meant to ask one of my co-workers if the flu was going around when I got to work, but got so busy 10 minutes into my shift that I forgot all about getting sick until the next morning.

This time, I made it to the bathroom before throwing up.

"Oh shit," I said, trying to think back when I had last had my period. "I can't be. This has to be the flu."

Nevertheless, I stopped at the hospital pharmacy before work and bought a home pregnancy test kit with two wands. I was nervous all day and wished I had someone I could confide in.

I got along OK with most of my co-workers, but I wouldn't say I was really friends with anyone I worked with. I was so focused on my patients and not making mistakes, that I tended to ignore everyone and everything else. Besides, having grown up with my parents, I wasn't too confident in my social skills. I knew my coworkers thought I was unfriendly, and I wished I could be less reserved but found it difficult to do much more than chat briefly when I ran into someone in the cafeteria or the break room.

Jason was in the back yard, playing with Roscoe when I got home.

I took the kit upstairs with me and into the bathroom.

The instructions on the box said the test worked best if you did it in the morning, after your bladder had time to accumulate urine during the night. I didn't want to wait, and since I hadn't urinated all afternoon, I decided to give it a try. Once I started peeing, I wasn't able to stop and flooded the stick before I thought to pull it out of the stream.

Then I sat on the toilet anxiously for 120 seconds, until two lines appeared on the test strip.

"Oh no," I said. "I can't be pregnant."

I wanted to cry, but decided to run the test again, just in case the results were skewered because I'd peed so much on the wand.

I squeezed out just enough urine to dampen the second stick and waited another two minutes, counting out the seconds anxiously.

The results were the same.

'Maybe it's a false positive,' I thought, knowing that it wasn't.

My period was 14 days late, I had morning sickness, and my breasts were getting tender.

As much as I wanted to deny it, I knew I was pregnant.

I went into the bedroom to change my clothes.

After I stripped off my scrubs, I felt an overwhelming urge to lie down.

I crawled under the covers and began to cry. I was still crying when Jason came in looking for me.

"What's the matter, honey?" he asked with alarm.

"I'm pregnant," I sobbed.

"That's great! I mean, I, oh honey, don't cry. Are you sure?"

"I did the test twice. It came back positive both times. What are we going to do?"

Jason sat down on the bed.

"Don't cry, honey. I know you're scared, but this is a good thing. We're going to be parents. I think this was meant to be."

Chapter 67

I went to my gynecologist, who did a blood test that confirmed I was indeed pregnant. After my exam Dr. Massey estimated I was seven weeks along. Jason was ecstatic and began estimating the due date.

He was so happy, I knew I couldn't even consider an abortion. I decided my best course was to do everything I could to ensure the baby would be healthy.

I took my prenatal vitamins, stopped drinking coffee, started eating salads with dinner and signed up for an exercise class for expectant mothers offered by the education department at the hospital.

I knew from work that the chances of having a miscarriage were higher in the early months of pregnancy, so Jason and I held off sharing the news with anyone until I entered the second trimester.

His parents were thrilled.

My father was excited when I told him the news, and my Grandfather, Eileen, Grandmother and Nana were all very happy.

Even Harold, my step-grandfather, was pleased and got on the phone to congratulate Jason and me. Uncle George, who knew about my fears more than anyone in the family, wished me well and asked me how I felt about being pregnant.

"I've got mixed emotions," I admitted. "I'm scared I'm bringing another schizophrenic into the world, and I'm scared I'll get sick, and the baby will have to grow up with a lunatic for a mother. But I'm excited, too. I love kids, and so does Jason. He can't wait for the baby to be born, and I know he's going to be a great, hands-on father."

"Then I'm really happy for you," George said. "I know you'll be a good mother. You're good at everything you put your mind to. And you definitely know what a mother shouldn't do."

"Thanks Uncle George. I really appreciate your support."

Jason and I started buying things for the baby's room; a crib, a changing table, a dresser and a mobile. We didn't want to know if we were going to have a boy or a girl, so we decided not to have a sonogram. We both agreed we wanted to be surprised, even if it meant everything we bought for the baby had to be either yellow or green.

We talked about names.

I wanted to name the baby George, if it was a boy, and Jason wanted to name the baby Kayla if it was a girl.

We picked some backup names as well.

I liked the names Isabelle, Madison, Jacob and Tyler.

Jason also liked Ashley, Andrew, Benjamin and Chloe.

We agreed to wait until the baby was born to decide what name fit best. In the meantime, we referred to the baby as CJ.

As my fetus grew, however, so did my fears of schizophrenia snatching me or my unborn child as another victim, until they developed into a full-blown obsession. Both Jason and my doctor urged me to see a therapist.

"I don't have time," I wailed. "I have to study and get ready for the baby."

Like many women of my generation who were pregnant for the first time, I had rushed to the bookstore for a copy of the book detailing what expecting mothers could expect.

I devoured the book and didn't stop there.

Sure I was so damaged by my upbringing that I'd be incapable of raising a child, I bought every book I could find on parenting, child development and how to raise healthy children.

I had thrown myself into a course of self-study, like I was cramming for a final exam I had to ace before I would be released from pregnancy and launched into motherhood. I signed up for every workshop and seminar the hospital offered for expectant parents and called Julie, who had given Aunt Beth and Uncle Ben their first grandchild nearly two years earlier, constantly to describe every symptom I had and ask for advice.

I talked to Aunt Beth at least once a week, since she was my model as a competent and compassionate mentally healthy mother.

I shared my fears with Nana and Eileen. Nana reassured me I'd be a good mother. Eileen, who had never had children of her own, was nonetheless patient with me as I vented concerns to her.

Finally, Jason, Julie and Aunt Beth held an intervention and convinced me, for the sake of the baby, that it was essential that I see a therapist.

I scheduled consultations with four different therapists until I found one I was comfortable with. Sondra reminded me of Clarissa, although the two looked nothing alike.

Sondra was in her 40s and was tall and heavy-set.

She had long, dirty blonde hair that she wore loose.

The most important thing to me was that she was calm, straightforward and knew how to gently draw me out.

She was well versed on the latest treatment advances for schizophrenia and encouraged me to visit the hospital's medical library and read some of the psychiatric journals.

Initially, I pooh-poohed her suggestion, insisting that my family experience had made me an expert in the disease. Later, I thought about her suggestion and about Dad, who had been doing fairly well since he moved into the group home, and decided to take her advice.

"Knowledge is power," Jason reminded me, when I told him about my plans.

He scoured the Internet for articles and information about schizophrenia while I struggled with the medical journals.

Jason printed out everything he could find that was published or posted within the past two years and highlighted the information he wanted to share with me. Jason was the optimist, always pointing out the most positive information he uncovered.

I was the pessimist and would respond with information I found that reinforced my fears.

"Listen to this Caitlin, from the British Columbia Schizophrenia Society web site. It says, and I quote, "schizophrenia is a highly treatable and manageable illness."

"Yeah, well this says, "schizophrenia has a tendency to run in families."

"Medication is highly effective in treating schizophrenia, however, oh never mind."

"Never mind what? Let me see that. "Medication is highly effective in treating schizophrenia, however it is difficult to keep individuals with schizophrenia on medication."

"Difficult but not impossible."

"Maybe not impossible, but that's one of the biggest problems. My

folks were always going off their meds, so was my brother. That only made things worse for the entire family. What if I get sick and refuse to take meds like
they did?"

"I don't know. I guess I'd try to convince you to take them."

"And I probably wouldn't buy any of your arguments, because I'd be psychotic. Schizophrenics are totally unreasonable when they're having a psychotic break. At least the ones I know are."

"Yeah, but look at what else this site says: "Schizophrenia is not the dreaded disease it was about 30 years ago. Now with early diagnosis, speedy initiation of treatment, careful monitoring of medication, regular follow-up care, proper residential, vocational and rehabilitation support systems in place, the long-term outcome is quite favorable."

"Quite favorable, but more than a full-time job. Who's got time for all of that? And again, if I get sick, how are you, or anyone for that matter, going to convince me to be a compliant patient?"

Although I countered almost everything Jason shared, his support helped me even more than the information we uncovered.

CJ was due in late July, and I had originally planned to work until the baby was born, then take a six-month maternity leave. By the end of June, however, I was so big that it was difficult to bend over a hospital bed to take care of patients. Tiffany, my manager, who had three children of her own, was very understanding when I told her I'd like to start maternity leave on July 9.

Just before the end of my shift, on my last day of work as a childless woman, Tiffany said she wanted to talk to me after work and to meet her in the break room.

I was worried that something was wrong; that either she had reconsidered my maternity leave or had decided she didn't want me to return at the end of it. I fretted as I completed my paperwork for the day and briefed my swing shift replacement on the status of our patients.

Finally, when I couldn't stall any longer, I went to meet Tiffany. The break room door was closed, which was unusual. When I opened it up, I saw all my coworkers, even those who had the day off, crowded in the room, which was decorated with green and yellow streamers.

"Surprise!" they yelled in unison. 'Surprised?' I thought as I froze in the doorway. 'Shocked and stunned is more like it.'

I'm sure my expression gave away my thoughts because Tiffany spoke up.

"We wanted to throw you a little baby shower before you start your maternity leave."

I looked around the room.

There was a white frosted cake on the counter decorated with pink, blue, yellow, red and purple balloons, and the words "Mama" written in green script. Next to the cake was a stack of presents wrapped in pastel papers and neatly tied ribbons.

"Thank you," I stammered. "Thank you all for being so thoughtful."

Chapter 68

Jason went off to work as usual the morning of July 27, leaving me propped up with pillows in bed with Roscoe lying atop the covers next to me. Ten minutes after he walked out the door, I felt my water break and a contraction cramp through me. I called Jason's cell phone and reached him before he had made it to work. He turned the car around and raced back home. He came bounding up the stairs and burst into the bedroom.

"Are you ready to go to the hospital, Caitlin? Where's the bag we packed? Should I call the neighbors and ask them to look after Roscoe? How close are your contractions? Don't forget to breathe."

I burst out laughing.

"Honey, I'm fine. My water broke, but I've only had two contractions so far. The baby is a long ways away from coming out."

We headed for the hospital at about three in the afternoon.

It was strange going to the hospital I worked at as a patient instead of an employee. I had called Julie and Aunt Beth after Jason got home to tell them I was starting labor and again just before we left for the hospital.

They joined us around five, after I had been admitted, examined, settled into the birthing room and was trying to calm Jason down in between contractions.

Six long, painful, sweaty hours later Kayla was born.

Dr. Massey laid her gently on my chest after Jason helped prop me up with pillows, and I wrapped my arms around my newborn child.

All the pain, all the worry, all the fears were forgotten momentarily as I was flooded with love for this squirming, red-faced little girl who was screaming her lungs out.

"She's beautiful," I said, with tears flowing down my cheeks. "I didn't know it was possible to love a baby this much. I'm overwhelmed."

"She's perfect," Jason said, as he sat down on the bed next to me, with tears in his eyes.

"Oh, Caitlin, she's perfect."

Later, after Kayla had gone to sleep, I asked Jason to bring me outside.

He went out of the room and came back with a wheel chair. Gingerly, he helped me out of the bed and into the chair.

He swaddled our sleeping daughter in a blanket, set her in my arms and draped a second blanket over her, then wheeled me to the elevator. We rode down to the first floor, and Jason pushed me and Kayla outside.

"Over here," I said, gesturing to the parking lot.

"Tell me when to stop," Jason said, pushing me down the ramp towards the lot.

I leaned back and scanned the sky until I saw the moon making its way towards the western horizon. "Here. Stop."

Jason locked the wheels and stood quietly. I looked up at the nearly full orb for a moment then began speaking.

"Hi Jon, it's me, Caitlin. I had a baby girl a couple of hours ago. I brought her out to show you. You're an uncle now. We named her Kayla Isabelle Kane, and when she gets older I'll tell her all about you and how wonderful you were. I wish you were here to see her and hold her and fall in love with her like Jason and I have. I love you, Jon."

Aunt Beth came home with Kayla and I the next afternoon.

I was tired, sore and grateful for her help. All the studying I had done about taking care of babies, along with all the training I'd had and the experience at work seemed to have disappeared from my brain.

Aunt Beth showed me how to hold Kayla while I nursed her and changed Kayla's diapers while Jason looked on. She made me chicken noodle soup from scratch and reminded me when it was time to take more ibuprofen.

I called Dad to tell him he was a grandfather and Granddad to tell him he was a great-grandfather. Beth got on the phone after I shared the news and assured them both that Kayla was the most beautiful baby in the whole world, with the possible exception of her own grandchild, and that Kayla and I were both fine.

I called Uncle George, who said he was thrilled with the news, and Nana, who was ecstatic.

I called my grandmother next.

She wasn't home, so I told Harold about Kayla's arrival.

Jason had called his parents early in the morning, about eight hours after Kayla Isabelle Kane was born and then called Alex to tell him he was an uncle. My cousin Billy came by shortly after we got home, to see his new cousin. He came into the bedroom, where I was feeding Kayla, with his arms full of packages.

Jason opened them.

There was a tiny, orange life vest in one, a baseball in a second, a tiny brown leather baseball glove in the third, and a extra-small Mariner's cap in the fourth.

I burst out laughing as each gift was unwrapped.

"Uh thanks, Billy," Jason said. "Uh, you do realize Kayla's only a day old and won't be able to use these gifts for awhile."

"Of course, Jason. I just wanted to get her off to a good start. I can't wait to take her kayaking and teach her how to play baseball. Let's put the life jacket on and see how it fits."

Jason held up the jacket. It was easily three times bigger than Kayla.

"Maybe we could wait a while."

Billy took off a little while later, after Kayla was burped and fell back asleep. Aunt Beth stayed until Renee and Mitchell arrived the following afternoon, driving off after showing Jason the fully stocked refrigerator and giving me a long hug.

Renee cried when she saw Kayla for the first time, and even Mitchell seemed moved. Neither Andrea nor Annette had children, so Kayla was their first grandchild.

Renee was especially moved that we had named her after the child she had lost to leukemia so many years before. She showered Kayla with kisses, thanking Jason and me over and over and over.

Chapter 69

My first three weeks of motherhood were a blur of exhaustion, nursing, diaper changes, burping, love and joy. Both Jason and I thought Kayla was a miracle, and neither of us could stop looking at her with amazement and pride, even when she was crying or throwing up. Jason changed quite a few of her diapers and got Kayla dressed and undressed each time she burped, pooped, drooled and got one of her tiny little outfits dirty.

I nursed Kayla every two to three hours, around the clock and tried to go back to sleep when she did, so I'd be rested for the next feeding, diaper change, bath or cuddle.

Even Roscoe seemed to be taken by Kayla.

I had been worried he might be jealous of her, even though Jason kept reassuring me that Labs loved kids.

Roscoe wanted to be as close to Kayla as we would allow.

He would lie down on the floor next to her bassinet when she was sleeping and sit patiently by the bed and watch me nurse her. When Kayla was crying, and Jason would hold her and walk her around the house to soothe her, Roscoe would be right behind them.

Before Kayla was born, Roscoe had reveled in visitors, automatically assuming that they were there to see him. Now he ignored Jason's parents, and even Jason and myself to some extent, in favor of the baby.

Renee helped out with the laundry, cooking meals for us, cleaning the house and holding Kayla as often as she could. Mitchell liked to hold Kayla, too, but would hand her to Jason, Renee or me when she cried, drooled, pooped or peed.

Although Mitchell made it clear he didn't do diapers, it was obvious he had fallen in love with Kayla. He would talk to her seriously, like she was an adult.

"How are you doing, little lady?" I heard him say to Kayla. "It's a drizzly day here in Washington State. Why don't you talk your parents into moving down to Oregon, where it only rains two days out of three instead of every day."

We had converted the guest room into the baby's room, even though Kayla was sleeping in a bassinet next to our bed so it was easier for me to nurse her at night.

So Renee and Mitchell stayed in a motel nearby.

I was grateful for Renee's help and for their generosity, buying us a stroller, baby blankets and several tiny outfits for Kayla, but I was glad it was just the three of us at night. Renee and Mitchell stayed for a week, basking in the presence of their first grandchild.

Two days after they left my Dad, Grandfather and Eileen arrived. Dad had gained weight since I'd seen him last, and his hair was starting to turn gray. He seemed fairly coherent, but I noticed his hands would tremble whenever he picked something up.

I was terrified when he wanted to hold Kayla and made him sit down on the couch between myself and Eileen before I let Jason set her down on his lap. Granddad never stopped smiling the entire time he was at our house and took dozens of pictures of Kayla.

He photographed her by herself, in my arms, in Jason's arms, with me and Dad, with me, Dad, Jason and Eileen. He recruited one of our neighbors to take pictures of all of us together, setting the camera's focus and exposure before handing the camera over to Kathy to push the shutter.

After each roll of film was exposed, Granddad would rush out to the one-hour photo counter at the nearby drugstore and wait impatiently until his prints were ready.

I asked him to order extra prints so I could send some to Nana and Uncle George. Dad overheard my request and commandeered some of Granddad's photos and mailed them to Mom.

Dad told me Mom was excited about being a grandmother, and that she wanted to come visit. I cringed when he said that and just shook my head.

"She misses you, Ava, and now that you have a daughter she was hoping you'd be willing to see her."

"No way, Dad. I don't want her up here upsetting me and my family. I want to be a good mother and protect Kayla from negative influences. And that includes Mom."

Dad tried to argue, but I just held up my hand and said, "Stop. I'm not going to talk about this anymore."

301

"But, Ava," he said.

I got up and walked away.

"Sorry, Dad, this conversation is over," I said over my shoulder as I left the room.

Jason and Eileen had been watching the interaction.

Jason followed me into the other room and wrapped me into a hug. I was trembling, just from the thought of having Mom around, and Jason held me until I stopped.

Dad, Granddad and Eileen left after a few days, promising to come back and visit soon.

Once again, it was just Jason, Kayla, Roscoe and myself.

Jason had taken three weeks of paternity leave, and before I knew it, he had to go back to work. I was terrified about being alone with Kayla and called Julie in a panic after Jason left. She reassured me I was capable of taking care of Kayla, reminding me that I'd already had three successful weeks of experience, and I worked as a pediatric nurse and had more experience with babies and young children than the old woman who lived in a shoe.

After calming me down, she reminded me she'd be reachable by phone all day and to call me if I needed to. I called her back later in the afternoon, just before Jason was due back home, to tell her both Kayla and I had survived.

She laughed, and said jokingly, "I told you so."

"I know you did, Julie, and you were right. And I appreciate your help so much that I'm not even mad you said 'I told you so.'"

I was glad I was on maternity leave and couldn't comprehend how mothers with newborns could return to work shortly after their children were born. I couldn't imagine being away from Kayla for more than the time it took to take a shower.

Adjusting to an infant was a lot of work, but I loved it. The first few months of Kayla's life involved getting up two, sometimes three times a night to nurse her. Even though it wore me out, I loved nursing Kayla at night, holding her close in my arms while she fed, just the two of us awake. I would talk to her while she nursed, softly so I wouldn't wake up Jason and tell her over and over again how much I loved her.

I had planned to breast feed Kayla for at least nine months, but had to stop after six months to go back on anti-depressants.

I was deliriously happy to be a mother and loved Kayla even more than I through possible. So I was shocked when I started feeling the darkness of depression beginning to send tendrils into my brain about six weeks after Kayla was born.

"It feels like a black fog is enveloping my head," I described to Jason.

"It's sucking the energy out of my body and draining some of my emotions. I don't feel sad as much as I do flat. Like I can't dial up my emotions more than one or two points on a 10-point dial."

Initially I tried to keep the darkness at bay, relying on some of the tricks that had worked for me in the past. I took Kayla for long walks with Roscoe trotting proudly next to her stroller during the day and went to Jazzercise classes after Jason got home from work to stimulate my endorphins.

I made a point of eating well, sending Jason off to work with the home baked cookies my neighbors would drop by and making sure I got my five-a-day dose of the fresh fruits and vegetables I bought twice a week at the Farmer's Market. I swallowed my vitamins every morning, and ate dry, cardboard-tasting cereal from the health food store with low-fat milk every morning for breakfast instead of the Fruit Loops I loved.

I talked to Aunt Beth and Julie regularly about my fears and resumed counseling. All those things helped a little but not enough. Jason urged me to see my doctor, as did Sondra, who as a therapist couldn't prescribe the medication she thought I needed.

Normally, I would have protested that I was fine and refused to go.

Now that I was a mother, however, with a baby to care for, I had to think about my family before myself. I made an appointment with my primary care physician, who diagnosed me with postpartum depression. I cried when she handed me a prescription for anti-depressants, which confirmed to me that I did indeed need to go back on the medication.

Kayla took to the bottle much more easily than I did. I missed breast-feeding her. I would hold her while she fed, but it wasn't quite the same. I missed the closeness of her suckling on my breast and wondered if this was the first of many separations my daughter and I would endure before she grew up and left home.

Chapter 70

I went back to work in February, on a point-seven schedule, which essentially meant I worked 14 shifts a month, instead of 20. I was glad that I had weaned Kayla earlier, after I had started taking anti-depressants again, because leaving her was hard enough. If I had still been lactating I don't know if I would have been able to stand the separation.

Jason and I both thought Kayla was too young for daycare, so I worked the swing shift so we could share child-care duties. Jason's boss was flexible about his office hours, more concerned that the work was completed on time than when it was done. So Jason went in to work early on the days I worked, so he'd be home before I had to leave for the hospital.

Both Jason and Kayla would be sound asleep, when I returned home shortly after midnight.

Jason would wake up when I climbed into bed, and we'd talk briefly before he drifted back to sleep. In the morning he'd get up before I awoke and would feed, change and dress Kayla.

Roscoe usually jumped up onto our bed when Jason left the room, only to be booted back onto his dog bed when Jason would put Kayla in bed with me before heading for work.

It was a little lonely, on workdays, seeing just snatches of my husband.

But we talked constantly. I'd call him on his cell phone after I'd gotten up, showered and was drinking my first cup of coffee. He generally would call me again during his lunch break, and we'd talk again mid-afternoon.

And of course, whoever was home with Kayla would call or text to report what amazing new milestone Kayla had achieved. Our conversations were short, generally under five minutes, but frequent.

It helped bridge the separation, which felt especially acute during my first few months back at work.

Occasionally Jason would get caught in traffic, or tied up in a meeting, and I'd have to bring Kayla to work with me.

I'd settle her down in an empty patient room, if there was one available, or in the break room, then call around to the different departments until I found a candy striper willing to watch her until Jason could pick her up. Watching the teenagers care for Kayla reminded me of my babysitting days.

Even when Jason got home in time to take over, my days were hectic, full and fulfilling. Although I missed spending all my time with Kayla, I enjoyed being back at work. It felt good to be bringing in a paycheck again, and I enjoyed interacting with my patients and co-workers. At least most of them, that is. There always seemed to be at least one co-worker who got on my nerves. I didn't have any close friends at work, but didn't realize until I was on maternity leave, how much I needed regular adult company and interactions.

Kayla was thriving and growing.

Some days it would seem like she'd gotten bigger while I was at work.

She said her first word Mama one morning while Jason was at work. She took her first step and promptly toddled over onto her butt, while I was working. I was so disappointed that I missed it that I wept when Jason told me.

Being busy helped me, well, not entirely forget, but keep my fears about developing my parents' health problems out of my mind.

Staying busy also made the time appear to fly by.

It felt like I was just getting used to being back at work when Renee called and asked if we had any plans for Kayla's second birthday, which was less than three weeks away. The realization that our daughter was nearly two got me thinking seriously about something I'd been mulling over since she was born.

One Sunday morning, when Jason and I were eating a late breakfast together I told him I was thinking about going off my anti-depressants.

"Are you feeling better?"

"I think so. I mean I've been feeling good for a long time, because they've been working so well."

"Have you been talking to your doctor about it?"

"Not yet. I wanted to talk to you first. I'd like to stop taking them, at least for a while, because I don't want Kayla to be an only child. I want her to have a brother or a sister, so she won't be alone in the world after we're gone."

Jason was overjoyed.

"Are you sure? I know how worried you were when you got pregnant the last time."

"I'll never be sure, and I'll always be worried. But I'm willing to take the risk if you are."

"You know I'm willing. Nothing would make me happier than having another kid."

The same day I stopped taking my birth control pills, I stocked up on home pregnancy test kits. Four months later, when the test was positive I cried tears of joy.

Jason cried, too, when I told him. He wanted to tell Kayla right away, but I urged him to wait.

"It's too soon. I haven't had the doctor confirm it. And besides…"

"I know. Anything can happen in the first trimester."

"Yeah. No point in getting her all excited, or all confused or whatever until we're sure."

"You're right. I'm just so happy I want to tell someone."

"Tell Roscoe then. He can keep a secret."

By the time I was three months along, we sat Kayla down and told her she was going to have a little brother or sister.

"Oh," she said. "I want a cookie."

Jason was disappointed that she didn't understand what the news meant. I just laughed.

"She'll figure it out eventually. We just need to keep talking about the new baby with her. It'll sink in."

"Yeah, when the baby is born. I want to her be prepared and be excited about it."

"Don't worry honey. When the new baby gets here, there will be more than enough excitement to go around."

A week or so later, Jason and I started talking about names.

We both agreed, as we had with my first pregnancy, that we didn't want to know the baby's gender until it arrived. So we talked about names for both boys and girls.

"Do you want to name the baby after someone in your family? We named Kayla after my sister. Maybe we should name junior after your brother. That is if he's a boy."

"No, I think it would be bad luck to name him after Jon. After all, Jon killed himself. It wouldn't feel right."

"Yeah, I guess you're right. But maybe we could name him after someone else in your family. Didn't we talk about naming Kayla George if she was a boy?"

"Yeah we did. And I would love to name him after my uncle. I think Uncle George may have saved my life when he let me move in with him. He certainly saved my sanity."

"So George if he's a boy, and what, Georgette if she's a girl?"

"No, Georgette a goofy name. She would get teased all the time. If it's a girl we could name her Taylor."

"Taylor, I like that. Now all we need is to come up with some middle names.

"You start thinking of middle names. I'm going to call my uncle."

Chapter 71

"Hello?"

"Hey, George, it's Caitlin."

"Hey there, honey. I was just going to call you."

"Really?"

"Yeah really. I've got big news."

"You signed a big record deal?"

"No, better. Trish and I are getting married."

"No way!"

"Yes way."

"I can't believe it. My bachelor uncle is settling down."

"Believe it. And I'm thrilled about it."

"What about Trish? Is she thrilled, too?"

"Well, she's getting used to the idea. No really, she's excited."

"Why now?"

"Why not? I love her, she loves me. She said, 'yes, it's time.'"

"Well, congratulations then. When's the wedding?"

"Well, that's what I wanted to talk to you about. And to ask you a favor. But we're thinking about June, in about four months."

"Cool, a June wedding. How traditional."

"I know can you believe it?"

"You're either heavily in love or have had a personality transplant. So what's the favor?"

"Will you be my best man?"

"Me? You want me?"

"You, yes you. I want you."

"Do I like have to have a sex change operation first? And throw you a bachelor party?"

"No and no," he laughed. "All you have to do is stand by me as my best friend and closest family member when I say I do."

"I can do that. And I'm glad you didn't want me to have a sex change operation. Cause it would be a little difficult to do now because, um, that's what I called you about."

"What, that you're happy to be a woman?"

"Well, that goes without saying. No, I'm pregnant. Other than Jason and Kayla, you're the first person I've told. I'm about three months along. If you get married in June, I'll look like I have a basketball under my shirt."

"Cool! We can shoot hoops after the ceremony. Seriously, though, Caitlin that's wonderful. That's great news. I'm really happy for you and Jason. That's incredible news. And yeah, if we go ahead with a June wedding you'll be my very pregnant best man."

"I'd be honored. And I've got some more news for you."

"What? Are you having twins?"

"No, at least I hope not. I wanted to tell you that Jason and I decided to name the baby after you."

There was silence from the other end of the phone. "George, are you still there?"

"I'm here. I'm stunned. After me? Are you sure?"

"Positive. It's a done deal."

"Wow. Is it a boy? Do you know yet?"

"We don't. But we're going to name him George if he's a boy, and Taylor if she's a girl. We've got you covered one way or another."

"Wow, Caitlin. Wow."

"Do you mind?"

"Do I mind? Are you kidding? This is the greatest honor of my life. I'm, I'm, like, overwhelmed. I don't know what else to say."

"You're welcome."

"Oh, thank you, honey. Thank you."

"So, like when are you going to decide what date the wedding will be? I might need to take some time off work."

"Well, I need to coordinate with you, so you won't have any reason to back out. Wow, I'm blown away. Thank you, Caitlin. I can't wait to tell Trish."

Chapter 72

The wedding was held in the back yard of Trish's friends, Emily and Amy. Trish's brother, Jim, was her maid of honor. I was seven months pregnant and waddled up to the makeshift altar in a maternity dress to serve as my uncle's best man.

Jason pushed Kayla, who was the flower girl, in her stroller.

There was a bouquet of flowers tucked into the back pocket of the stroller, where I normally kept spare diapers. A second bouquet started out on her lap, but she tossed it to the ground as soon as the ceremony began.

Trish's dog Rusty was the ring bearer, with the wedding rings tied to his collar with blue and white ribbons.

George and Trish swore to love and cherish each other before a friend of one of Trish's cousins who had a certificate proclaiming he was authorized to perform marriage ceremonies.

He pronounced them man and wife.

Nana, Mom, Trish's mother, stepfather, ex-stepmother and sister witnessed the festivities. So did George's friends Matt, Rick and four guys from two of his bands, as well as a handful of Trish's friends, who got drunk before the ceremony. Her friends pelted Trish and George with rice and confetti as she and George walked down the grassy aisle.

After the "I dos" were said, rings donned and the newly wedding couple kissed each other, George's friends broke out their guitars and serenaded the crowd while Amy started barbecuing fresh salmon and hamburgers.

Emily brought out big bowls of coleslaw, potato salad and fruit salad out of the kitchen and put them on a picnic table set up by the back door.

I helped her carry out paper plates, plastic wear, napkins, juice and cups, while Rick poured more ice over the cooler of sodas and beers.

Everyone filled their plates, then settled down on the grass or in lawn chairs to eat. Rusty ran around the yard and snatched a piece of salmon off Jim's plate and swallowed it before Jim realized he had been robbed.

Before George and Trish cut the cake, I stood up and made a toast to "King George" and his new queen.

Kayla fell asleep in her stroller. Emily offered to let us lay Kayla down inside, but I was reluctant to let her out of my sight. So we pushed her stroller into the shade where we could keep an eye on her and prevent Mom from waking her up.

Nana did a great job of keeping Mom on her best behavior.

As expected, Mom fussed over Kayla, who she was meeting face-to-face for the first time, when we arrived.

Mom let everyone within earshot know that this was the first time she'd seen her granddaughter, implying that I had been insensitive for keeping them apart for so long. I did my best to ignore Mom, while Jason kept a close eye on Kayla to make sure Mom didn't overwhelm her.

My reunion with Mom had been somewhat awkward.

She was both happy to see me and angry that I had avoided her for so long. Fortunately my role in the wedding kept me busy, so we didn't have much time to talk. And Mom was so taken by Kayla that after the wedding was over she was more interested in gazing at her granddaughter than talking to me.

I couldn't avoid her forever, though.

Nana and Mom were staying at the same motel we were.

We were all tired, and Kayla was fussy when we got back to the motel after the wedding, so we went into our separate rooms after making plans to meet for breakfast the following morning.

Mom was chatty at breakfast, talking about her recent paintings and an upcoming art and wine festival she had been invited to participate in.

She told us she had her paintings in several galleries now, including one in Portland, and that she and Nana planned to swing by the gallery before returning to Cumberland to see about having a show there. She talked about Dad and lamented the fact that they were living apart.

"It feels like we're dating again, like when we were teenagers and lived with our parents. He's got a curfew, and I'm not allowed to spend the night in his room. So we have to watch the clock when we're together, to make sure he gets back in time."

"But," she reassured us, "that hasn't stopped us from sleeping together. In fact, we have sex more often now than we did when we were living together. In fact, just last Friday your Dad came over and we…"

"Nana, can you pass me the syrup," I interrupted.

311

"As I was saying," Mom continued. "Your father and I."

"What are you painting these days Nana?"

We talked about Nana's artwork until Mom completely forgot what she had been so eager to share with everyone.

We finished the meal in peace and started saying our good-byes after the waitress brought the check to our table. Mom wanted to spend the day with us, but Jason had to work the following day, so we told her we needed to get on the road. She pouted for a while, but recovered by the time we walked out of the restaurant to lavish more attention on Kayla, kissing her forehead repeatedly until Kayla squirmed and cried.

Jason picked her up and cuddled her while Nana, Mom and I said goodbye.

"It's great to see you, Ava," Nana murmured as she hugged me. "You're looking great, and you and Jason seem like wonderful parents."

"Thanks, Nana. It's been great seeing you, too. Did you ever think George would settle down and get married?"

"Not in a million years," she said with a laugh.

"Me neither. If I hadn't been at the wedding myself, I still wouldn't believe it. I love you Nana."

"I love you, too, Ava."

No sooner had Nana stepped back than Mom embraced me in a hug.

"Good-bye, darling."

"Good-bye, Mom."

"Don't be a stranger, honey. I miss you."

"Take care, Mom. Give my love to Dad."

Chapter 73

Taylor Gwendolyn Kane was born on Aug. 28, three years, one month and one day after Kayla entered the world. Jason and I had expected a second child would keep us twice as busy as we'd been.

We were wrong.

We were much busier.

Kayla was still in diapers, and at three could race around the house faster than we could keep up with her.

She wasn't happy when Taylor was born and wasn't shy about letting us know it. She seemed to regress back into her terrible twos, and along with saying "no" to just about everything Jason or I said, she also seemed to have forgotten how to feed herself, wash her hands and needed help putting her clothes on.

Whenever I was nursing Taylor, Kayla would suddenly get needier, demanding juice, a cookie, or knocking over something to get my attention. Jason and I tried to give Kayla as much attention as we did Taylor, but she never felt it was enough.

We tried all the tricks to get Kayla to adapt to having a little sister. We told her she was a big girl and asked her to help with the new baby.

She said, "No."

We told her we loved her so much that we wanted to give her a little sister.

She told us to "take her back."

We gave Kayla her own baby doll to care for when Jason or I cared for Taylor. Kayla tossed it in the closet.

Finally, we took another tact.

We stopped trying to convince Kayla that Taylor was a welcome addition and just went about our business, lavishing love, attention and care on both our daughters.

It amazed me how different the two were. Taylor looked a lot like Kayla had as a baby. Both had round faces, small ears, a button noses, huge blue eyes and a shock of brown hair. Kayla's eyes turned brown after a few months, and I was hoping Taylor's would stay blue like her father's.

It was their personalities that were so different.

Kayla had been fussy and cried often, sometimes for reasons we couldn't discern. Taylor was calm and smiled most of the time.

She'd cry if she was hungry, tired, or needed a diaper change, but her tears would stop as soon as she was picked up as if she knew she was going to be tended to, and there was no longer any need to sound the alarm. Kayla had slept just two to three hours at a time for her first 18 months. Taylor slept through the night by the time she was a month old. Kayla had been a grabber, wrapping her little fingers around my hair when she nursed, or my hand when I reached down into her bassinet. Taylor waved her hands and feet and would wrap her fingers around one of my fingers only if I put it in her hand.

The only thing that was the same about our two daughters was how deeply I loved them both.

With two children to care for, my days were busier than I thought possible. I was on the go from the minute I awoke in the morning, to the minute my head hit the pillow at night, nursing Taylor, feeding Kayla, bathing the girls, getting them dressed, changing diapers, playing with Kayla, cleaning the house and running errands and shopping for groceries with both in tow.

Kayla had outgrown the use of her stroller, but once we put Taylor in it, she suddenly decided she wasn't going to walk with us anymore.

We bought a double stroller to take the kids to the park, where I'd sit on a bench with Taylor and watch Kayla while she played. As I had with Kayla, I took maternity leave after Taylor was born.

Jason envied me for all the time I got to spend with the girls, while I envied him, on the busiest days, for being able to get out of the house and go to work. I also felt a little tug of envy, along with great pleasure at the way Kayla would greet him when he came home.

She'd run to the front door shrieking "Daddy, Daddy, Daddy" with excitement when she heard him open it and say "Hello." She'd wrap her arms around his legs in a hug, then reach up for Jason to pick her up and give her a kiss. I knew she loved me, too, but since I was home with her all day she took me more for granted.

Chapter 74

I went back to work six months after Taylor was born, again working the swing shift so we could share child-care. Taylor hadn't been weaned, and I would pump my breasts before I left for work. It was a hassle, and I would occasionally start to leak at the hospital, but I was determined to nurse her for at least nine months. I still felt bad that I hadn't been able to nurse Kayla that long, as I wanted to give the girls the best possible start in life.

I'm sure all parents want to give their children an optimum start in life, but for me, it took on huge importance. I had been bracing for my hormones to trigger a return of my depression after Taylor was born and was relieved that it never materialized.

What came in it's place, however, was a low-grade anxiety about the family curse. I had never been able to completely stop worrying about developing schizophrenia myself, or passing it onto my children.

After Taylor was born, however, the anxiety ratcheted.

Instead of giving into my fears, I decided to take a more positive tack, and provide my daughters with an optimum foundation for their lives.

That way, if my biggest fears came true, and I became mentally incapacitated, they might have the strength to cope with my illness much better than I had coped with my parents' diseases. Jason, who loved his daughters more than any man I've ever known, also took Kayla and Taylor's early development seriously.

While he downplayed my fears, he agreed their physical, mental and emotional well-being was especially critical while they were young.

He read to the girls every day, talked to them constantly, played with them and helped prepare nutritious meals for all of us, even before Taylor was ready for solid foods.

We started Kayla in preschool two mornings a week, once she was out of diapers. She balked initially when we took her for her first day, and I was concerned that at 3 1/2 she was too young. By the end of the morning, however, she was having so much fun she didn't want to leave when I came to pick her up.

That was a turning point for her.

From then on, she was proud of being a big girl, who went to school. She wanted to go to school to play with her friends everyday after that, and bugged us constantly until we let her go four mornings a week after her fourth birthday.

Time may have dragged on slowly for Kayla, who practically counted the days until she turned four and then started counting them again until she turned 5, but they whizzed by rapidly for Jason and myself.

Before I knew it, it was time to sign her up for Kindergarten.

Kayla knew all her colors and shapes, how to count to 10, and some, but not all, of the alphabet. She loved being read to and would "read" along with the books she knew well.

She was eager to start "real school" and insisted on going with me to Culver Elementary School, which was three blocks from our home, when I enrolled her.

I put Taylor in her stroller, took Kayla by the hand, and we walked to the school. Rather, I walked, Taylor rolled, and Kayla skipped with excitement.

I lifted Taylor out of her stroller when we arrived at the campus, and we walked up the six front steps, with Kayla counting out each step, and into the school.

As soon as we walked through the door, I was flooded with memories.

The inside of the building was cool, which was especially welcoming on a hot August day, and smelled like glue and floor wax.

I spotted a piece of white poster board on the bulletin board opposite the door, which had a big red arrow and the words "Kindergarten Registration."

Kayla and I followed the arrow and walked down the hall to the Kindergarten classroom. I picked up an enrollment form and sat down to fill it out with Taylor on my lap.

Kayla ran over to a small group of children who were playing with blocks, stuffed animals and dolls. I kept glancing up at her to make sure she was OK while I answered all the questions on the form.

I heard her talking to the other kids and smiled.

My daughter wasn't shy, and I was glad she took to other kids so easily.

Out of the corner of my eye, I saw another woman about my age walk in with two little boys.

At first I thought they might be twins, but when I turned my head I could clearly tell one was much older than the other.

They were obviously brothers, dressed in matching shorts and T-shirts and sharing the same red hair, blue eyes and freckles dotting their faces, arms and legs. The older boy, who was missing his two upper front teeth, looked around the room and zeroed in on the toys. The younger boy, who was clinging to his mother's leg, was looking anxiously up at her.

"Come on Brady," I heard the older boy say to his brother. "Let's go play with those toys."

Brady looked at his mother.

"Go on honey," she said. "Go play with Aaron while I sign you up for Kindergarten."

Aaron skipped over to the toys, with Brady following slowly. Aaron picked up a couple of toy trucks and motioned for his brother sit down on the floor. Aaron handed one to Brady, and the two started rolling the trucks around the floor, going.

"Your boys are cute," I said to their mother, who sat down across from me.

"Oh thank you. They're a handful to be sure, but I just adore them."

I finished with the paperwork, handed it to a woman who looked like she was in charge and waited while she scanned the form.

"Looks good," she said finally. "We'll see Kayla here on September 16th."

"Thank you," I said, tucking Taylor more securely against my hip and turning towards Kayla.

"Kayla, it's time to go."

Kayla was so engrossed in play, she either didn't hear me or was pretending not to. I walked over to her and caught her attention.

Taylor kicked her legs, and one of her little booties flew off.

It landed near Brady, but Aaron was the one who picked it up and brought it over to me.

"Why thank you," I said. "That was really nice of you."

Aaron broke out into a big, gap-toothed grin.

"She's cute. What's her name?"

"It's Taylor. How did you know she's a girl?"

He pointed to the pink knit bootie he had just handed to me and said, "I'm Aaron, and that's my brother. His name is Brady."

"I'm pleased to meet you. How old are you Aaron?"

"I'm eight," he said with pride. "I'm going to be in the third grade."

Aaron grinned again, then turned to walk back to his brother.

I took Kayla's arm and led her out of the room.

Chapter 75

I couldn't stop thinking about 8-year-old Aaron, or more accurately, 8-year-old Jon taking me to school to sign me up for Kindergarten. Jon, who should have been playing with toys while Mom or Dad enrolled me in school. Jon, who had assigned himself an adult responsibility before he reached four feet in height, because it needed to be done. Because he realized if he didn't do it, nobody would.

As a child, I had always looked up to Jon.

As an adult, looking back, I was in awe of what he had been capable of at such an early age.

Unfortunately, those memories inevitably triggered anger and anguish: anger at the unfairness of life. Anguish at how schizophrenia had captured my brother and ultimately destroyed him.

For years, I had done my best to come to terms with mental illness, and the impact it has had on my family. I had long lamented that the disease had robbed my brother of an adult life. Now I realized it had also thoroughly robbed my brother of his childhood as well.

The realization saddened me.

When the sadness failed to ease, I knew it was time to resume counseling again.

"I don't know why it's hit me so hard now," I told Sondra. "After all these years. I thought I was over it, you know, been there, done that. I didn't know there was anything left that I hadn't analyzed and come to terms with."

"Schizophrenia is a life sentence, even for survivors like you. All it took was a reminder, like the one you had at the school to trigger a flashback."

"This is more than a flashback. It's like a reoccurring nightmare. I can't stop thinking about Jon and my family and all the chaos and turmoil. And how unfair it was. It is. I don't know. It's, it's, I don't know. It sucks."

We talked for a while, Sondra asked me if I'd consider going to a support group for people who had schizophrenic family members.

"I did that. Back when I was a kid. Jon and I went to a children of schizophrenics support group. It was kind of lame."

I paused and thought about the group and the dorky facilitator.

Then I remembered how comforting it was to talk with the other kids, who had similar experiences to mine.

"It wasn't all lame. Some of it was good. I remember being so relieved that there were other kids who knew what I was talking about. And who didn't get freaked out when I talked about my dad lining all his hats with tin foil, and my mom smoking cigarette butts she picked up off the ground."

"Why don't you think about it, Caitlin. There's a group that meets regularly in Seattle. If you'd like, I could get you the information."

Chapter 76

Kayla loved Kindergarten. Her teacher told me she was outgoing and friendly. "She's socially adept," was how the teacher put it. "She not only knows how to handle herself with her classmates, but she's also sensitive to other kids who may be struggling a little. On several occasions, I've seen her invite classmates who are sitting off to the side at playtime to join her and her friends. She shows real leadership abilities."

"She must have gotten that from her father," I said with a laugh. "She certainly didn't get that from me."

What Kayla did get from both Jason and myself was a love of reading.

She quickly mastered the alphabet once she started school and began to understand how letters went together to form words. When Jason or I read to her, which was one of her favorite activities, she would use her finger to follow along with the text.

If neither Jason nor I was available to read to Kayla, she'd pick up a book and "read" to Taylor or, if her sister was sleeping, to Roscoe.

At first she was just reciting words she'd memorized from books we'd read to her over and over and over. Occasionally, if she was "reading" a book she wasn't familiar with, she'd make up stories to go along with the illustrations.

One day, however, Jason and I realized with surprise that she could actually read.

Once she started reading, there was no stopping her.

Kayla read all the books we'd gotten for her, and loved picking out new books during our weekly visits to the library. Not being shy, she also loved to tell people about her new skill. When somebody called on the phone, she would beg me to put it on speaker so she could share her news.

"I can read, Gramma, I can read," she told my mother shortly after Easter.

"That's wonderful, Kayla. I can read, too."

"But, Gramma, you're all grown up. I'm in Kindergarten, and I can read."

"Well, I'll have to send you some books then. I'll send you my favorite books, and we can talk about them together."

I rolled my eyes when I heard that and joined back in the conversation.

"You don't have to do that, Mom. We've got books coming out of our ears here, and what we don't have the local library does."

"Hmmpt. I'm her grandmother, and if I want to send my granddaughter some books, I'm going to do it."

"OK, Mom, just don't go overboard. I know you don't have a lot of money."

"When are you going to send them?" Kayla asked. "When are my books coming?"

I forgot all about that conversation until a week later, when a big, fat padded manila envelope came in the mail addressed to Ms. Kayla Kane.

Kayla was excited when I gave it to her and began pulled at the tape that sealed the envelope.

"Is it from Gramma? Is it a book? It's big and heavy. Maybe it's six books. Moooom, I can't get the tape off."

I opened the envelope for her and handed it back so she could take out the contents. She struggled unsuccessfully to yank out them out, finally turning the open side down and shaking it until a big, hardback book fell out onto the floor.

Kayla's face fell as the book dropped out.

"It's a grownup book! I don't want any grownup books! That's not fair."

"Let's see what book she sent you honey."

"I don't care what book it is," she wailed.

"It's too big! Do I have to read it? I'll never be able to read it. And it smells," she added before dissolving into tears.

"Honey you don't have to read it. It's not a schoolbook. It's the kind of book people read for fun. If you don't want to read it, you don't have to. When you're reading for fun you can read or not read anything you want."

I bent down to pick up the book and got a whiff of mold. Mom had obviously sent Kayla a used book.

"Oh, you're right it does smell. Yuck."

I knew before I flipped the book over and saw the title what it was.

Sure enough, Mom had sent my 5-year-old daughter "The Clan of the Cave Bear," a 373-page volume that she wouldn't be interested in reading for at least 10 years.

"I think Gramma sent you this because it's her favorite book."

"I don't care. It's yucky."

"Let's put it on the book case, and you can read it when you get older. A lot older."

"No! It stinks. It smells like old rotten boogers. Throw it away."

"OK, honey, I'll get rid of it. Then why don't you pick out one of your favorite books, and we can read it together."

"I don't wanna read. I wanna call Daddy and tell him about the big old stinky booger book."

Chapter 77

The members of my support group laughed when I told them about Mom's gift to Kayla, then moaned in sympathy when I told them Mom had named me after the protagonist.

"She actually put Ayla on your birth certificate?" Susan asked.

"Yup. It cost me $25 to get a new birth certificate issued after I changed my name."

"My mom starts calling me Zygore when she's having a psychotic break," John said. "But at least it's not on my birth certificate. And she usually starts mumbling when she starts losing it, so nobody can understand what she's saying other than the family. And they know better than to tease me about it."

"My sister's hard to understand when she has a breakdown," Rachael agreed. "She doesn't really mumble, but it's more like verbal kung fu. She has about six conversations at once and mixes them all up liked tossed salad."

"Don't you mean like a Waldorf salad?" Bob asked, and the group cracked up.

Generally, there was a lot of laughter at the Family and Friends of Schizophrenics support group I'd been attending for the past eight months. The group met twice a month in a church basement in the outskirts of Seattle. I took me an hour to get there from home, if the traffic wasn't bad, and an hour to get back home.

Initially, when I realized how long the commute would be I hadn't wanted to take the time to attend. Now, I tried to schedule my life around the meetings, because I hated to miss them.

At work, in the neighborhood, at the store, even around my kids, I was always guarded, worried my old anger would resurface, or that I'd say something inappropriate or share a childhood memory that would freak people out.

I hadn't realized how guarded I'd become until I started meeting with what I called other schizophrenia survivors.

There were nine people in our support group, ranging in age from 19 to 69, but not everybody made every meeting. Generally, there were five or six survivors, including Charles, a therapist with a schizophrenic father and sister who volunteered to serve as the facilitator.

Although it's always been hard for me to make friends and relax in social settings, I felt a comfortable sense of ease with this group of people immediately, because all of them had grown up with at least one schizophrenic parent. Surprisingly, two others in our group, Jeff and Crystal, both had a mother and father who were mentally ill. In Crystal's case, however, her mother was bipolar.

Like me, most of the members had developed a warped sense of humor to deal with their loved one's illness. And like me, all of the members had deep scars.

"I used to look at my mother's eyes every time I came home from school to try to gauge what state she was in," Amber said.

"When they went from dead to demonic, I knew I was in trouble. Usually she'd start with the verbal abuse and tell me I was worthless, a nobody and a burden. Then she'd start hitting me. When she was deep in a psychotic state, she would often feel threatened by me and come after me with her hands, clothes hangers, belts, whatever she could get her hands on. When she was really bad, she'd chase me around the house and into the yard with a knife. It was a pretty nerve wracking way to grow up."

Everyone nodded knowingly.

Even those of us who were lucky enough not to have had physical violence or emotional abuse inflicted on them recognized the horror of situation, and how helpless we were as children in dealing with a schizophrenic parent.

Most of us have self-esteem issues, and all of us, at one time or another, suffered from depression.

We had long talks about the pros and cons of various anti-depressants.

Although I'd never taken an MOI inhibitor, as my doctors had always prescribed me SSRIs, or selective serotonin reuptake inhibitors, I knew the potential side effects of every MOI drug on the market.

The subject of anti-anxiety medication also came up regularly, and members were divided into separate camps.

Some believed Valium was the most effective drug, while others preferred Xanax or Ativan, or various different tranquilizers. I avoided tranquilizers as I was terrified of being induced into a zombie state.

I also tried to avoid all anti-anxiety medications because, though they were effective in stopping my occasional panic attacks, they tended to increase my depression symptoms if I took them too frequently.

I was always worried about developing a dependence on them, so I tried to avoid them except when it was obvious that taking a warm bath, going for a nature walk or thinking serene thoughts wasn't going to cut it.

Each meeting was different.

We generally started by going around the room and listening to one another as we shared our most recent experiences.

Sometimes the conversations would be intense, like when Bethany related how she had to call 911 when her brother, who was a paranoid schizophrenic, tried to attack her during a psychotic break.

Bethany broke down in tears describing the incident, then sobbed when she talked about how guilty she felt after the police arrived, wrestled her brother into handcuffs and took him to the mental health unit where he was involuntarily committed on a 72-hour hold. That hold, like the ones my family experienced, turned into to an indefinite stay.

"I don't know if he'll be released tomorrow or next year," she cried. "I feel so horrible about taking away his freedom."

Everyone in the room nodded in sympathetic understanding.

"Every time my mother has to be hospitalized I feel horrible too, even if I'm not the one who signed her in," Tom said.

Bethany nodded through her tears.

"I know it's hard, but you did what you had to do," Charles said. "You might have even saved his life."

Often the biweekly updates would be emotional.

"Schizophrenia is the gift that keeps giving," Roger remarked after describing how his low self-esteem had doomed yet another dating relationship.

"Sometimes I think I'm just destined to be lonely. I can't blame her for not wanted to go out with me anymore. Sometimes I'm so needy, I wouldn't want to be around me either, if I had a choice."

If the conversation lagged, Charles would jump start things by talking about some of his experiences.

"I hate to admit this," he said once. "But sometimes I think my father and sister would be better off if they were dead. Has anybody ever felt like that?"

Judging by the tears streaming down everyone's faces, it was obvious that we had all had that thought, most more than once. I was especially distraught by the subject because of Jon.

I broke down and sobbed when I told the group about his suicide, and what he had written in his farewell note.

"I'm so torn," I cried. "I miss my brother so much that sometimes it feels like a physical ache, even after all these years. But he was so tormented. I hate to admit it, even to myself, but he probably is better off dead. I just pray that he's at peace."

A few months later, Charles brought up another universal emotion.

"I can't stop thinking about the statistics. You know what I'm talking about. The ones that say if you have a schizophrenic parent, you've got a 10 to 15 percent chance of developing schizophrenia, too, and if you've got a schizophrenic sibling you've got a 9 percent chance of getting sick. And that if you've got multiple family members with the disease, your chances increase. That means I've got almost a one in four chance of getting sick, even though the numbers go down the longer I stay healthy. You know, the onset of the disease generally happens between the ages of 16 and 30."

"I'm 42, and I'm still worried about getting sick," said Roger.

"I'm 25, and I'm definitely worried," said Sarah. "It shows up much later in women. I won't be out of the woods until I'm in my late 30s. And I'll probably still be worried about it. Who knows? I could be one of those rare cases that begin after I'm 40."

"I'm not worried, I'm terrified," I admitted. "Most studies indicate if you've got two schizophrenic parents, your chances of getting it increase to 50 percent. And since my brother was sick, too, I think that raises the odds up to 59 percent. I don't like those numbers. I think about it all the time. I've got two kids, and the thought of developing schizophrenia sometimes leaves me paralyzed with fear. I'm always monitoring myself to see if I've got any symptoms, and I'm always worried about my girls. I just keep praying we'll all stay healthy."

"Me too," four people said in unison.

After an intense meeting, I often cried nearly all the way home, pulling myself together before I pulled into the garage.

Somehow, the tears would stop when I was a mile away from home.

I'd daub my eyes and blow my nose at every stop sign and red light and wash my face with the cleansing wipes I kept stashed in the glove compartment.

Jason could always tell when I'd been crying, but fortunately the girls seemed oblivious.

Chapter 78

One of the signs of paranoid schizophrenia is that the patient thinks people are always talking about them behind their back. Although worrying about developing schizophrenia has practically become an obsession that's not one of the things I worry about. I know that my coworkers talk about me behind my back.

If I were them, I would, too. Today I walked into the break room, and the conversation suddenly stopped. There were three people in the room, including a new nurse named Carmen who has only been on the job for about two weeks. Maria, one of the older nurses, tried to cover it up by launching into a conversation about the Seattle Seahawks.

I'm sure that Carmen had been asking about me, as in "what's up with her? She seems so cold."

I suspect everyone I've worked with has wondered the same thing at one time or another.

I've also overheard coworkers refer to me as a "control freak."

And once, I heard two of my coworkers discussing whether or not I was just plain weird, or had OCD. I can understand why people might think I'm obsessive-compulsive.

Sometimes I wonder myself.

I have rituals I follow to help myself cope with the inherent chaos of working in a hospital.

I meditate in my car for 10 minutes before I walk into the hospital.

I hate getting my clothes dirty, so I keep extra scrubs in my locker to change into if anything spills on my clothes.

At the end of each shift, I walk around the outside perimeter of the hospital, rain or shine, and shake my hands as they dangle at my sides to release the tensions and frustrations of the workday out of my body before getting in the car and going home to my family.

Whether those practices make me obsessive or not doesn't bother me. I just know my routines work for me, and that's what's important. Overhearing those kind of criticisms used to bother me, but I've come to terms with the fact that I'm never going to make a good first, second, or even 10th impression on people.

Schizophrenia, like my support group members had pointed out, is the gift that keeps giving.

Having grown up with two mentally ill parents had forced me to find ways to cope with constant chaos. Being a neat freak, even a possible obsessive-compulsive one, gives me some control over my environment.

I can't do much to change my personality, but I can find ways to compensate for the turmoil I endured in my formative years.

That turmoil turned me into a survivor and taught me some useful skills. I was reminded of that fact yesterday when Karen, one of my co-workers stormed out of a patient's room visibly distraught. I knew immediately what had made her so frustrated. It wasn't the patient, a 5-year-old boy who had had an emergency appendectomy the day before. It was his overbearing, overly needy mother, who was turning her son into a manipulative, spoiled, whiny, overly dependent monster. Karen caught my eye and said, "Hey, Caitlin?"

"Sure," I replied. "Do you want my pregnant 13 year old with nephritis, my jaundice baby, or my new diabetic?"

"I don't care. I'll take them all if you'll take the mother from hell off my hands." Later that day the charge nurse came up to me and told me I was a real team player."

"I know we can rely on you to help your fellow nurses out when they reach the end of their rope," Ron said. "You're the only one who has the balls to stand up to the neuroticparents."

"It's not so much I'm brave," I said with a smile. "It's more that I just don't give a damn if they like me or not. My job is to take care of the patients, not make friends with neurotic parents."

Chapter 79

Taylor and I were at the park, waiting for Kayla to get out of school. Or rather, I was waiting and Taylor was playing in the tot lot, blissfully unaware of the fact that we were going to have to leave in seven minutes so we could get to the elementary school by the time Kayla's second grade class was dismissed for the day.

When it came to Taylor and the park, she always felt like we left too soon. I was looking at my watch, so I could tell Taylor when we had five minutes of playtime left when I heard my cell phone ring.

I began digging in my bag looking for it.

It rang four times before I pulled it out, two rings short of going to voice mail. I saw Jason's cell phone number on the caller ID and flipped open my phone.

"Hi, honey."

"Caitlin?" Jason said in a choked voice that let me instantly know something was horribly wrong. He got out the words "my dad" before starting to cry.

"Honey, what's wrong?" I asked, felling a wave of panic wash over me. "Are you all right?"

"I'm, I'm OK," he cried. "My dad had a stroke."

"Oh, honey, that's terrible. I'm so sorry. No wonder you're upset. Is he, is he" what I wanted to ask was has he died, but settled for "is he stable?"

"I don't know. He's in intensive care. My mom just called."

I glanced at my watch and motioned for Taylor to come over to me. She ignored me, pretending she didn't see my gesture. I got up off the bench and walked over to her, while trying to comfort Jason.

"Honey, I'm so sorry. I hope he's going to be OK. Do you want me to call the hospital and find out what's going on? Do you want to go down to Salem to see him? Your mom must be so worried."

Jason struggled to get control of himself.

"Can you get me a flight? For later today? And call Andrea and ask her to meet me at the airport?"

"Of course, honey. I have to pick up Kayla right now, but I'll do it as soon as I get home. Do you want me to tell Annette, too? Does she know what's happened?"

"I think so. I don't know. Maybe you should wait, and I'll call her when I get home and have my flight plans."

"OK, honey. Do you want me to pick you up? Are you OK to drive?'

"No, yes, I'll be OK. I mean no I don't need a ride. I'll be OK."

"Drive carefully, honey. I love you."

"I love you, too, Caitlin."

Taylor started crying when I told her it was time to leave.

I hadn't given her the usual warnings.

Normally I told her we were going to leave in "five minutes," then "two minutes" then "one minute" before telling her "it's time to leave."

I picked her up, not an easy task and carried my squirming, angry 4-year-old to the car and strapped her into her car seat.

"I don't wanna go," she wailed. "It's not time to leave. I wanna play some more."

"I'm sorry, honey. I lost track of time talking to Daddy. We need to pick up your sister."

Kayla was waiting impatiently on the sidewalk in front of the school when we pulled up. She opened the back door, climbed in and announced, "You're late."

"I know, sweetie, and I'm sorry. Put your seatbelt on."

"I don't like it when you're late."

"I know, Kayla, and I don't like to be late. But sometimes we can't always get what we want."

"Hmmpt."

Kayla pouted all the way home. Taylor, who had finally stopped crying just before we arrived at the school, started up again.

"What are you crying about?" Kayla asked her. "Was Mom late to pick you up, too?"

I switched on the computer as soon as I walked in the door and led the girls to the kitchen before Kayla could start complaining again. I fixed them both a snack, poured them some juice and went back to the living room to log on.

I was comparing flight information when Taylor, who had finished her crackers, climbed up on my lap.

"Can you read to me Mommy?"

"Not now, Taylor. Daddy needs to go visit Grandmom and Grandpa today. I need to help him get ready."

"Then will you read to me?"

"Later. I have to book him a flight and help him pack, and then we'll all drive him to the airport. Then, after we get back home, and have dinner and get ready for bed then I'll read to you. Will you get my wallet out of my purse for me?"

Kayla and Taylor were uneasy with Jason gone. So was Roscoe. I had a hard time getting the girls to bed. They had never spent a night away from either of us and kept asking when Daddy would be back home.

"I don't know." I told them. "Grandpa is sick, and Daddy went to Oregon to help take care of him. We don't know yet how long Daddy will be there. But he'll call us, and we can all talk to him on the phone."

"I wish Daddy was home," Taylor said.

"Why is Daddy taking care of Grandpa and not you?" Kayla wanted to know. "He's not a nurse."

Roscoe kept looking at the front door, as if expecting Jason to walk in at any time. He was restless, no doubt because he could sense all three of us were upset, and he kept walking around the house to see what Taylor, Kayla and I were doing. Every time I moved, he was underfoot. I was annoyed and kept telling him to "go lay down." Roscoe would look mournfully at me, lay down on the floor, then get up a minute or two later.

Finally, after the girls were asleep, and I was sitting on the couch with a book in my hand, waiting for Jason to call, did the dog start to relax. I invited him up on the couch with me and stroked him as he leaned against my body. Roscoe fell asleep with his head on my lap, and I dozed off, only to be jolted awake when the phone rang.

Mitch was in intensive care, in a coma, and the doctors said they'd run a lot of tests and would know more in the morning.

In the meantime, it was a waiting game, waiting to see if Mitch would wake up and what kind of condition he'd be in if and when he did. Renee was distraught, the twins were sniping at each other, and Jason was completely drained. Alex was at the hospital with him, and they were planning to spend the night in the waiting room because the staff wouldn't let them sleep in Mitch's room.

"Go home, honey, and get some rest," I advised. "You won't be able to do anybody any good tomorrow if you pull an all nighter."

"I don't think I'll be able to sleep."

"Maybe not. But you'll have a much better chance of getting some rest at your mom's house. At least you'll be able to lie down. It'll be much more comfortable than spending the night in a hard plastic hospital chair."

"But I want to be here in case, in case anything happens."

"Someone will call you if anything happens, honey. Go home. You won't be able to do anything from the waiting room."

Chapter 80

J ason stayed in Salem for five days. Mitch was still in a coma, and the doctors said, essentially, it was in God's hands. He could wake up in an hour, a week, a month or die at any time. Jason was distressed, and the uncertainty of his father's situation was difficult for all of us.

My heart ached, and I wished I could be with Jason to try to comfort him. Renee was distraught and spent most of her time at the hospital, generally with one or more of her children, and with one or more members of her great circle of friends by her side.

Jason called home three, four, sometimes five times a day, to give me updates, share his fears and to talk to Kayla and Taylor. We had told our daughters that Granddad was sick and in the hospital but didn't give them any details.

As the days went by without any change in Mitch's condition, Jason decided to come home and go back to work. Annette had returned to Portland after three days. Andrea was still living in Salem and had gone back to work two days after Mitch's stroke.

The girls wanted to take Roscoe with us to the Seattle Airport.

"He misses Daddy, too," Kayla said.

"Yeah," agreed Taylor. "I bet Daddy misses him, too, almost as much as he misses me."

We left Roscoe in the car and made our way to the baggage claim area to wait for Jason.

Kayla saw him first, as he came down the stairs and began running towards him before I had a chance to stop her. Taylor started after her sister, and I caught up with her and grabbed her hand.

Jason scooped Kayla up in his arms and gave her a big hug. Taylor pulled away from my hand and raced to her father and hugged his legs. Jason set Kayla down, hugged Taylor, then me.

He held me tight and let his head rest on my shoulder.

"Oh, Caitlin, it's so good to see you. I've missed you so much,"

"I've missed you, too, honey. So have the girls."

"Roscoe missed you too, Daddy," Kayla said.

Roscoe demonstrated how excited he was to see Jason when he heard us approaching the car. Roscoe tried to squeeze out of the back window, which we had left partly open for him. He got his head out and was straining to try to get more of his body out, all the while with his tail thumping frantically.

Jason opened the car door, and Roscoe leaped out and nearly knocked Jason down in his enthusiasm to greet him. The girls laughed as Roscoe spun excitedly around and around Jason, circling him at least half a dozen times before Jason got him to sit down so he could pet him.

Taylor wrapped her arms around Roscoe's neck, and Kayla reached up and grabbed one of Jason's hands. It took a while, but we eventually got both girls and Roscoe in the car.

Jason helped Kayla with her seatbelt, even though she didn't need any help and secured Taylor in her booster seat. Roscoe sprawled on the seat between them. I loaded Jason's bag into the trunk and got into the driver's seat. It wasn't until Jason finally sat down in the front passenger seat did I notice how exhausted he looked.

His eyes were bloodshot, and they were rimmed with black. There were crow's feet on his face I'd never seen before. I reached over, put my hand on his arm in a wordless gesture of support. He looked at me and smiled wanly.

"Oh, honey, you have no idea how good it is to be home."

"We're not home yet, Daddy," Kayla piped up. "We're still at the airport."

Jason's cell phone rang three times on the way home.

His mother called to say there was still no change in Mitch's condition. His sister, Andrea, called to ask him when he was going to come back. Finally, Alex called to see if Jason had gotten home OK and tell him he was planning to spend the following evening at the hospital with Renee.

I could see clearly that although Jason's body was back in Washington, his heart and mind were still in Oregon.

Jason had planned to go to work the following morning, but I talked him into sleeping late and heading into the office in the afternoon.

He was still sound asleep when I got up back from dropping Kayla off at school and delivering Taylor to preschool.

Jason finally stumbled downstairs around 11 a.m.

He checked his cell phone for messages while I poured him a cup of coffee, then called his boss and said he wouldn't be in until the following day.

"I'm wiped out. And I haven't done anything for days."

"You've been through a lot, honey. It's exhausting to spend that much time at the hospital, waiting and worrying."

"Waiting, worrying and not knowing what's going to happen. I just wish someone could tell us if my dad is going to get better, or if he's not going to make it. I just can't stand this uncertainty. It's like walking around holding your breath for days on end. I wish there was something I could do."

"It doesn't get much harder than this, honey. It's a tough, tough time."

"You know what's the worst part, Caitlin? I don't know if my Dad has enough fight in him. He's been slowly drinking himself to death since my sister died. It fucking pisses me off that he drank himself into this condition. And I feel bad for being so pissed off at him."

I wanted to argue with Jason and point out his father had had a stroke and wasn't in an alcohol-induced coma, but I knew he was right. Mitch had put on weight, unhealthy belly weight, since I first met him and was at least 100 pounds overweight. His blood pressure and cholesterol were both high, and the most exercise Mitch got was going from the living room into the kitchen for another beer.

I just shook my head.

"It sucks, honey, that he didn't take better care of himself. Maybe this will be a wake-up call for him."

"Yeah, if he wakes up."

When the phone woke us up three days later at 2:30 a.m. Jason and I

337

both knew, before he answered it, that Mitch had passed away. We cried for a good 20 minutes after Jason hung up.

"I can't believe he's gone. I can't believe I'll never get another chance to talk to him again," Jason lamented. "I'll never get a chance to finally hear him say he was proud of me."

"He was proud of you, honey. I know he was."

"No, he was just critical. He never forgave me or the twins for surviving after Kayla died."

Chapter 81

Katie graduated from college with a degree in business and moved down to Cumberland to work at Granddad's hardware store. Grand-dad was delighted. Neither Dad or Beth were interested in taking over the family business when he retired, so he had hoped at least one of his grandchildren would. Katie wasn't making him any promises, but she was eager to give it a try.

"How do you like it so far?" I asked her on the phone after she'd been in Cumberland for two weeks.

"It's OK. I like working with Granddad, but I'm getting tired of doing the janitor stuff. I'll be a lot happier when he lets me wait on customers."

"Be patient. He made me do the same thing when I started out. Then I had to work as a stock clerk for months before I got to the cash register."

"I know. He's told me all about it. And all about how he made your brother do the same thing. And your dad. And how he would have made my mom do that, too, if she'd been dumb enough to work for him. And he told me all about how his dad made him sweep and mop the floors for months when he first started."

"So you get the idea then."

We both laughed.

"At least it will give me time to get familiar with the store and everything. I don't know much about hardware. We didn't study that in college."

"How are you getting along with my dad?"

"OK. I think. Well, kinda OK. But..."

"But he freaks you out?"

"Sort of. Not really, but I don't know what to think. It's hard to understand him some of the time. He kind of mumbles, and I can't tell what he's saying."

"Welcome to the family. I'm not even sure if my dad understands half of the things he says."

"How do you deal with him?"

339

"I don't. Remember, I moved to Washington State. My dad's pretty harmless these days. He may be a little strange, but he's got a good heart. And Granddad deals with him pretty well."

"Yeah, it's amazing. Granddad seems to be able to read him pretty well and communicate with him."

"Yeah, Granddad knows his cycles."

"Cycles? What do you mean?"

"Dad's on a couple of different medications. Most of 'em he takes every day, but he also gets an anti-psychotic injection every 21 days. He's usually pretty pissed off right after he gets his shot, because it makes him feel that he's losing his grip on reality when it starts working."

"Losing his grip? Isn't it supposed to give him a grip?"

"Yeah, it quells all the voices in his head, but that kind of freaks him out initially, 'cause it changes his own unique view of reality. Then a couple of days later, he gets used to being so-called normal and likes it. He's usually happiest then until the shot starts wearing off."

"How do you know when the shot is wearing off?"

"It's easy. It's when he starts talking louder and louder. When the medication starts wearing off, the voices in his head start getting louder and louder, so my dad starts talking louder and louder to try to drown them out. Kayla and Taylor call it "when Grandpa is talking speaker phone" because he gets so loud when he's talking to me on the phone, they think he's on speaker. A couple of times they tried to talk back to him, not realizing he wasn't."

"Wow, that's a bummer. I guess he's about ready for another shot then, because he's been talking pretty loudly for the past couple of days. Granddad's got him working in the stock room, so he doesn't bother the customers."

"That sounds about right. If he hasn't already, he'll start getting depressed next. That'll go on until he gets another shot and gets pissed off again."

"Poor guy. What a horrible thing to go through."

"Yeah, it sucks. But believe me, my dad's better off with the shots than he was before. At least it allows him to have more of a life."

"Well, thanks for the info, Caitlin. Now that I know more about what's going on with your dad, it's, it's, um…"

"Not so weird?"

"Well."

"It's OK, Katie. I know what my dad's like. He's pretty fucking weird, but I still love him. I'm just glad I don't live with him anymore."

"He's lucky he's got the family."

"Yeah, I don't know where he'd be without Granddad especially. Probably out on the streets or in jail."

"Wow."

"Yeah, I guess they didn't teach working with a schizophrenic uncle in business school did they?"

"No, they didn't. But that's OK. I'll learn. Besides, he may be sick, but he's still family."

Chapter 82

Kayla, the family socialite, had yet another birthday party to attend. There were 23 other kids in her third grade class, and if this year is like last year, they'll all wanted Kayla to help them celebrate getting a year older. Sometimes I thought I was going to have to pick up an extra shift each week just to pay for all the birthday presents we needed to buy for Kayla's friends.

Jason had a soccer game and Taylor and I had planned to go watch him play. But it was raining, and Taylor was getting over a cold, her second since starting Kindergarten five weeks ago, so I decide to stay home and make brownies. Taylor adores and looks up to her older sister, but she loves having one-on-one time with either myself or Jason.

She was quiet in the car when we drove Kayla to her party, letting Kayla do all the talking for both of them. But she chattered happily with me all the way home. Sometimes I wonder if she's overshadowed by her older sister, or if she's just happy to hear what Kayla has to say.

The differences between my daughters continues to grow.

Kayla is outgoing and loves to be around people; the more the merrier. Taylor is a little shy and prefers to play with just one kid at a time. Kayla is physically active and is the fastest runner on her soccer team. She's an enthusiastic player, even though she's not the most coordinated kid on the field.

Taylor prefers indoor activities. She's especially fond of drawing and coloring and is a dreamer who loves to make up stories to go with her pictures. Every time we've asked her if she wants us to sign her up to play soccer, or softball like her sister, she's said no.

When we got home Taylor ran into the house looking for Aerial, the gray-striped tabby cat that adopted us two months ago. Aerial appeared on our front porch one afternoon, and the girls were enchanted. I let them pet the cat, but refused to let them bring it inside or put out a saucer of milk for it.

"We've got a dog," I said. "We don't need another pet, and if you feed an animal, they'll keep coming back."

Aerial didn't get the message, because she was back on the porch the next morning and again the next night. She kept up her vigil until Jason broke down and let her into the house. The next thing I knew, the girls and Jason had come back from the store with a little pink collar, a pink feeding dish and a bag of kitty chow.

Kayla and Taylor were so in love with the kitty by then, I didn't have the heart to protest. And I knew it would be a losing battle if I did.

Aerial must have been asleep in the girls' bedroom, because she usually comes looking for the kids when she hears us come in the house. Taylor ran upstairs, then came back down a minute later with Aerial in her arms. They settled on the couch, with Aerial snuggled up on Taylor's lap, getting stroked and talked to.

Roscoe lay down on the floor in front of them, looking mournful.

Before Aerial moved in, Roscoe would jump up onto the couch when any of us sat down, looking for attention. After Aerial swiped him with her claws, a day or two after she was officially "adopted," Roscoe started keeping his distance from her.

I went upstairs to get the dirty clothes out of the hamper in the bathroom. When I came back down Taylor was "reading" to the animals, making up her own story to go with the illustrations in the book she was holding.

I put a load of laundry into the washer and went back into the kitchen. I found the brownie recipe in the cookbook I'd bought last year when Kayla's school—now Taylor's school as well—was doing a fundraiser. I pulled out the ingredients and put them on the counter, along with two mixing bowls and a baking pan.

"Taylor," I called out. "Do you want to help me make some brownies now?"

"Yeah, Mom," I heard her say to me, followed by "We'll finish this story later," to Roscoe and Aerial.

I pulled a chair next to the counter for Taylor to stand on while she washed her hands.

"Can I do the measuring, Mom?" she asked as she clambered up on the chair.

"You sure can," I said, handing her a measuring cup and a box of sugar. "We need two cups of sugar. That's all the way to the top red line."

Taylor spilled sugar all over the counter, the first of many spills we'd experience before the brownies were in the oven. It was slow baking with my daughter, but I wouldn't have had it any other way.

Taylor loved helping, and I loved her company.

She giggled and chattered while we worked, growing silent with concentration as she measured out the specific ingredients, then laughed with glee as she added each ingredient to the mixing bowl.

I creamed the sugar and butter together and let her mix the flour, cocoa, baking powder and salt together. She stirred vigorously, sending clouds of powder into the air and settling on the counter, floor and her clothes.

"Oops," she said, looking dismayed.

"Don't worry, honey, we'll clean everything up when we're done. Just slow down and don't stir so hard."

"OK, Mommy."

Taylor "helped" me clean up the counters and sweep the floor after we put the brownies in the oven to bake. I rinsed out the bowls and utensils and put them in the dishwasher. When Taylor was finished cleaning, I told her she had been a big help, which made her grin, and sent her upstairs to change her clothes.

When she left I picked up a sponge and wiped down the counter, then swept the floor again. The broom seemed to just spread the mess around, so I pulled out the mop and decided to give the floor a good cleaning. I was thinking that maybe Taylor was a little too young to "help" out in the kitchen.

I was wondering if I had made a mistake when I heard the front door open, and Jason calling out "anyone home?"

"Daddy, Daddy, Daddy," Taylor squealed as I heard her thump down the stairs. "Mommy and I made brownies. I helped. You can eat some when they're ready. It was fun. Mommy let me measure everything and mix it all up."

"That's great, honey. I can't wait to eat some."

"It was better than great, Daddy. It was super super special."

344

Chapter 83

A re you coming up to bed, Honey?" Jason asked as he leaned down the stairs.

"In a minute. I just want to finish tidying up down here."

"See you in an hour, Sweetie."

I wandered through the living room, picking up toys, sweaters and books. I stacked the books neatly on the bookshelf by the door and hung the sweaters up in the hall closet.

I tossed the toys into the basket next to the couchwaking up Roscoe who was laying on the floor next to it. I walked into the kitchen, rinsed the empty glasses on the counter and put them into the dishwasher.

I opened the refrigerator and noticed Jason had forgotten to pack the girls their lunches for the following day. I made sandwiches and packed them into their lunch boxes, along with an apple and two cookies secured in a little plastic baggie.

I filled plastic bottles with juice, apple for Kayla and raspberry for Taylor, and put them in the freezer.

I found the girls' backpacks and put them by the door, with a note on each one reading, 'Don't forget your lunch and your juice.'

I took the clothes out of the dryer and folded them.

I pulled out the ironing board and ironed my scrubs, then put two sets in my own bag, which I placed by the door. I whistled for Roscoe and send him outside to do his business.

After I let him back in, I locked the back door, then I checked the locks on the front door and the door connecting the garage to the house.

I checked to make sure the water bowl that Roscoe and Aerial share was full of fresh, clean water and swept up a few stray pieces of kibble that Roscoe scattered while he ate. I made another circuit through the downstairs rooms, to make sure everything was in order. Then I sat on the couch, closed my eyes and reflected on my day.

I gave thanks for my life, for my husband, my children, my extended family, our home and my career.

Then I played back the mental tape of my day, thinking about what I did, said, heard and saw.

Only after I analyzed the events and was sure that there were no strange sights, odd sounds, or anyone, especially Jason, asking me if I was OK, did I give thanks for my health and for the powers that be for allowing me to escape the family's genetic curse for one more day.

Finally, I walked upstairs, followed by Roscoe, tiptoed into the girls' room, kissed their foreheads gently so as not to wake them, then went into my bedroom and climbed into bed next to Jason.

Acknowledgments

Writing can be a lonely profession, and my computer isn't exactly great company. However, I was fortunate enough to have the support and assistance in various different capacities from many great people. They include:

Ina Kandel
Jon Morgan
Nina Morgan
Sally Morgan
Tyler Morgan
Chris Reed
Dian Duchin Reed
Gary Neville Sandstrom
Stacey Vreeken
Deborah Washofsky
Jim Wood
Carol Kozlovich
and Alejandra Zamudio

Special thanks to Katja Coulter for designing both the cover and the interior of this book.

Mahalo
and my apologies to anyone I have inadvertently overlooked.

For information about Schizophrenia

The Genetic Lottery is a work of fiction, but schizophrenia is a very real disorder that affects one out of every 100 people across the globe. That means just about everyone has a family member, close friend, or close friend with a family member who is living with schizophrenia. And everyone who loves someone who lives with this devastating mental illness, as the protagonist of my novel illustrates, is affected.

Despite that, many people feel like their situation is unique because of the stigma surrounding mental illness. Even in this day and age when people go onto television and share their innermost secrets with the world the stigma prevents many people from talking about schizophrenia and other mental illnesses like bipolar disorder and depression and sharing their experiences. That in turn prevents many people from seeking the help they need.

I hope my novel has shed a little light on schizophrenia, and prompts readers to start talking about mental illnesses. By encouraging conversations, hopefully more and more people will recognize that mental illness is a disease, like cancer or diabetes and that it's nothing to be ashamed of. There are a lot of great people and great organizations that mental health consumers and their loved ones can turn to for information, resources and support. I've listed the ones I found most helpful when researching schizophrenia and the impacts it has on people along with their URLs. Many of these organizations have local chapters that offer support groups, meetings, and face-to-face conversations, and many address all types of mental illnesses.

The great thing about the internet is that you can access information from any part of the globe. The not-so-great thing is that web addresses, as well as organizations and associations, can and do change. While these addresses were current in May, 2015, if you find a link no longer works, please email me at terri@terrimorgan.net so I can update this information. If you know of an organization that's not included, please send me information as well.

National Alliance on Mental Illness http://nami.org

Schizophrenia Society of Canada www.schizophrenia.ca

Sane Australia www.sane.org

Rethink Mental Illness www.rethink.org

Mental Health America www.mentalhealthamerica.net

National Alliance for Research on Schizophrenia and Depression www.narsad.org

Schizophrenia and Related Disorders Alliance of America www.sardaa.org

Embracing My Mind www.emminc-recovery.org

Psych Central online resources http://psychcentral.com

Mental Health Association Australia www.mentalhealth.org.au

International Schizophrenia Foundation www.orthomed.org/isf/isf.html

SZ Magazine www.mentalwellnesstoday.com

Compeer www.compeer.org

National Institute of Mental Health www.nimh.nih.gov

http://schizophrenia.com An online community providing information, education, support and forums

Bring Change 2 Mind (working to end the stigma and discrimination) www.bringchange2mind.org

Lightning Source UK Ltd.
Milton Keynes UK
UKOW01f1023220218

318318UK00002B/439/P